D0961929

MICHAEL ARNTFIELD
AND MARCEL DANESI

MURDER IN PLAIN ENGLISH

FROM MANIFESTOS TO MEMES—LOOKING AT MURDER THROUGH THE WORDS OF KILLERS

Ⓟ Prometheus Books

59 John Glenn Drive
Amherst, New York 14228

Published 2017 by Prometheus Books

Cover design by Nicole Sommer-Lecht
Cover design © Prometheus Books

Inquiries should be addressed to
Prometheus Books
59 John Glenn Drive
Amherst, New York 14228
VOICE: 716–691–0133
FAX: 716–691–0137
WWW.PROMETHEUSBOOKS.COM

21 20 19 18 17   5 4 3 2 1

Library of Congress Cataloging-in-Publication Data Pending

ISBN 978-1-63388-253-9 (hardcover)
ISBN 978-1-63388-254-6 (ebook)

Printed in the United States of America

Dedicated to the innocent victims of criminal violence everywhere.

CONTENTS

PREFACE

There are a great number of people to thank for having generously helped provide the inspiration, support, and source materials for this personally daunting book. We feel compelled, however, to call some people out for less felicitous reasons. We are not sure who first decided that the study of criminal violence should be relegated strictly to specific branches of criminology, as little more than adjuncts of psychology and sociology at their most banal and doctrinaire. Such individuals may take issue with our approach, impelling us to identify what "school" we subscribe to. We wish to make it clear from the outset that we subscribe not to any one particular school of thought or theory but to many. Above all else, we want to make it clear that our approach is based on a humanistic-literary view of murder—that is, a view that sees murder as understandable through language, discourse, and stories—by fictional authors and murderers alike. In this book, we have charged head-on into a different and new territory in the study of murder. It is a methodology that, in our view, is overdue. Thus, in so doing we have chosen to follow an approach that offers a synthesis of high concept ideas and street smarts, with takeaway knowledge gleaned from and informed by a combination of primary and secondary sources in order to bring about a change in how murder is treated by fields such as criminology and forensic psychology, among others.

In building this ambitious book from the ground up, we have sought out ideas, feedback, and other intellectual contributions from scholars who have a like-minded, flexible, and strongly interdisciplinary approach to murder as we do. In particular, we offer special thanks to Tom Hargrove for his tireless work with the Murder Accountability Project (murderdata.org) along with the entire board of directors. These members include Enzo Yaksic, who also merits special mention for his founding and heading of the Northeastern University Listserv for Atypical Homicide, a remarkable cadre of experts who rank among the world's leading luminaries in the field of murder investigation and criminal investigative analysis. Their collective wisdom is inscribed in the chapters that follow. We would also like to thank Dallas Drake of the Homicide Research Institute and Dr. John Olsson of the British Institute for Forensic Linguistics, as well as Dr. Bob Barsky at Vanderbilt University and Percy Walton at Carleton University, all of whom have demonstrated a commitment to the study of criminal violence through a variety of academic and practical lenses and always with the best of public and intellectual intentions. This, unfortunately, cannot be said about most crime writers and even conventional criminologists.

On the law-enforcement side, we offer thanks to Detective Ken Mains of the American Investigative Society of Cold Cases, Deneen Hernandez of the FBI's Forensic Cryptanalysis Unit, Constable Cam Shea of the London Police Service, and Constable Grant Worrall of the Waterloo Regional Police Service. Special thanks also go out to retired Assistant Commissioner Cal Corley of the Royal Canadian Mounted Police and retired Detective Sergeant Pat Postiglione of the Nashville Metro Police Department, both now spearheading new initiatives and helping to change the dialogue on policing from the private sector.

A large portion of the research for this book was also compiled with the assistance of five research assistants at the University of Toronto. We wish to thank them all for their consistent and effective work. They are Emma Findlay-White, Nadia Guarino, Alex Shenouda, Soli Doubash, and, in particular, Stacy Costa. We would also like to thank research assistants Kevin Shaw and Katherine (Kay) Reif at Western University, as well as the members of the Western Cold Case Society. Last, but not least, we would like to acknowledge the dedication of our literary agent, Grace Freedson, as well as Steven L. Mitchell, Mark Hall, and the rest of the editorial team at Prometheus Books. We thank them heartily for their support and their recognition of the timely importance of this book.

With thanks,
Michael Arntfield and Marcel Danesi

PROLOGUE: PEN NAMES AND CRIMINAL MINDS

"I say a murder is abstract. You pull the trigger and after that you do not understand anything that happens."
—Jean-Paul Sartre, *Dirty Hands*, 1948, English version
(London: Rutledge, 2015), act 5, scene 2

In July 2016, a spate of viral videos quickly came to pervade the online world, simultaneously replayed on an endless loop reel on all global television newscasts and on nearly every portable screen conceivable. The images were visceral and kindled already-simmering tensions between the police and the African American community in the United States, tensions which were later transferred to the public at large. The provocative footage was amateur, to say the least, and it depicted the often questionable and at times incendiary sights and sounds of young and usually unarmed black men being shot and killed by (usually white) police officers. Amidst the controversy and escalating rallies, protests, and divisive rhetoric in every major city in America that followed, not to mention the retaliatory ambush and murder of five police officers in Dallas that same month, a deeply troubled US Marine Corps veteran named Gavin Long made a one-way trip to Baton Rouge, Louisiana, with the intention of getting even. He began the over 700-mile trek in a stolen rental car from his hometown of Kansas City, Missouri, within days of the mass murder of officers in Dallas and with the intent to up the ante, hoping to start what he called a "revolution."

Long likely had no idea that he followed in the line of countless deranged killers before him, with their empty platitudes of "revolution" and "rebellion" to justify their cowardly crimes. Not coincidently, many of these same killers, like Long, were failed writers of one kind or another. The difference is that Long's murders, like his accompanying manifestos, would go on to mark a disturbing turning point in the historical link between murder and the written word—between murderers and storytellers—and even of murderers themselves *as* storytellers.

On the morning of July 17, after having scouted the city of Baton Rouge for several days, Long finally set out on his mission to hunt down and murder the city's police officers at random. He is not the first cop killer to embark on such a hate-fueled, seek-and-destroy mission; nor is he the first deranged and disaffected malcontent to go to war against the state with the intention of indiscriminately aiming and shooting at any uniform to cross his path. He is, however, likely the first to integrate these into a larger story—a serialized arc traversing numerous media formats and dating back to earlier events otherwise unrelated to his final showdown.

It's a twisted story that began years earlier and one that took Long on a cross-country journey to Baton Rouge because of its symbolic importance to an unconscious narrative of revenge and of perceived redemption. It's the same city where, less than two weeks earlier on July 5, a black man named Anton Sterling was shot and killed by local law enforcement, touching off widespread international condemnation once footage of the shooting was made public. That same footage and the story it told was the justification Long had been waiting for, the catalyst he felt could be used to give his own story a convenient ending—one that made sense. Like most self-proclaimed and ill-fated "revolutions," however, the police officers later targeted that fateful morning had nothing to do with the earlier shooting of Sterling. In fact, one of the officers ambushed by Long was black himself, and by all accounts—like the other two victims that day—an exemplary officer and humane person.

In the end, Long attacked and murdered three officers who were simply in the wrong place at the wrong time, two with the already-besieged Baton Rouge PD and another patrolman with the East Baton Rouge Parish Sheriff's Department. Long was eventually killed by SWAT officers who had been on standby amidst recent unrest, and who arrived in short time to the scene before Long could kill any additional victims. Long died in a hail of gunfire and, no doubt in his mind, went out in a proverbial blaze of glory. It was the punctuation mark on a deranged life defined by equally deranged stories—a life constructed through fantasy and fiction and one that left no shortage of clues that he was teetering on the edge—clues that went, as usual, unnoticed by the experts. Prior to the killing spree, he had adopted the pseudonym Cosmo Ausar Setepenra—likely an acronym or anagram—and claimed affiliation with a variety of groups, some of which are recognized political factions while others are what have been historically described as "imagined communities," some of which we will discuss later. Long's alias was, however, more than just a garden-variety nickname. It was, in fact, his *pen* name.

Known as a *nom de plume* in literature, the adoption of a pen name by a killer has become a significant phenomenon, crossing over from the literary domain to the criminal one. In his hack writing endeavors, the divorced, unemployed, and overmedicated cop killer, Long constructed a literary alter ego. Having self-published a series of nonsensical books about mysticism and spiritualism through Amazon's CreateSpace print-on-demand service under his pen name, as well as a series of online essays in which he discussed rambling topics ranging from race to masculinity, Long saw himself as a self-avowed literary-intellectual celebrity. A more-detailed manifesto about the murders he was planning, including what he saw as a secret civil war between "good cops" and "bad cops," was later sent to an amateur rap artist whose own self-promotional materials published to the Internet apparently drew Long's fatuous admiration, and who, as a mutual online pseudo-celebrity himself, ultimately and unwittingly became the administrator of Long's last will and testament—the custodian of his story of murder.[1]

The complete materials contained in Long's manifesto have not at the time of writing this book—thankfully—been made public. Long's extant collection of written materials does, however, reveal a perverted sense of himself as a literary genius. Long's case is not exceptional. As we discovered in researching for this book, it is rather common.

Over two thousand miles north of Baton Rouge, in the tiny water-tower town of Woodstock, Ontario, Canada, a fifty-nine-year-old registered nurse named Elizabeth (Bette) Wettlaufer was uploading and curating the poem "Inevitable" to the open-access wiki site allpoetry.com under the pen name Betty Weston, while Gavin Long was planning his massacre of law-enforcement officers. In her awkward stanzas that discussed how a "heart beats then sprays" while "the victim pays," Wettlaufer was in effect leaving a poetic transcript of the eight elderly patients she would soon be arrested and charged with murdering over a ten-year period while working in area nursing homes.[2] As Canada's first known "Angel of Death" healthcare serial killer, Wettlaufer wrote the dark poetry from the perspective of a psychopathic serial killer over the course of her nursing career, which stood in stark contrast with her seemingly harmless and frumpish exterior. It was a banal façade that concealed a murderous rage, one that she was compelled to release on her helpless and bedridden elderly victims on the one hand and through the writing—and anonymous publication—of junk poetry on the other. Indeed, mass murderers, terrorists, and serial killers alike, regardless of education or literacy level, all demonstrate a consistent narrative impulse to both document and rationalize their grisly crimes. Yet this linkage between writing and murder has, until now, undergone very little expert scrutiny or analysis. In a digital world where all things vapid and vexatious rule, where the bizarre and often crass written content perpetrated by countless troubled people pollutes nearly every online forum, we are almost desensitized to the type of foreboding and deranged material that Long and Wettlaufer thought they were publishing as literature under their respective pseudonyms. Whether these writings served as progenitors and disinhibitors to the murders they committed, whether Long's failure as a commercial writer somehow accelerated his descent into homicidal madness, or whether his pen name, like Wettlaufer's, somehow allowed his already-disordered mind to turn him into something more than he really was, will likely never be known for certain. What is for certain is that the Internet and countless social-media platforms draw killers like Long and Wettlaufer to them, providing a truly discerning source for understanding their crimes. Now, while the digital writings of today serve as detailed road maps to criminal intent, the pen name—the killer as celebrity author—dates back to much earlier times.

Consider what is arguably the most infamous homicidal pen name on record: Jack the Ripper. There is no question that the heinous murders and mutilations attributed to the killer or killers known as Jack the Ripper in the East London slum district of Whitechapel in late 1888 actually occurred. The problem is that it is principally a set of letters that embedded the Ripper story into the popular imagination. In other words, the Ripper letters served to establish a public expectation that serial killers should enter into a correspondence with a larger audience. As it turns out, they created a mythology about serial killers, one that, as we will argue in the second chapter, has little grounding in reality.

The Ripper story as it is known today is rooted in the wrongful assumption that the murders in Whitechapel abruptly stopped by the end of 1888. In fact, it is that one key element of the Ripper myth around which every theory of the killer's identity has been built; it is also the timeline by which potential suspects have been established. As the saga goes, there were five murdered prostitutes that could be linked to the Ripper—Mary Ann Nichols, Annie Chapman, Elizabeth Stride, Catherine Eddowes, and Mary Jane Kelly. These women, all indigent prostitutes, were indeed slain and defiled in horrific fashion over the course of late 1888, as both the history books and half-baked works of true crime have detailed. However, it is unlikely and actually improbable that they were murdered by a single person, an inconvenient truth that suggests the figure of Jack the Ripper was little more than a literary fabrication of the popular press.

First, Scotland Yard has a total of *eleven*, not five, unsolved cases that to this day constitute the "Whitechapel murders" on file with the Public Record Office. There are likely to be additional murders not documented in the file, corpses found immediately outside the geographic boundary of Whitechapel with indications that a similar modus operandi was used. There are also suggestions, given the escalating nature of the mutilations, that there might be even more victims whose bodies have never been found at all. Furthermore, although the murders began in 1888 and were carried out through 1891, the first two victims, prostitutes Emma Smith and Martha Tabram, have been arbitrarily excluded from the set of Ripper victims for reasons that no one—experts and self-styled pundits alike—seems to ever agree on. This is perhaps because Smith survived her attack long enough to describe her assailant as being not one but two men, a fact that has proven inconvenient for those espousing the lone Ripper theory.

Beyond the role played by false linkages and inconsistent victimologies regarding the Whitechapel murders, the most important factor was, and continues to be, the role played by the media with respect to the communiqués purportedly written by the killer himself. Consider the role of Thomas John Bulling of the British Central News Agency in all this. He was, as it turns out, an opportunist, con artist, and degenerate alcoholic. Amid a burgeoning and hypercompetitive newspaper market where tawdry penny dreadfuls and respectable dailies battled it out, Bulling knew that the working-class British public of 1888 couldn't resist a new breed of crime story—the more lurid and sensational the better. He was also well aware of the popularity of urban legends that were circulating at the time, including the Hammersmith Ghost story between 1803 and 1804, a mysterious apparition reported to have attacked several people in the West London borough of Hammersmith. The reports soon ignited a widespread frenzy that led to armed night patrols scouring the streets in search of the elusive specter. It came to a head one night when a plasterer, covered head-to-toe in white dust from his work, was mistaken for the ghost and shot and killed on sight by an unruly and drunken mob. By the fall of 1888 Bulling would have presumably also known of the legend of Spring-heeled Jack, an uncanny, winged, yet distinctly humanoid creature first reported stalking mothers and their children in 1837, and whose sightings by 1888, while on the wane, were still trickling into the British newspapers. With growing panic and the body count climbing in Whitechapel, Bulling knew that the timing was right and the market primed for a new mass hoax.

With the signature "Jack the Ripper" (no one knows for sure where this pen name came from), Bulling published the first two presumed letters by the killer—the "Dear Boss" letter, postmarked and received September 27, 1888, followed by the "Saucy Jacky" postcard letter on October 1. Both detailed basic facts of the Ripper murders along with an array of cryptic statements. A third letter, popularly known as the "From Hell" letter—which contained a severed piece of what was thought to be a human kidney—was sent on October 15 to a man named George Lusk, head of the Whitechapel Vigilance Committee. A lesser-known note was later sent on October 29 to Dr. Thomas Openshaw, a pathologist at London Hospital. While the first two were clear forgeries concocted by Bulling, the last two remain of unknown origin. Whether written by the killer, by Bulling, or by someone else, they were simply two of the hundreds of known or suspected hoax letters received by the Yard and the London media during that same period of a few months in 1888 when the Ripper hysteria was at its climax. In a similar fashion to what was depicted in a final-season episode of the acclaimed HBO series *The Wire*,[3] where an equally unscrupulous newspaperman concocts a serial-killer myth in modern-day Baltimore by claiming to have received calls from the murderer, Bulling was a desperate man opportunistically taking advantage of a gullible public in order to make a name for himself.

The idea of a single attacker, an elusive "Ripper," fully crystallized in October 1888 when, amidst the public spectacle surrounding the letters, the Yard's forensic pathologist, or police surgeon as he was then known, Dr. Thomas Bond, was asked to provide an opinion on the murders for Assistant Police Commissioner Sir Robert Anderson. Although his opinion was to be based on the wounds found on the five victims, Bond had actually only observed wounds and conducted an autopsy on the most severely mutilated victim, May Jane Kelly. That was in November 1888, while the four other women had been murdered in October; Bond simply reviewed the notes made by others with respect to those earlier victims. His report had been solicited in the hope that it would provide investigators with some sense of whom they were dealing with, in terms of weapon choice, dominant hand, height, and any other useful information based on the verifiable physical evidence. Bond essentially used the opportunity to indulge in some navel-gazing conjecture and wild speculation, underscoring the limited criminological understanding and often crude nature of the forensic science of the period.

In what is generally considered to be the first offender "profile" and psychological mock-up of an unknown suspect created in the modern era, Bond came to the conclusion that all five victims had been killed by the same suspect. Bond used mainly the notes of other pathologists and the forgeries created by Bulling under the Ripper pen name, going on to surmise that the nature of the wounds—the slashing of the women's throats in particular—suggested a right-handed attacker in each case (90 percent of the population today), an attacker of significant physical strength, and an attacker who had used a straight knife of at least six inches in length.[4] But Bond didn't leave it at that. Speculating that the killer was a man of great aplomb, he went on to theorize that the killer would be "neatly and respectably dressed," even during the commission of the crimes. This was in spite of the fact that the impoverished and gang-controlled area where the murders were committed was a place where such a well-dressed society man would not only stand out but also likely be the target of attack himself. Bond additionally hypothesized that the killer was "solitary and eccentric" and hiding in plain sight among "respectable persons" despite having no fixed source of income or stable employment. How he was able to extrapolate such specific and individuating characteristics after examining the bloodied remains of a single victim is still something of a mystery. No one ever got to ask him—Bond threw himself out of a window and plunged to his death a little over a decade later. Yet, today, his flawed 1888 profile lives on to sustain the mythology and related tourist industry around the Ripper case. The legend of a single, mysterious, and meticulously attired killer being responsible for the last five victims in Whitechapel—a respectable but eccentric man leading a double life—in effect validated the hoax letters authored by Bulling and sent to Central News. And so was born the myth of Jack the Ripper as we continue to believe today.

But by the end of November 1888, conventional Ripper lore suggests that the murders stopped as the killer either emigrated to America, went forever into hiding, or else simply died. While there are also scores of other theories ranging from the coincidental to the mostly ludicrous and laughable, the stark reality is that the murders back in Whitechapel and the surrounding area continued well beyond what the myth allowed. In December 1888, Rose Mylett was found strangled in an alley; in July 1889, Alice McKenzie was discovered with her throat slashed ear to ear and with evidence showing that she suffered from nearly identical stab wounds to the abdomen as some—but not all—of the previous victims; in September 1889, an unidentified, mutilated, headless, and dismembered Jane Doe, the "Pinchin Street Torso," was found under a railway arch. The modus operandi, or MO, in the Pinchin Street mutilation also matched three other dismembered victims, at least one from Whitechapel, going back to 1888. Then, in February 1891, prostitute Frances Coles was located, also beneath a nearby railway arch, with her throat cut. The police foot patrol apparently missed the killer by a matter of seconds, thereby preventing any additional postmortem mutilations.

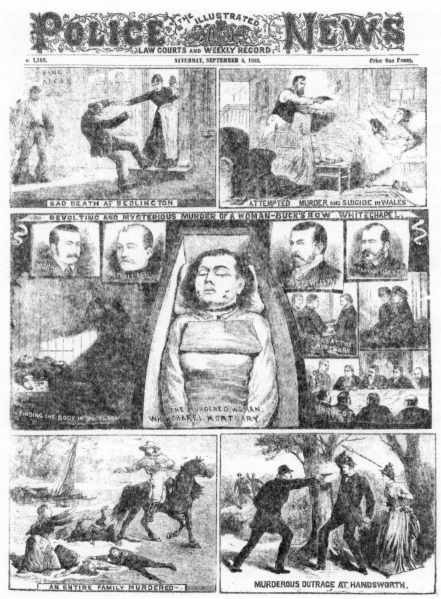

Fig. P.1. A September 1888 edition of the British crime tabloid *Illustrated Police News*, an example of a so-called penny dreadful that luridly glamorized the murders in Whitechapel attributed to Jack the Ripper.

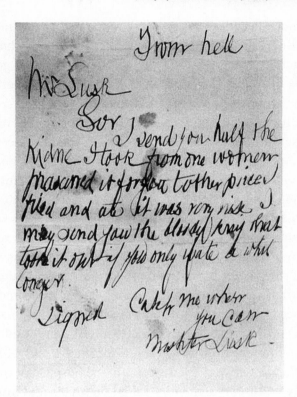

Fig. P.2. The third and arguably the best known of the four purportedly genuine writings sent to the police and press by one or more authors claiming to be Jack the Ripper. The "From Hell" letter depicted here is thought by many to have also been written by sleazy reporter Thomas Bulling, the man who masterminded the scheme to sell newspapers and who likely coined the pen name Jack the Ripper.

Today, Jack the Ripper is less a pen name than it is a contrivance for cultivating a populist hysteria related to serial murder as an industry all its own. There are Ripper walking tours of East London, Ripper paraphernalia—what's known as murderabilia—for sale in stores across England and online. There are Halloween costumes, sports mascots, and media parodies all devoted to the iconography that owes its origin to the pseudoscientific pronouncements made by Dr. Bond in late 1888. Without question, it was in Whitechapel that same year where the construct of murderer as author, as autobiographical raconteur controlling the narrative, emerged for the first time. The question is, why? Why is there a link between murder and narrative—between killing and writing—that seems to be so instinctive, so visceral? Moreover, how might we go on to use the writings of murderers to identify them, to catch them and stop them, as Dr. Thomas Bond first tried to do in vain?

Is there a dominant story to murder? Is there an archetypal narrative and set of literary conventions among specific breeds of murderers that today, with these materials immediately and publicly available in most cases, might allow for the development of predictive modeling—a kind of early-warning system? What would such a model do to the imagination of crime-fiction writers who create stories of murder as cultural artifacts, and what is the relationship between crime fiction and crime as it actually happens in the real world? The stark truth is that while the expectation of the murderer as a storyteller—a self-published author using a pen name—dates to the Ripper hoax, murder as connected to some internal narrative mechanism in the human species dates to antiquity and may actually be hardwired into our DNA, even forming a part of the human brain. People have always used stories to make sense of the world. It is why every culture in prehistory relied on myths and fables—from cave paintings to oral traditions—to explain and rationalize the good, evil, and sheer randomness of their worlds. It is why, as the Aarne-Thompson classification system suggests, there are about 2,500 basic plots and accompanying stories in world history, all of which show up in similar versions across hundreds of disparate language systems—both ancient and modern—and among societies who otherwise have had no direct contact with each other.[5] It suggests that there are only a handful of tale types and motifs that are common to the human imagination, and that everything beyond that is pure imitation. Organizing these myths and legends by number and description, renowned folklorists Antti Aarne and Stith Thompson created what might be described as the periodic table of stories and, in so doing, identified that much of what we today recognize as Disney classics actually existed as fables in several societies simultaneously. "The Sleeping Beauty" (the basis for *Sleeping Beauty*) and the "The Persecuted Heroine/Cruel Relatives-in-Law" (the basis for *Cinderella*) are just two examples of how universal archetypes of consciousness have been realized into specific stories for commercial audiences today. The most common theme in all tales ever told is, not surprisingly, murder. Stories in all languages have attempted to explain it, to rationalize it, to deter it—to try in some sense to come to grips with why it exists in our species in the first place.

Murder dominates the list of the Ten Commandments and the Nielsen Ratings alike. Why do we kill, especially in a world where survival does not depend on killing? Why are we so obsessed with crime dramas on television, most of which involve murder as the main plot device? Why are we constantly seeking to understand murder—psychologically, socially, and morally? Religions, philosophies, and the modern-day criminal sciences have all developed their own perspectives for explaining murder. Yet no single explanatory theory can be found, unless of course we subscribe to a theological interpretation of murder as a deadly sin and its source as evil.

Often, the problem is actually just defining murder. Murder is illegal everywhere, yet *killing* is not. Soldiers "kill" (not murder) for political-military reasons; executioners put prisoners "to death;" in most countries people are allowed to kill in self-defense; and so on. But murder is something totally different. It reverberates with different meanings, one of which is control over others—the Mafia enacts murders as part of its overall strategy of control; terrorists kill for various ideological reasons; some states perpetrate genocide to tailor human populations to their own liking; and so on. As the French biologist Jean Rostand (1894–1977) observed, there is a hidden irony in all this, which he articulates eloquently as follows: "Kill a man, one is a murderer; kill a million, a conqueror; kill them all, a God."[6]

Great writers have also explored murder, from Homer to Shakespeare, Dostoyevsky to Capote. They are the luminaries who have collectively and individually made efforts in their work to understand what it is about murder that fascinates us, what it is that we find so compelling and so alluring. The truth is that the written word has allowed us to penetrate the meaning of murder through the creative mind of the writer, at the same time that it has allowed us to reflect on the human condition. Pop culture has also embraced murder as an entertainment industry, with its many *CSI*-oriented and crime-heavy programs—a zeitgeist that has provided many subtle insights into how we, as a modern society, perceive murder—from "hot" murders vis-à-vis passion killings to "cold" serial murders. Programs like the now-defunct *Dexter* have even introduced a new twist to the Gothic and foundational Jekyll-and-Hyde story of the contemporary murderer, suggesting that we all have the instinct for murder within us—that it is only society's moral strictures that block us from acting on that instinct.

Our fascination with this deadliest of all deadly sins in a secular age may also be due to the fact that murder is still felt to have spiritual consequences in the grand scheme of things. This is the subtext of our book, one that aims to penetrate the raison d'être of murder here and now. Through fictional and semifictional tales alongside the actual words of murderers themselves, we will take a look at murder through two sets of eyes—those of the literary writer and those of the murderer-as-writer. We will look at classic texts about murder from the Bible and the Greek dramatists to current-day novelists such as James Ellroy, Michael Connelly, and Stieg Larsson. Alongside these, we will examine the words of actual killers, thus drafting an overall "tale of murder." We will also take a deliberate and critical look at a comparatively new and powerful platform for murder and its enactment—the Internet. What will we conclude? In the style of a murder mystery, we set this question aside for now, leaving it up to the reader, as in a detective story, to come to his or her own conclusions. But we also offer a road map—a legend of sorts—for the reader to see what hides in plain sight all around us—our collective tale of murder.

We call our approach *literary criminology*—defined as the study of crime through the lens of literature and language.[7] As we have seen in notable cases ourselves as researchers in this field, it is in the words of the murderers that we can get a truly insightful glimpse into the nature of murder and why we as a society have become so engrossed by it—we fear it and loathe it, yet it transfixes us. Literary criminology therefore also includes the study of the puerile and flimsy attempts at creating literature by the murderers themselves. Like narrative medicine, literary criminology is becoming a well-established field[8] used to teach everything from criminal investigative analysis and offender profiling carried out in the field to more abstract ideas like the epistemology of punishment and deterrence. The approach is part of a more general one that we have previously called the "criminal humanities," which, like the medical humanities, also requires the participation of scholar-practitioners with those who have a direct field experience of crime, so as to validate the credibility and sustainability of the approach.

We sincerely hope that the reader will enjoy our trek through the many vicissitudes of murder and what these tell us about the human condition. We have no particular ax to grind intellectually; we genuinely want to get at the truth of the matter. We do not exclude the traditional criminological techniques; we simply intend to supplement them with an approach that is based on a simple psychological hypothesis—the words people use not only reveal their immediate thoughts but also those buried deeply inside. If nothing else, we hope the reader will come out of this with some insights that he or she may not have had previously.

Chapter 1

THE TALE OF MURDER

"The line between thinking murder and doing murder isn't that major."
—Oliver Stone, *World Weekly News*, September 6, 1994

"Then she struck his neck twice with all her might, and cut off his head. Next she rolled his body off the bed and pulled down the canopy from the posts."

Quite a gruesome murder, isn't it? It reads like something plucked from the pages of some lurid crime tabloid, scandal rag, dime novel, or penny dreadful—perhaps something from the Whitechapel "Ripper" era. But as contemporary as the above graphic depiction reads, it actually appeared in the Old Testament. The whole passage is as follows:

> She went to the bedpost near Holofernes' head, and took down his sword that hung there. She came close to his bed, took hold of the hair of his head, and said "Give me strength today, O Lord God of Israel!" Then she struck his neck twice with all her might, and cut off his head. Next she rolled his body off the bed and pulled down the canopy from the posts. Soon afterward she went out and gave Holofernes' head to her maid, who placed it in her food bag. (Judith 13: 6–10).

Tales about murder that mirror the narrative tropes of today's obsession with true crime date to antiquity, from ancient hieroglyphic and cuneiform stories to biblical tales of violence; and they all have diverse meanings etched into them. All species kill instinctively for survival or for territory. Only the human species, however, carries out intentional murders for some reason other than survival—malice, jealousy, financial gain, lust, hatred, revenge, patriotism, a warped sense of justice, gang solidarity, and even pleasure. Victor Coppleson's "rogue shark" hypothesis based on the 1912 Jersey Shore shark attacks on vacationing swimmers, which inspired both the 1974 Peter Benchley novel and subsequent blockbuster film *Jaws*, suggests that some Great White sharks, like the "Jersey Man-Eater," as it became known, might kill humans for sport, rather than for survival. This theory, if true, would imply that murder with malice might actually jump the species line and apply to nonhuman animals as well. Today, Coppleson's theory gets solicitous treatment and generous replay every year as part of Discovery Channel's famed Shark Week, but it has otherwise been widely discredited by science. The truth is that humans are the planet's outliers when it comes to murder. We are, needless to say, also the only species that has the ability to document our experiences associated with murder through the written word.

The Book of Judith is one of the longest standing examples of a murder tale, telling the story of the humiliating defeat of the imperious Assyrians at the hand of Judith, a brave Hebrew woman. Her beheading of the Assyrian general Holofernes, in his own tent and with his own sword, was thus hardly seen as an assassination, much less a criminal act of murder; rather, it was viewed as an act of valiant heroism. Clearly, as this and many other similar tales—both religious and secular alike—emphasize, murder is more than killing, depending on historical context and setting. Murderers can, in fact, be perceived and portrayed either as villains or as heroes. There is no one single tale of murder. It all depends on who, where, when, and why murder is committed and, most important, who gets to tell the story—and how he or she does so. Some stories are told in courts of law as prosecutors and defense attorneys grapple for control of the master narrative, which may or may not reflect an accurate and truthful account of events. Others are told in our many modern arenas of spectacle, from the commercial press to the theatrical stage and even the Internet. Some are told by the murderers themselves, who chronicle their versions of events so that their actions might find some legitimacy and social meaning—some carry-forward value as parables or cautionary tales to others. In all cases, though, the murder of another human being evokes a powerful emotional reaction in everyone, from writer to reader. The only thing to conclude at this early point is that murder is, for some mysterious reason, an intrinsic part of the human condition.

We begin our trek on the meandering trail to understanding murder by looking first at various stories and accounts of murder. The study of crime, typically relegated to traditional schools of criminology and their proponents past and present, often turns out to be pedantic and proscriptive—with few real implications for understanding the role of murder in human life. In fact, the self-avowed experts in crime and violence populating various academic and media circles are, in many cases, individuals who have had little or no field experience, nor any direct exposure to violence, victims, or offenders, fiddling with dated statistics or artificially collecting data that do little more than muddy the waters. We intend to use a "humanistic" approach instead, as mentioned in the prologue, examining murder stories in the same manner as a literary critic might analyze novels or plays—that is, by critically analyzing murder as a narrative performance. Our perspective, as pointed out, is known as literary criminology, or the study of murder through texts about murder. The Book of Judith is therefore an ideal starting point; it is a perfect example of how this kind of approach unfolds hypothetically. Modern-day scholars view Judith's narrative as a historical romance written for didactic purposes, that is, as a story imparting some historical and/or moral lesson, not as factual reportage on an ancient heroic murder. Its author is unknown and actually seems to have skirted around several historical facts about the real incident upon which the story is based. But this is irrelevant to those who read it in the context of patriotism and liberation from domination. Such a

reading leads, conversely, to the inescapable conclusion that, sometimes, we perceive murder as justifiable, legitimized by what we now
term "mitigating circumstances." As Richard Slotkin, a noted historian of the Old West, puts it, the context of a narrative "can help us
make sense of the history we have lived and the place we are living
in,"[1] regardless of whether that narrative is fact or fiction.

A literary criminological approach is all about how factors such
as history, cultural interpretation, and modes of storytelling overlap
with biological instincts and psychopathic traits—disordered and
dangerous frames of mind. We will not ignore the scientific facts.
Indeed, we believe that science and the humanities have been artificially separated for too long, especially in the study of crime.
We need them both to gain meaningful insights into a horrific life-
denying act that has, in many ways, driven both the great plots of
history and the plots that make up everyday life.

WHAT IS MURDER?

Murder isn't easy to define. It is not equivalent to killing (as briefly
discussed). Taking a human life is not always defined as murder. This
is why so many types, or more accurately "degrees," of murder are
distinguished in America and throughout the Commonwealth legal
system of the western world. Also, calling murder a "crime" is a comparatively modern practice. In medieval society, murder was perceived as one of the seven deadly sins, a moral failing that seriously
interfered with living a spiritual life committed to God. As the role of
religion in everyday life started declining by the outset of the Renaissance, sins started being recast as crimes, both legally and socially.

But crime did not become instantly immune to moral interpre-
tations (or more exactly misinterpretations). In the not-too-distant
past, women were accused, convicted, and punished for practicing
witchcraft, since it was seen as being a corollary of devil worship
and black magic. Under this interpretive rubric, an estimated five

hundred thousand people in Europe—mostly women—were burned alive at the stake between the fifteenth and seventeenth centuries alone. Now, while the theological explanation that murder was a manifestation of evil forces at work in corrupting the soul, in a secular world criminologists would explain it variously as the effect of mental dysfunction, an impulse-control disorder, the result of an aberrant upbringing, and so on. But the sense that murder is a transgression of some moral code has not disappeared. It continues to prevail even among modern societies.

The relation between sin and crime was explored brilliantly in the 1995 film *Se7en*, which details the hunt for a Los Angeles serial killer of the mission-oriented subtype (as we shall see), and who both models and rationalizes his crimes on the seven deadly sins, each grisly slaying intending to serve as a warning to a decadent world that has become morally relativistic, interpreting sins solely in clinical terms. The final scene is about (literally) the deadliest of all sins—wrath—as the lead detective summarily executes the suspect in retaliation for the murder of his own wife. A similar tale of the relation between sin and crime is found in the 1990 film *Mister Frost*, about a serial murderer who presents himself to the police and society as the devil incarnate, engaging in a brilliant philosophical dialogue about morality with a psychiatrist who, by the end, starts to believe that he may indeed be who he claims to be. As these films suggest, the act of murder defies all secular or rational explanations, whether the narrative is contoured by the killer or by society at large.

It was in the eighteenth century that the western (secular) view of murder began to move away from spiritual or moralistic evaluations toward psychological-sociological ones. At that time, jurist William Blackstone put forth a definition of murder that has shaped our modern view of it ever since. Murder occurs, Blackstone wrote, "when a person, of sound memory and discretion, unlawfully kills any reasonable creature in being under the king's peace, with malice aforethought, either express or implied."[2] Although we might read the language and some of the details as being somewhat antiquated today, it enfolds several tenets that are part of our contemporary definition and view of murder, including the notions of malice and aforethought. But despite all attempts to define it, murder still remains a slippery notion, having been part of everything from patriotic strategy (as we have seen) to a brutal act to satisfy sexually deviant urges. There can be no one definition or theory of murder just as there can be no one tale. Most other crimes, such as robbery or fraud, might have a conspicuous socioeconomic motivation. However, murder seems to transcend any attempt to constrain it to any single or dominant social-theoretical paradigm. While our goal here is hardly to pontificate on the causes and origins of murder per se, as others with various motives and with equally varying accuracy have done, it is important nonetheless to make some specific technical and legal distinctions as we move forward to discuss how the *act* of murder and the *tale* of murder cross-pollinate each other.

Intent is what principally distinguishes murder legally from other acts of killing. Modern law, as mentioned, differentiates between degrees of intentional murder, as opposed to manslaughter, defined instead as unintentional killing, however reckless or unsympathetic. Most criminal and penal codes across the United States and other western nations are based on British common law, discriminating between two degrees of murder. The first is defined as a deliberate, premeditated act to cause the death of a human being; and the second, as any intentional act causing someone's death without such premeditation or deliberation. There are, however, some notable exceptions. Most jurisdictions in the United States classify a homicide that occurs during the commission of another felony as first-degree murder by default, even though premeditation is absent. In some states, any behavior that is imminently dangerous to others, such as throwing an incendiary device into a crowd or a brick off of a rooftop causing death, is also classified as first-degree murder. Prosecution for murder—a felony—is by indictment, and the maximum punishment in some states is death by execution, carrying out a contemporary biblical eye-for-an-eye form of retributive justice, as well as one that harkens back to the role of frontier justice in shaping the fabric of the American courts. In other circumstances, if an act of killing is seen as "necessary," it is sometimes described as justifiable homicide. Examples include killing someone in self-defense or in a fit of provoked anger. The latter can also be classified, more specifically, as voluntary manslaughter. If death results from reckless driving, on the other hand, the offense is generally known as involuntary manslaughter. Contentious "stand your ground" laws adopted recently by various states—a modern iteration of the medieval "castle doctrine" perspective—represent yet another example where homicide is deemed permissible.

Judith's murder of a ruthless tyrant would hardly be read, even with today's eyes, as a transgression of another's right to live or the unlawful killing of a reasonable creature, as Blackstone postulated. But had Judith killed the Assyrian general as an act of vengeful retribution for, say, infidelity, it would be perceived differently as a more commonplace form of murder for revenge—a common iteration of what is now known as a *personal-cause* homicide. This suggests that morality might itself be a contextually variable and a historically relative measure of right and wrong. John Wilkes Booth, Jack Ruby, and Timothy McVeigh all considered themselves patriots and as having acted morally and even righteously. Society disagreed, viewing them as assassins, traitors, or terrorists. In that same vein, the self-proclaimed New Year's Gang—a group of domestic terrorists who blew up a collegiate building (Sterling Hall) at the University of Wisconsin–Madison in 1970, as a protest against the university's research affiliation with the military during the Vietnam War—went on the run as wanted murderers. However, with the passage of time, three of the four bombers ended up returning to Madison as prodigal sons widely acclaimed as "student combatants." Evidently, how we decipher an act of killing—the meaning of murder—is really a matter of context, of subjective interpretation. It all depends on the timing, the target, the reason, the provocation, and who tells the story.

Our fascination with the chameleonlike nature of murder has

led to legions of books, websites, scholarly treatises, and now even an online encyclopedia—a type of macabre kissing cousin to *Wikipedia*—known as *Murderpedia* that feeds our instinctive and insatiable need to know as much as possible about our deadly acts and those who carry them out. Bank robberies, Ponzi schemes, and even serious sexual assaults garner very little, if any, of the attention that murder gets, online or elsewhere. With the exception of what are sometimes known as "caper films" that depict high-stakes heists (*Ocean's Eleven*, *The Sting*, and so on), which are throwbacks to the socially destructive force of robbery in the Old West, there is really no other crime—in fact, no other subject matter—that has inspired as many commercial films in contemporary cinema as murder has. Since the early 1980s, when the expression "serial killer" became a household term, with its particular definition and policing mandate, the number of slasher films glorifying serialized murder grew by an extraordinary measure, with a 600 percent growth in murder-oriented films over the subsequent two decades.[3] On television, crimes like bookmaking and extortion have no ongoing series of their own. Murder does. In fact, it might be argued that murder, and by extension all true crime, is resuscitating television as a medium. From documentary serials such as *Dateline* to *Making a Murderer*, *The Jinx*, *O.J.: Made in America*, along with the rise of cable network channels, such as Identification Discovery and Crime & Investigation, that are committed almost exclusively to the subject of homicide, murder is arguably engendering television's renaissance—and its transformation from appliance to art form.

Statistics are often used to develop theories of murder. We will use them as well throughout this book, doing so sparingly and always in context. In themselves, statistics are mere tools for drafting any realistic theory (or tale) of murder. That is to say, they can be used to supplement any decipherment of the underlying story of murder. They can be viewed as telling a kind of implicit tale about murder, providing an empirical inroad to understanding why this act rejects the simplistic "one size fits all" theories that have been historically espoused by criminologists, politicians, and policy makers. Murder reaches deeper into the human psyche than other types of crime, often defying rational explanation, much less statistical compartmentalization. The FBI has broken down murder into four distinct categories for the purpose of assessing principal motive—the personal-cause homicide (revenge, avarice, jealously); the group-cause homicide (furthering or protecting the interests of a conspiracy, cult, cell, and so on); the sexual homicide (killing to satisfy disordered sexual desires and twisted fantasies); and the criminal-enterprise homicide (killing on official order from, or in service to, an organized crime group or other syndicate). These are useful, of course, but they provide us with only a general causative framework for penetrating any underlying cause of murder.[4] It is an important starting point, nonetheless.

MOTIVES FOR MURDER

All murders upset the social order, producing a temporary sense of emotional chaos or imbalance. In many cases, where innocent victims are involved, we empathize with the loved ones who are left behind. TV programs, in fact, provide a public platform and electronic locus for grief to be expressed. The judicial system later steps in to restore the balance through systemic punishment of the murderer, from long-term incarceration to execution. In premodern societies, such punishments were frequently meted out by the affected kinship group. If someone murdered, for instance, an uncle, then it was up to a member of the family to enact their preferred brand of justice and closure through a retributive form of punishment. The same kind of thinking underlies the rationale for the murders perpetrated by gangs and criminal organizations. "Getting even" is a basic strategy for righting the emotional imbalance created by murder.

In all cases and at all times throughout history, *killing* is seen as a fact of life, *murder* as something anomalous. The Aztecs believed that regular offerings of blood to the sun god Huitzilopochtli were necessary to enlist his protection; otherwise, they believed, he would destroy them. In the nineteenth century, vendetta was part of the legal code in Corsica and other Mediterranean locales. It required family members to kill anyone who wronged the family honor. Vendetta is central to the operation of Mafia and gang culture generally.[5] It reflects what Paul Lunde, a preeminent expert on Islamic literature and symbols, calls "a pan-Mediterranean ideal of manhood, going back to the ancient Stoic tradition of ancient Greece and Rome," which is bound up "with the larger category of *onore* ('honor')."[6] The code demands a retributive killing against anyone who dishonors a Mafioso or his family. The true "man" must defend family honor—no exceptions. In such communal environments, the killing of the person who has defiled that honor is hardly considered an act of homicide.

Analogously, the murder of a child, a pregnant woman, or a police officer, or one motivated by ethnic or racial hatred, invariably elicits in all of us a similar demand for retributive justice—it provokes blood lust in even the most benign and restrained of people. Anthropologist René Girard saw the revenge killing as an "inevitable exchange" in various societies.[7] These had surrogate victims whose lives and deaths represented communal interests and values—they were surrogates, like a police officer as a reflection of the community he or she serves, of entire populations. Whether through tragedy or sacrifice, surrogates could be killed to restore balance through the laying of blame and the subsequent punishment (typically execution) of a ritual victim, whether it be the genuine culprit or simply a patsy. This cycle of killing, from surrogate victim to ritual victim, in turn became something integral and even sacred to a society that required that death beget death, blood beget blood.

Overall, as we will argue, we tend to perceive the murderer as a character in some ongoing narrative (a tale of murder) while the murderer, as we explain ahead, also inevitably identifies his or her victims as characters in a deranged unconscious story that he or she has concocted. Murder is the extrinsic manifestation of the story's plot. We will develop this notion subsequently. For now, let's look at various categories for classifying murder, found typically in the criminological and police literature:

passion and revenge murder: betrayal, dishonor, envy, jealousy, and any kind of "getting even" killing (as, for example, the murder of a cheating spouse or lover by the one offended and hurt by the betrayal—a common topic on reality crime TV programs);

planned murder: gang killings, assassinations, contract killings (as, for example, those by the cold-blooded Mafia hit man Richard Kuklinski, known as the Iceman, who kept his violent profession a secret from his own family[8]);

ideologically based hate murder: mass murders, genocide, and any killing where hatred of a specific group is the trigger (as, for example, the murders that characterized the Holocaust);

ritual murders: such as those of some serial killers, and some gang murders (such as the serial murders of Ted Bundy and the gangland murders of the 1930s and 1940s, respectively, to be discussed subsequently);

cause murders: whereby the murderer sees his or her act as part of some greater cause; this includes the murders perpetrated by suicide bombers and any individual or group who carries out murder in the name of some cause (as, for example, the murders perpetrated for reasons of survival, as portrayed by the fictional film The Purge, in which the government sanctions an annual twelve-hour murder spree to allow our instinctive need for killing a legal outlet);

thrill murders: murders committed to satisfy a disordered need for attention or pleasure seeking, or to fulfill a dangerous restlessness generally indicative of psychopathy (as, for example, the murder committed by Dinh Bowman of Seattle, dubbed a "student of murder," who killed an innocent motorist in 2012 just for the thrill of experiencing the act of murder and how it would feel to get away with it[9]);

cover-up murders: committed by a perpetrator to cover up some other major crime, such as rape, so that he will not be caught (as, for example, in the rape and murder of seven-year-old Megan Kanka by her neighbor, Jesse K. Timmendequas (a sex offender) in 1994, who killed her to cover up his rape; the case led to Megan's Law, which makes it obligatory for law-enforcement authorities to make information available to the public about registered sex offenders[10]);

pathological murders: committed by psychopaths, sexual sadists, and other deranged individuals suffering from a major personality disorder who have no empathy for their victims (as, for example, the serial murders of deranged psychopath Richard Ramirez—discussed subsequently—who apparently killed his victims for the thrill of it);

control murders: murders enacted to control someone, as in certain kinds of serial murders where the murderer desires to exert control over his or her victims (as, for example, the case of Jeffrey Dahmer—also to be discussed—who desired to gain control over his victims' bodies);

bravado murders: killing in order to prove oneself to someone, such as the killings carried out by peers in gangs as part of initiation rites (as is typical for many factions of the Mafia and similar organizations);

fame murders: murder as a means of gaining fame or notoriety (as, for example, the fictitious murders portrayed in the movie *Natural Born Killers*);

vigilante murders: murder by citizens who take the law into their own hands or to pursue an ideological cause (as for example, the case of the New York Subway shooter Bernhard Goetz, discussed below, whose actions were remarkably reminiscent of those of Charles Bronson in the *Death Wish* movie franchise, based on a pre-Giuliani crime-plagued New York City);

infanticide: murder of a child by a parent or caregiver; or else the practice of killing unwanted children soon after birth (as in the famous case of Celine Lesage, who admitted to strangling two of her children with a cord and choking four others between 2000 and 2007 in Cherbourg, France[11]);

femicide or *uxoricide*: killing of a female spouse or paramour because she has betrayed her male partner; or simply the killing of women because they are women (as in the case of the East London murder of Mumtahina Jannat by her abusive husband, Abdul Kadir, in 2011, after having become enraged by her independence[12]).

Killing a spouse or paramour for cheating, betrayal, or even just hatred is one of the most recurring motives seen in both popular culture (such as on reality TV crime programs) and the historical record on murder. In Roman law, daughters and their lovers who committed adultery could be killed by their fathers; the law also permitted a cuckolded husband to murder an adulterous wife's lover. Most of the episodes of true-crime television programs reflect this historical reality and ongoing psychological and emotional fixation we have with uxoricide. Films and television luridly depict these crimes of passion, not only blurring the lines between fact and fiction, but also highlighting the marketability of the cause murder in in the popular imagination—perhaps because it hits close to home in many cases. The Identification Discovery series *Fatal Vows* salaciously depicts marriages that end in murder; *Scorned: Love Kills* is about love triangles that also end up in murder; and *Wicked Attraction* is about murders committed by two people as a pair who are usually in a romantic relationship. What is most interesting is that these series, like their prime-time antecedents on conventional network television, still follow a storytelling blueprint known as "Poe's template," in reference to American crime and horror writer Edgar Allan Poe, the father of the narrative treatment of murder, and arguably the inventor of true crime as a cultural narrative.

In his 1842 short story *The Mystery of Marie Rogêt*, Poe presented a semifictionalized account of the murder of a young Parisian socialite named Marie Rogêt, who is a rather transparent stand-in for a real woman named Mary Rogers, herself murdered in New York City a year prior and in identical fashion to Poe's fictionalized murder. Perhaps the first example of a story for mass audience consumption that has been "ripped from the headlines" (as the crime series *Law & Order* would later distinguish itself in its promotional materials), Poe's narrative is essentially a roman à clef—a true story or biographical work disguised as fiction—with Poe outlining the details of a murder that, while still officially unsolved, was widely believed to be the work of a jilted lover who later committed suicide.[13] The main elements of the narrative treatment (known as Poe's template) include: the "body drop" (the revelation of the corpse or other evidence of death); the "summons" (investigators arriving at the scene); the "lineup" (where family and friends react to the death and offer leads and theories); the "rewind" (the facts of the case are recapped through procedural details); the "reveal" (the killer's identity is uncovered); the "encounter with evil" (the killer speaks about his crime and his motives are revealed); and the "restoration" (life returns to normal, even if briefly).[14]

Many of the characters in programs or productions using Poe's template today are common, involving everyday people engaged in high-stakes love triangles, betrayals, and related financial entanglements—murders that would have been interpreted, in the past, as being motivated by the deadly sins of adultery and greed. Those that involve celebrities either as victims or perpetrators, again drawing on Poe's template (which can be considered a nineteenth-century equivalent of a reality-television script), will invariably create heightened interest and media sensationalism. Examples range from the Aaron Hernandez, Oscar Pistorius, and O. J. Simpson cases as murder stories transformed into tales about fallen heroes, to the brutal murder of NFL star quarterback Steve "Air" McNair, shot and killed in his Nashville apartment by his girlfriend on Independence Day 2009 before she later turned the gun on herself.[15]

Mafia hit man Richard Kuklinski, on the other hand, best exemplifies murder by a third party, thereby changing both the narrative format and the motive—murder for hire. Kuklinski was nicknamed the Iceman because he often froze his victims in order to obscure the time of their deaths. After being apprehended in 1986, the ruthless hit man gave media interviews, bragging about his exploits. He lived a double life, hiding his gruesome profession from his family, who remained oblivious to his true vocation while he carried out his heinous acts. The persona of the professional hit man has great appeal in pop culture, as can be seen by the proliferating film depictions that have become highly influential across other media, including *The Day of the Jackal* (1973), *Prizzi's Honor* (1985), *Pulp Fiction* (1994), *Desperado* (1995), and *No Country for Old Men* (2007), just to name a few.

Ideologically based hatred murders include everything from the mass killings of coworkers, caused by feelings of revenge, to the calculating Beltway sniper murders of 2002 perpetrated by someone— John Allen Muhammad, executed in Virginia in 2009—who had an intrinsic hatred of all humanity.[16] Some murders, such as the senseless one of twenty-four-year-old Daniel Zamudio in 2012, are particularly poignant and unsettling.[17] Zamudio was attacked, tortured for hours, and eventually beaten to death in downtown Santiago, Chile, simply because he was gay. His murder has become symbolic of the hate crimes committed against homosexuals across the globe. Indeed, such homophobic murders reveal an often dangerous undercurrent of anger among those rallying against models of living that are felt to "bring down the moral order." Restoring order in this case has a perverted twist to it.

Ritual murders are routinely highlighted in films and documentaries about serial killers, which we will discuss in detail in the next chapter. Such murders have always existed beyond the context of contemporary serial murder, from sacrificial killings to those that function as initiation rites for those entering criminal gangs. In the latter case, the murder marks a criminal's entry into a new life—a violent metamorphosis and a type of crossing over galvanized through violence. To be eligible for acceptance into the Mafia, for example, the initiate might have to participate in a killing, a process known as "making bones." The initiate may then be asked to attend a special meeting of the clan. After answering the clan's questions successfully, the process of being "made" in the mold of a virile Mafia warrior is complete. And then a new chapter begins.

Murder for an ideological or self-styled heroic cause returns us to the origins of human history, as we saw with the story of Judith at the start of this chapter. Sometimes the cause is purely in the head of the individual, not part of a social mind-set such as patriotism. The best-known novelization of this type of murder is Fyodor Dostoyevsky's iconic magnum opus, *Crime and Punishment* (1866). The novel's protagonist, Rodion Romanovich Raskolnikov, by murdering an innocent victim, attempts to shake people out of the spiritual lethargy of their banal, repetitive, and unexamined lives. So, he decides to kill a friendly old woman, but, regrettably, he also has to murder her half sister, who happened to arrive at the crime scene by chance. Soon after, Raskolnikov becomes despondent and physically ill, remaining in his room in a semiconscious state for days. He goes out only to read about his crime in the newspapers. In a qualm of conscience, he then confesses to Sonya, a young woman with whom he had become close. After ultimately surrendering to the authorities and being sentenced to eight years in a Siberian prison, he begins his spiritual rebirth with Sonya's support, becoming aware that murder is a transgression of the human spirit, not an antidote to social ennui. Just before the publication of *Crime and Punishment*, Dostoevsky had written another masterpiece, *Notes from the Underground* (1864). The protagonist of that story begins the narrative by proclaiming: "I am a sick man. I am a spiteful man. I am an unattractive man."[18] The same sense of worthlessness, or alienation, is what motivates Raskolnikov to kill in *Crime and Punishment*, emphasizing the senselessness of murder—literally.

The Unabomber, former mathematics professor Theodore Kaczynski, is a Raskolnikov-type figure—an ideologically motivated serial killer who committed murder not to shake humans out of their spiritual lethargy but to punish the moguls of technology and thus to teach us all a moral lesson about the dangers of industrial society. Kaczynski was a lone anti-technology fanatic, a veritable neo-Luddite, who mailed and planted bombs from the late 1970s to the mid-1990s targeting specific victims, mostly university-level computer researchers and airline executives (hence "UN-A," a blend of *university* and *airline*) in order to wake people up from their indifference toward what he saw as the abiding dangers posed to human freedom by technology. On April 24, 1995, he sent a letter to the *New York Times* promising "to desist from terrorism" if either the *Times* or the *Washington Post*, America's two official newspapers of record, published his manifesto, "Industrial Society and Its Future." In the rambling 35,000-word screed, Kaczynski argued that his campaign of letter bombings was extreme but necessary—a righteous "revolution"—to draw attention to the erosion of liberty that had come about as a result of the rise of modern technologies. The manifesto was published, and it was Kaczynski's own brother who recognized the idiosyncrasies of the writing style and its ideological contents as being consistent with those of the troubled Theodore. He subsequently alerted the FBI, who found a reclusive Kaczynski holed up in a one-room Montana cabin and living in squalor. The official UNABOM Task Force assembled by the FBI had been completely unaware of his existence previously, much less considered him a suspect. His published essay, however, changed that. It also served as a harbinger of how future crimes should and would be assessed—and also how murderers would come to identify themselves—namely, through writing.

Thrill murders have always existed, such as the brutal and genocidal killings perpetrated by Vlad the Impaler, who ruled in Transylvania in the fifteenth century, impaling his enemies seemingly for the thrill of it. More recently, infamous cases of thrill kills include one committed on October 4, 2009, by Steven Spader, who, along with Christopher Gribble, murdered a mother and severely maimed her young daughter during a home invasion in Mont Vernon, New Hampshire. Both victims were viciously slaughtered with a machete simply for the excitement of it, as was later admitted by the remorseless murderers themselves.[19]

Fig. 1.1. A preliminary and later widely parodied composite sketch by the FBI of the Unabomber, based on a lone witness description of a "suspicious" male observed delivering a package at a US Post Office.

NOT THIS ONE...   THIS ONE!!!

Fig. 1.2. The FBI booking photo of the actual Unabomber, Dr. Ted Kaczynski, who had been living in the Montana hinterland and writing his manifesto for several years prior to the composite sketch in fig. 1.1. The dichotomy between the two public images remains a key point of contention about the accuracy and investigative viability of both composite sketching and eyewitness descriptions.

The most iconic fictional tale of thrill murder is likely the 1994 film, *Natural Born Killers*, directed by Oliver Stone, which depicts two young serial killers who become celebrities, thanks in large part to the sensationalistic press coverage of their murder spree of fifty-two people. The film suggests that the source of the serial-killer phenomenon in the modern world is a culture of violence that breeds a lack of respect for moral structures. The rise of mass and serial murderers may indeed be connected to the influence of the mass media on human behavior. Stone's film is one part portrait of the criminal mind, one part cultural satire and moral condemnation. There is little doubt that the two killers are psychotic rather than psychopathic, a trait more common among mass murderers than serial murderers and one of countless errors of nomenclature in the film, but so too are, in some sense, the media who glorify them. Ironically, though perhaps not surprisingly, the film has inspired a number of copycat thrill killings. The most famous was no doubt the case of bottom-feeding and drug-addled couple Sarah Edmonson and Benjamin Darras, who drank LSD and watched the film several times before going out and shooting victims at random soon after.[20] The same film was apparently also a spark for the Columbine massacre that claimed the lives of thirteen high-school students in Littleton, Colorado, in 1999, as the phrase "going NBK" (*Natural Born Killers*) appeared in the journal entries of shooters Eric Harris and Dylan Klebold and was used as their shared cipher to describe their rampage while it was still in the planning stages, as will be discussed later on.

Cover-up murders, along with pathological, bravado, and control murders, need little elaboration here. The former are committed to hide some other crime, such as rape; pathological murders are carried out by psychopaths who may have a clinically diagnosable psychological disorder (these will be discussed subsequently). Bravado murders occur almost exclusively at the hands of members of gangs and criminal cliques who feel that they have to prove their mettle or manhood by killing someone for whatever senseless reason they might conjure up. Lastly, control murders are perpetrated by sadists, typically psychopaths, who need to exert power over others; the need is especially evident in many subtypes of serial murder.

Another motive that has now become a topic of interest among both criminologists and pop culture theorists alike is murder as a means of staking a claim to fame. The murderers in this case are looking to get their "fifteen minutes of fame," as Andy Warhol famously put it.[21] As we shall see, a great number of serial killers, showing no qualms of conscience, admitted during interviews that fame was their principal motive for murder.

The vigilante killer, such as the aforementioned Bernhard Goetz, is someone seeking to take justice into his or her own hands. Goetz came to be known as the Subway Vigilante after shooting four young men on the New York Subway as they were allegedly trying to mug him. Although none of them died, Goetz was charged with, and found guilty of, attempted murder. The case sparked a national debate on race and crime, since the young men were African Americans and Goetz was white. Yet Goetz later consistently denied that race was a factor in his actions; he claimed that it was a need to gain control over and tame the dangers posed by the modern city that spurred him on. Following his eventual arrest, he was quoted as saying: "You can't let yourself be pushed around. You can't live in fear. That's no way to live."[22]

Regardless of the specific type of cause murder at hand, one recurring emotion seems to be imprinted in most, if not all of these homicides: hatred. Even planned and thrill killings reveal a form of hatred—a hatred (or spiteful disregard) for human beings in general. Another overarching motive seems to be boredom. Endemic boredom, which existentialist philosophers called *ennui*, inheres in a deep abiding sense of meaninglessness to everyday life (or life in general). Thus, killing someone bears no moral consequences under such circumstances for the perpetrators, or so they believe. Murder is felt to be an antidote to ennui. The fact that there is no documentary evidence of boredom until the nineteenth century, where it is discussed perhaps for the first time in Charles Dickens's novel *Bleak House* (1853), may lend some credence to this hypothesis. In the novel, boredom is connected to meaningless habits of everyday life in an ever-expanding industrialized urban society. Some sociologists have since come see the ultimate source of ennui as rampant capitalism and its bourgeois materialistic worldview, which requires the adoption of tedious habits and acquisition of useless items, as French philosopher Marcel Mauss emphasized, to carry out the tasks of everyday life. This rigmarole in turn renders life meaningless by way of a lack of hope or belief in some spiritual reward or larger meaning to it all.[23] This whole line of thought derives ultimately from the notion of alienation—a term coined by Karl Marx to describe a sense of estrangement from other people that he claimed was endemic to capitalist societies, and which he saw as shallow and depersonalizing.[24] French sociologist Émile Durkheim similarly suggested that alienation stemmed from a loss of moral and religious traditions.[25] He used the term *anomie* to refer to the sense of irrational boredom that results from this loss. It may not be far-fetched to envision boredom as a spark for some types of murders, such as various serial and thrill killings—an antidote to ennui, alienation, and anomie all at once, and in the most debased and selfish sense.

As Phil Chalmer argues in his book, *Inside the Mind of a Teen Killer*, a case in point is the murder of Christopher Lane, a twenty-two-year-old Australian who was living in Oklahoma to play college baseball, and who was shot to death by three jaded adolescents as he was jogging.[26] One of the three accused later told police, "[we were] bored and didn't have anything to do, so we decided to kill somebody."[27]

It stands to reason that there is not and in fact *cannot* be one consistent motive for murder. Contrarily, in the medieval period the source of murder was indeed singular—evil. Even neuroscientists cannot really locate the propensity for murder in any specific part of the brain. Some studies suggest that a murderer's brain has a significantly reduced prefrontal cortex, also known as "the executive function" of the brain, with respect to the general population. But the relevant research is inconclusive and highly speculative. We shall return to this topic in the final chapter, where we seek to turn the tale of murder into a more scientifically rigorous theory of murder—but one still grounded in writing, storytelling, and narrative identity. The attempt to explain crime biologically began with Cesare Lombroso in the late 1870s.[28] Lombroso studied convicted criminals and their behaviors, describing what could be construed to be distinctive criminal traits, such as above or below average height, projecting ears, thick hair, thin beards, enormous jaws, a square chin, large cheekbones, and other visibly marked features. They also had recognizable behavioral characteristics—they felt apart from others; they needed to leave their mark through victimization; and so on. Basically, Lombroso painted the picture of an archetypal Hollywood villain—a textbook criminal monster. But murderers come in all shapes, sizes, and appearances. It is our imagination, ensconced in mythic tales of evil and the uncanny, that has generated this physical and behavioral "profile" of the vicious killer, not the structure of the brain or of the body.

MURDER AS TRAGEDY

One of the first tales of murder in history is the story of Cain and Abel in the Book of Genesis in the Old Testament. It is an example of murder framed as tragedy. The most relevant and revealing biblical passage of the tale is the following:

> Now Abel was a keeper of sheep, and Cain a tiller of the ground. In the course of time Cain brought to the Lord an offering of the fruit of the ground, and Abel for his part brought of the firstlings of his flock, their fat portions. And the Lord had regard for Abel and his offering, but for Cain and his offering he had no regards. So Cain was very angry, and his countenance fell. Cain said to his brother Abel "Let us go out to the field." And when they were in the field, Cain rose up against his brother Abel and killed him.[29]

This is a story of sibling rivalry gone awry—a variation and early iteration of the personal-cause murder, as well as perhaps the earliest tale of fratricide, or the murder of one's brother. Cain was the eldest son of Adam and Eve, a farmer who cultivated the land, while Abel, the younger son, was a shepherd. Both brothers, as the story tells us, made an offering to God. Cain's offering was rejected, which caused him to become obsessed with jealousy, which, as result, induced him to kill his brother.[30] When God asked Cain where Abel was, Cain made the remark that has now become part of proverbial language: "I know not: am I my brother's keeper?"[31] As punishment, God turned Cain into a wanderer, placing a mark on him to prevent anyone from killing him (which would provoke God's vengeance). Parallels to the story of Cain and Abel are found in an earlier Sumerian legend in which a farmer and a shepherd compete for the love of the fertility goddess Inanna.[32]

The biblical tale sets the moral tone for the manner in which we perceive some events in life as tragic, revolving around a sense of calamity and fatality that is narratively irreversible. Killing someone for envy and hatred is a disruption of divine law, however it happens to be defined or perceived. It is also an act of hate-based hubris. Sigmund Freud would later, in a psychoanalytical context, define hate as an overpowering urge to destroy the source of one's unhappiness.[33] This describes the Cain and Abel story with a remarkable clinical exactitude. In the New Testament, the Gospel of John also portrays hatred as the basis of murder: "Whosoever hateth his brother is a murderer and you know that no murderer hath eternal life abiding in himself."[34] The story of Cain and Abel is tragic because we expect brothers to love each other. Hatred and wrath are always harbingers of tragedy of some sort or other.

In his book the *Poetics*, which dates to roughly 335 BCE, the Greek philosopher Aristotle argued that we have invented tragedy as a dramatic genre to stimulate the emotions of pity and fear, which he considered to be morbid and unwholesome, so that that we can be purged of them.[35] This *catharsis*, as he called it, makes us emotionally healthier and thus more capable of achieving happiness. Most, if not all, classic tragedies revolving around murder are typically cathartic. This is why everyone in Aristotle's day—from the aristocrats to the peasants—flocked to the tragic plays of great writers like Aeschylus, Euripides, and Sophocles, which engaged audiences in emotional participation through tales of murder. Today, the psychologically liberating and cathartic function of tragic plays like *Antigone* and *Oedipus Rex* has simply been replaced with that of episodes of *Forensic Files* and *How to Get Away with Murder*. The dramatic platform for tragedy might have changed, but its psychic sources and its cathartic value have not.

In these same Greek tragedies dating back to Aristotle, hatred within families leading to murder is a recurring, dominant theme. The stories of Jason and Medea, Atreus and Thyestes, Agamemnon and Clytemnestra, among many others, are all essentially tragic forensic essays on hate as a motive for murder—blueprints for the personal-cause homicide. The hatred is typically provoked by acts of betrayal or dishonor. In the *Iliad*, the Trojan War forms the background for the central plot of the story, the wrath of the Greek hero Achilles. When his companion Patroclus is slain, Achilles, filled with fury and remorse, turns his wrath against the Trojans and kills their leader, Hector. But there is a moral dénouement, as there always is in such tragic tales. This occurs when Achilles surrenders Hector's body for burial, recognizing a shared sense of humanity with the Trojan king as they both faced the anguish of mortality and bereavement.

Greek tragedy flourished in the fifth century BCE, when more than one thousand plays were written, even though only thirty-one remain today, all penned by Aeschylus, Sophocles, and Euripides. The plays deal in large part with the moral aftermath of murder as a shared social phenomenon. The story of Medea (431 BCE), by Euripides, is a marvelous treatment of the horrific and tragic repercussions that murder for revenge and for vengeance invariably brings about.[36] Medea was the princess and sorceress who helped Jason obtain the Golden Fleece. She killed her children, fathered by Jason, as revenge for his infidelity; the narrative today reads like an episode of *Deadly Women* on the Identification Discovery network. We can truly sense the collective tragedy that emerges from Medea's wrath and her quest to avenge Jason's betrayal. In their 2012 book, *What Makes Love Last?* John Gottman and Nan Silver offer a contemporary rendition of the Medea tale by suggesting that betrayal is "a noxious invader, arriving with great stealth,"[37] as it does in Euripides's play.

Oedipus Rex (430–415 BCE), by Sophocles, similarly addresses how murder leads to catastrophic consequences on a grand scale.[38] Hubris is the spark for murder in this tale, since Oedipus refuses to yield to destiny and circumstance, conceding instead to some inner compulsion that leads him to an agonizing revelation and, ultimately, to unimaginable tragedy. As is well known, Freud saw in Oedipus—the king who was abandoned at birth and then unwittingly killed his father and married his own mother—a mirror for probing hidden abnormal sexual desires and how they unconsciously guide human actions, particularly in males. Murder is a way to quell a devastating inner turmoil and is thus a means of release. As Ralph Waldo Emerson aptly remarked in 1844: "Murder in the murderer is no such ruinous thought as poets and romancers will have it; it does not unsettle him, or fright him from his ordinary notice of trifles; it is an act quite easy to be contemplated."[39]

The classic tragic tales of ancient Greece continue to raise profound philosophical questions about morality, the human condition, and the control human beings seek to exercise over their own actions—including the control, if only illusory, over life and death. Murder is always justifiable to the betrayed murderer. We can see it in the very words of Medea.

> Oh, what misery! Cursed sons, and a mother for cursing! Death take you all—you and your father.[40]

Here Medea is venting her odium at anyone associated with her philandering husband, including the fruit of their ill-fated love—her children. Fate be damned, she is thinking. Medea acts on impulse and emotion, rationalizing her killings to herself. It is not a calculating and devious form of murder; it is revenge, pure and simple. Indeed, betrayal, hatred, and revenge continuously crystallize as motives for murder throughout the ancient tragedies. The intended victim may be a philandering spouse or an entire nation, but the motive is the same. And the same motive drives many modern-day narratives about crime on television programs. These are the modern descendants of classic tales of murder.

MURDER AND FREE WILL

Early medieval people were wholly unaware of the progressive Greek views of murder and tragedy—hence the term Dark Ages, which refers to the insularity of Western society that remained effectively in a black box during that same period. Early medieval European society cut itself off from the past—a past with which it would reconnect only later in the Renaissance. The medieval period starts, according to most historians, with Saint Augustine (354–430), who was born in Algeria and became bishop of Hippo (now Annaba, Algeria) in 395, an office he held until his death. One question he posed and one that still haunts us to this day was: Why does God not intervene to block murder and thus remove tragedy from human life? The problem, St. Augustine answered, is free will, God's gift to humanity to decide a course of action on its own, without God's intervention.[41] Free will is a burden, since we have to respond to murder on our own terms. No other species has this burden. And it cannot be transferred to our machines—this is the reason why we do not hold machines, such as automobiles, responsible for the deaths they cause. They have no free will, even if sometimes the machine simply breaks down and can bring about a tragic accident. In those cases, we look to assign blame to the people behind the machines—a ritual victim.

Psychologists have difficulty recasting the concept of free will in more scientific terms, having recognized that the element of spontaneity might lie outside of natural law. This spontaneity is, clearly, equivalent to free will, or at least a measure of self-determination that people possess and by which they make moral judgments.

Free will is the dominant subtext in the mystery or morality plays of the medieval period. These plays were highly popular and were performed in public squares from the fifth to about the fifteenth century, each story dealing with aspects of everyday life that affected common everyday people. The typical play revolved around an allegorical figure known as the Everyman, who represented common people and their souls. His antagonist was Vice, who often appeared as the devil incarnate, full of tricks and disguises. Everyman was easily deceived by Vice and needed to vanquish him in order to gain salvation. But despite the moral warnings of these plays, people still killed each other for the same reasons as at any other time. Free will always has a dark side, no matter who the individual possessing it might be—it's unstable; it's mercurial; it's potentially lethal. The death of Arthur of Brittany in 1203 was caused by King John, who (as the legend tells us) stabbed Arthur to death in a drunken rage. Arthur, John's nephew and heir to the throne, was the leader in a rebellion against John that was aiming to grab the throne before John's natural death. After Arthur was captured by John's forces, legend has it that John drank heavily and proceeded to stab the sixteen-year-old to death in his prison cell. He then personally tied a large rock to Arthur's corpse and dumped the body into the Seine River, where it was discovered later by fishermen and then buried secretly at Bec Abbey.

The murder of Thomas Beckett in 1170 has been the stuff of legend from the medieval period to today, and it was immortalized into contemporary lore by T. S. Eliot's 1935 play *Murder in the Cathedral*.[42] Beckett was Archbishop of Canterbury under Henry II, with whom he argued constantly over tyrannical laws. The climax to their feud occurred in December of 1170, when four knights arrived at Canterbury Cathedral to arrest Beckett. After refusing to submit to the arrest, one of the knights sliced the top of Beckett's head off, just above the eyes, with a blow of his sword. The knights had arrived with orders to kill.

Betrayal is a negative consequence of free will—love robots do not cheat on each other, unless we humans program them to do so. The story of the love affair between Paolo and Francesca in the thirteenth century, immortalized by the poet Dante in Canto V of his best-known work, *Inferno*, is a medieval tale of how freedom of choice leads to inevitably tragic consequences. The story details the life of Francesca da Rimini, whose hand in marriage was given to Giovanni Malatesta (also known as Gianciotto) in order to solidify the peace between warring families.[43] Francesca's father knew that she would spurn the ugly and deformed Gianciotto. So, he asked Gianciotto's younger and handsome brother, Paolo, to retrieve Francesca. But the opposite of what the father desired occurred. Francesca fell instantly in love with the attractive Paolo, as the two kissed passionately—an image captured indelibly by Rodin's awe-inspiring sculpture of 1886,

The Kiss. Realizing that Paolo was not going to be her spouse, Francesca became enraged. Her love would not be denied. According to Dante, it was kindled after the two lovers had themselves read the story of two other star-crossed lovers of medieval lore, Lancelot and Guinevere. The tragic ending comes when the jealous Gianciotto, rapier in hand, is about to kill Paolo. Francesca throws herself between the two brothers. The blade passes through her, killing her instantly. Gianciotto, completely beside himself, for he loved Francesca more than life itself, then kills his brother. The two lovers were buried in the same tomb, symbolizing their union beyond mortal life.

Paolo and Francesca's love story is overwhelmingly sad and tragic. It is about love that transcends life and death, even though the society of their era saw their act as a sin. As Juliet tells Romeo in Shakespeare's version of the medieval tale of Romeo and Juliet (*Giulietta e Romeo* in Italian), "Then have my lips the sin that they have took," to which Romeo answers, "Sin from thy lips? O trespass sweetly urged! / Give me my sin again."[44] Today, this subtext is found throughout pop culture narratives of love, betrayal, and murder, from mainstream movies to Harlequin bestsellers. The sway of romantic love to change people's lives and chart their destiny from that moment onward draws us inexorably to these tragic tales of murder.

MURDER AS MEANS

Justifying murder as a means to gain or maintain power also fills the pages of many classic tales. It gains concrete articulation as a political means to power with Niccolò Machiavelli, in his book *The Prince* (1532), in which he advises rulers that obtaining power may necessitate unethical methods, including murder, turning his name into a synonym for treachery, cunning, and duplicity today. Machiavelli believed that a ruler is not bound by traditional moral and ethical norms, since he is above the common fold. A prince should be concerned only with power and be bound solely by implicit rules that lead to political success, whatever they may be. Murdering your enemy or anyone who stands in the way of success is simply one of many rules available to the prince.

Machiavelli might have been influenced by Greek philosopher Heraclitus's view that humanity was divided into two classes—a moral and intellectual elite, known as the *aristoi*, and those who belonged to the unthinking and conforming masses, known as the *hoi polloi*. The ruler is a member of the aristoi. He is above the moral codes by which the hoi polloi live, which are intended to keep them from killing each other to extinction. Murder as weapon of Machiavellian power and control is everywhere today, from terrorism to gang warfare on the streets of urban centers. In a fundamental sense, Machiavelli was more of a psychologist than an evil-manifesto maker, identifying a trait of the dark psyche—murder for control. After all, war is nothing if not a means to control and gain power over others, albeit even if part of defense.

In the same time frame, Shakespeare emerged as a throwback to Greek tragedy and its view of murder as morally portentous, because it was used so frequently as a weapon of choice, that is, as a Machiavellian means to an end. One could say that in the eyes of the murderer the weapon is a moral one; it is in the eyes of others that it is an amoral instrument. This is a theme in all the great Shakespearean tragedies, although it is rarely identified as such by critics. It is in *Hamlet* (ca. 1601), perhaps his most famous play, where murder comes to the surface more than in any other tragedy of revenge, decrying the enigmatic sordidness of the human condition. The following exchange is between the Ghost and Hamlet, before Hamlet discovers that he has to kill the king:

Ghost: Revenge his foul and most unnatural murder.
Hamlet: Murder?
Ghost: Murder most foul, as in the best it is, / But this most foul, strange, and unnatural.
Hamlet: Haste me to know't, that I, with wings as swift, / As meditation or the thoughts of love, / May sweep to my revenge.[45]

Hamlet's actions were bound to end in tragedy. So too are those of the bard's other tragically flawed characters. For instance, *Othello* (ca. 1604) portrays how unjustified jealousy provokes a forlorn lover to use murder as the only means for him to escape from his emotional prison. Othello's own fate ends in similarly tragic yet predictable fashion. In a nutshell, vengeful murder also destroys the murderer—mutually assured destruction. This is perhaps the greatest moral dilemma of all, and why to this day we seek to find answers to the tragic ubiquity of murder in everyday life.

GOTHIC TALES OF MURDER

Post-Shakespearean tragedies bring murder down from its moral pedestal to the level of a senseless banal action, perhaps because they aim to tap into the decadence of contemporary society. Critics disagree about whether any true tragedies have been written since Shakespeare, given that the contemporary ones seem to lack the moral, philosophical, or religious subtexts found in the classic tales of murder, from the Greeks to Shakespeare. Perhaps the modern portrayals of murder mirror the secular world's view that it is part of the repertoire of human vengeance, not any transgression of the moral order. This is why most modern tragedies do not have the classic hero—typically they have an antihero.

But there is one modern-day genre where the hero figure makes a renewed appearance—the Gothic tale and its descendant, the detective story. As we have mentioned several times already, Edgar Alan Poe's influence on our views of murder as a means to solve larger questions of human existence cannot be overstated. His short story *The Murders in the Rue Morgue* (1841), which is the first of three narratives set in Paris that depict the character of his brilliant hero investigator C. Auguste Dupin (the second of these stories is *The Mystery of Marie Rogêt* as discussed earlier), is widely considered to be the first modern detective story. Writers as diverse as Robert

Louis Stevenson and Dostoevsky have used the hero-detective format established by Poe to launch their own fictional experiments, as did Charles Dickens in *Bleak House* (1852–1853), featuring fictional police detective Inspector Bucket of Scotland Yard. Dickens also pursued the same detective fiction conventions in his unfinished novel, *The Mystery of Edwin Drood*. So too did Wilkie Collins in *The Moonstone* (1868), which was at once an early detective story and a Victorian sensation novel that would establish a nexus between murderous biographies and celebrity scandal for twentieth-century audiences. Sherlock Holmes and his sidekick, Dr. John Watson, made their first appearance in 1887, in Sir Arthur Conan Doyle's *A Study in Scarlet*. Holmes is the most famous, universally recognizable detective hero of all time, despite the fact that the hero-detective character with a sidekick and raconteur builds on Poe's earlier, albeit lesser-known narrative format. In the end, it seems that Holmes simply proved to be a more likeable and marketable figure than Poe's Dupin, along with the fact that his creator was a more prolific author than Poe was. The murderers in the Conan Doyle tales also proved to be more galvanizing—characters who captured the essence of the nineteenth-century Gothic tale.

The image of an unknown murderer as a shadowy and terrifying figure, who commits a homicide intentionally while motivated by some inner dark force, rather than spontaneously by such passions as revenge or envy, dovetails with the rise of the Gothic novel and the detective story. These nineteenth-century stories catered to an increasingly secular and industrialized society's need for an imaginary engagement with evil outside of purely theological terms—a phenomenon that manifests itself in the Gothic technique of the uncanny. Gothic tales of murder came, rather prophetically, just before the birth of psychoanalysis in the 1890s as probes of the "dark regions" of the human psyche through the eyes of a detective hero. Often, the Gothic tale and corresponding advances in forensic science fed on each other. The polymath Dr. Abraham Van Helsing, in Bram Stoker's 1897 novel *Dracula*, is a literary construction of the real-life forensic psychiatrist Dr. Richard von Krafft-Ebing, whose pioneering work on sexual perversion and paraphilia would lay the groundwork for how sexual offenders, up to and including sexual murderers, are both investigated and assessed today.[46] The fascination with sinister Gothic stories and characters among both intellectual and laypersons in the late nineteenth-century was, according to some literary historians, a reaction to the depressed social conditions created by the Industrial Age. Others see them instead as stories that simply recycled the classic myths of monsters and demons into new popular narrative genres and in commercially printed form. The stories about real and fictional murderers have, in fact, merged into an overarching über-tale, as it can be called, for common people trying to make sense of an increasingly uncertain and dangerous urban world that may have plunged into moral nihilism.

It is no coincidence that the scientific study of real crime, or forensic science as broadly defined, matured at around the same time as Gothic literature was booming in popularity and influence, forming an ideational entanglement with it. Indeed, many practices used in the criminal investigations of the period were modeled on those employed by fictional detectives. As professor, author, and historian Ronald Thomas has persuasively argued, a specific crime-solving technique or technology (such as fingerprinting) was more often than not inspired by detective fiction; vice versa, as new forensic techniques came forward, these same techniques were quickly incorporated into detective and mystery fiction by writers aiming to make their stories more realistic.[47] The contemporary view of murderers as "monsters" also comes from the Gothic tradition that, itself, is based on the medieval view of monstrosity as being the earthly manifestation of evil. Many modern-day serial killers characterize themselves, in fact, as "monsters." The self-avowed Son of Sam serial killer David Berkowitz, who killed six victims in New York City between 1976 and 1977, referred to himself as "the Duke of Death," "the Monster," and "Beelzebub" (see chapter 2). When he was eventually identified, he was seen for what he really was—a pathetic man with no sense of purpose in life. Dennis Rader, the serial killer who murdered his victims in and around Wichita, Kansas, between 1974 and 1991, also known as the Bind Torture Kill (BTK) Strangler, claimed under interrogation that it was a "monster" that "entered [his] brain," provoking his bizarre and cruelly sadistic slayings of entire families in some cases (discussed in chapter 2). Rader was also a quintessential underachiever, eventually concocting the BTK alter ego and later reveling in the attention his murders received in the media. Rader, like Berkowitz, was also compelled to put pen to paper between his crimes—to be both killer and raconteur, much like Dupin's unnamed narrator in Poe's short story murder mysteries. Both of these killers' respective written works—the prose of Rader and Berkowitz—will be discussed and analyzed in the following chapter.

Does life really imitate art, as Oscar Wilde once put it?[48] Or is it perhaps the opposite? Psychological imbalance and a disordered sense of self, as Freud and his Swiss protégé Carl Jung certainly understood, both have their roots in a morally unstable world. It is unlikely that Rader would have been seen as insane in the medieval period—that is, he would have been seen as a real "monster," just as he described himself.

It is no coincidence, in our opinion, that Freud and his psychoanalytic methods arrived on the coattails of both industrialist society and Gothic literature. Freud may have, arguably, been directly influenced by the latter to construct his theory of the unconscious mind and especially of the "id." The id is the part of the mind where instinctive impulses are harbored and seek gratification. Because they cannot be expressed freely and must submit to the demands of society, they produce a darkness that, in some people, is vented in a murderous fashion. The darkness of the "repressed id," to use Freudian terminology, may underlie the storyline in both Gothic literature and real-life murder. The ego, on the other hand, is the sense of awareness that mediates between the conflicting demands of the id and the superego (the inner voice of conscience). As we will see, serial killers in particular seem to be incapable of controlling the id, as they reject the safeguarding mechanisms over the id that operate for most other people.

Rader's phrase that there was a monster in his head recalls the original meaning of *monster* as a "warning." The word *monster* derives from Latin *monstrum*, meaning an "aberrant occurrence," usually physical (such as a birth defect), that was interpreted in medieval times as a sign of punishment from God for some sin of the parents. The root of *monstrum* is *monere*—which means "to warn and instruct." So, the monster is a warning from God. We learn constantly that murderers tend to be abandoned children who become monsters ultimately because of a traumatic childhood. We do indeed produce monsters through upbringing, and also take upbringing as a warning, much like medieval people. The monster figure was a central one in Gothic literature, beginning with the novel *Frankenstein* (1818) by Mary Shelley, which tells the story of Victor Frankenstein, a scientist who tries to create a living being for the good of humanity but instead produces a monster, by assembling parts of dead bodies and then activating the creature with electricity. The creature is actually gentle and intelligent; however, everyone fears and mistreats him because of his hideous appearance. Frankenstein himself rejects his creation, refusing to similarly engineer him a mate so he won't be alone. The monster's terrible loneliness in turn drives him to seek revenge by murdering his creator's wife, brother, and best friend. The creature is, thus one of the first fictional serial killers, motivated by the alienation that Marx would later argue as being central to the despair of modern life. Subsequent Gothic novels such as *The Partisan* (1835) and *The Monks of Monk Hall* (1845) similarly detail the monster figure, and as author Philip Simpson remarks, all "present multiple body counts and Shadow villains in which one can see the literary prototypes of the contemporary American serial murderer."[49]

The monster figure is, however, rivaled in Gothic fiction by another literary surrogate of the contemporary serial killer—the vampire. In many Gothic tales, the act of murder is traced to some inner passion or lust for blood, as it is in the vampire stories that began not with Bram Stoker's *Dracula* (1897) but with the lesser-known 1872 novella *Carmilla*, by Irish author Joseph Sheridan Le Fanu.[50] The theories of both the monster and the vampire figures have modern-day psychological counterparts. As mentioned, the early theorist Von Krafft-Ebing describes, in his 1886 book *Psychopathia Sexualis*, the case of a French serial killer in the 1870s, named Eusebius Pieydagnelle, who murdered six people in order to drink their blood.[51] There is little doubt that the Gothic personae of the monster and the vampire are still operative in the modern imagination. Without such figures of thought to describe some killers, most murders would not be envisaged as tragic tales of moral mayhem, just as banal acts of senseless criminality.

NARRATIVE PERSPECTIVES OF MURDER

The connection between real-life murder and fictional, semifictional, and factual tales of murder is a recurring though not necessarily obvious one. It began, as we saw, in biblical times, subsequently uniting scripture, Gothic literature, and the contemporary news media's narrative treatment of murder. Such connections additionally reveal an inner compulsion among both the creators and the readers of this content to come to grips with murder through narrative-expressive means. Murder has, in fact, spawned its own narrative genres, including those crafted by investigators, criminologists, and the murderers themselves. We seem to be entangled in an overriding universal über-tale—the over-story, or the story beyond the story—as we have called it, every time a specific murder makes it to print or dominates the headlines or Nielsen ratings. Groundbreaking research by forensic psychologist David Canter and his associates in the United Kingdom in recent years has actually suggested that not only acts of murder but also all major crimes spark some internal narrative mechanism for coming to grips with the tragedy and horror of crime. Even among offenders of limited literacy and those murderers who do not commit their thoughts, fantasies, or braggadocio to writing, there appears to exist a latent sense of story structure and awareness of character in their verbally expressed motives that can be generally interpreted as operating within a narrative structure.[52]

Relying in part on the detailed analysis of hand-drawn maps created by murderers in police custody, allowing them to re-create their crimes as part of their confession or to help authorities locate a concealed body or other evidence where the specific address or GPS coordinates are not known, researchers have been able to extract four character archetypes from murderer manifestos, writings, confessions, and sketches of crime scenes. Each of these categories can be defined as the narrative means through which perpetrators recall and retell their murders, revealing their innermost motivations. The maps and crime-scene reproductions constitute complementary "point-of-view tales" filled with intricate landscape details or bird's-eye views that suggest an aloof relationship with the crime scene, rather than an emotional connection with the victim or the act of murder. In other words, the drawings, confessions, and writings of murderers suggest that there exists a connection among: (a) the source or motivation for murder, (b) an inherent "narrative mechanism" in the human psyche (a proclivity to express something meaningful in storytelling form), and (c) the murderer's rationalization of his or her act. All of this leads us to posit a *narrative theory of murder*, which we believe will help explain the raison d'être of murder, at least in part. The main idea here is that we can gain access to the motives for murder by analyzing the expressive constructions that murderers have produced to rationalize (interpret, explain, etc.) their actions. The theory can be put into diagrammatic form as follows:

Motives for Murder → Narrative Mechanism → Rationalization

The model implies that in order to unravel the motives for murder, we need to decipher the rationalizations of the murderer encoded in linguistic, narrative, or any other expressive form. In other words, the literary criminologist starts with the words (in "plain English," as we have characterized them colloquially in this book) and other expressive artifacts, such as maps and drawings, so as to discern any intrinsic character archetypes in them for reconstruction of both the motives and potentially the meaning of murder itself.

The model suggests that murder sets off an internal storytelling mechanism which, like all significant life events or memories, frames or contextualizes the crime as part of an ongoing life tale. For this reason, everything in the murderer's confession, from the location of the crime, which is part of a narratively perceived setting, to the perception of the victim as a character in his or her own life, unfolds as a story. As the perpetrator replays the events mentally time and again, the context of the crime and the nature of the characterizations may change, but the mechanism remains constant—the perpetrator either elevates or diminishes their importance as he or she seeks to rationalize, justify, or fantasize about the crime. As Shakespeare proclaimed in *As You Like It*, first published in 1623, "all the world's a stage."[53] Nowhere does this maxim seem to be more accurate than in analyzing the stories of murderers as imagined theater, wherein they see themselves as the writers and stage directors of those stories. Supporting this narrative theory is the data on the drawings or sketches that the perpetrators themselves create, often as part of their story. Variants in the stories come down to how far the murderer is prepared to go to portray himself or herself in the story structure. The main murderer-character archetypes connected with the narrative mechanism can be summarized as follows.

> *The Hero*: a perpetrator who conceives of his or her crimes as a quest or as a self-righteous adventure to be pursued, playing the imaginary role of an embattled protagonist who feels impelled to follow a calling. The Hero's storyline is also embedded in drawings or sketches that depict ground-level POV (point of view), complete with graphic details and individuating features. The Hero archetype can be retroactively associated with some of the most sadistic, self-entitled, and psychopathic murderers in history, including

sexual and thrill murderers such as the Zodiac Killer, the Toolbox Killers Lawrence Bittaker and Roy Norris, James Holmes, and many more.

The Professional: a perpetrator who conceptualizes his or her crimes as either a vocation or a practical exercise, that is, as a means to earn money or ensure survival—including emotional survival or to exercise physical or mental control over his or her world. The Professional's stories and corresponding drawings or sketches provide aerial views of crime scenes with limited personal or individuating details. The Professional often holds grandiose delusions about being a master strategist or a meticulous operator in areas of non-criminal life as well. Examples are the Unabomber, the Iceman, the unidentified murderer of JonBenét Ramsey, and others.

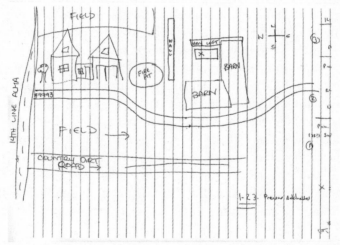

Fig. 1.3. A map created by a co-conspirator and accessory to murder, entered as evidence in a 2013 Canadian murder trial. The aerial POV and near-scale distribution of landmarks is generally indicative of the detachment of the "professional" murderer who mentally re-creates the narrative circumstances of the crime.

The Revenger: a perpetrator who rationalizes crime as a necessary response to the injustices of his or her own life, justifying murderous actions as righteously getting even with a specific victim, type of victim, or institution. The Revenger typically creates stories, drawings, and sketches that depict his or her crimes with little or no detail, that is, with a diminished use of the available writing and drawing spaces. Revengers may be suffering from various psychological disorders, including borderline personality disorder, schizoid personality disorder, or clinical depression, whether diagnosed or undiagnosed. Examples are Seung-Hui Cho, Elliot Rodger, Eric Harris and Dylan Klebold, and many others (to be discussed later on).

The Tragedian: a perpetrator who defers personal responsibility to some preordained cause to rationalize his or her actions, and who adopts a crime-neutralization strategy through an almost uncanny (in the Gothic sense) or even a cosmic view of events. The Tragedian is a kind of "Othello" or "Hamlet" killer who sees his or her crimes and self-destructive behaviors—and eventual downfall—as fatalistic, unavoidable, and irreversible. The drawings or sketches in this case are similar to those of the Revenger, providing a "Petri-dish scenario" where people and places are reduced to miniscule, indeterminate dots. Tragedians perceive their life story and the world at large as miniaturized entities controlled by unconscious forces, and their victims as collateral damage in their irreversible descent into tragic revenge. Ironically, the Tragedian also shows an aptitude for theatricality that differentiates him or her from other archetypes, suggesting either an affectation or a significant mental disturbance. Examples include Son of Sam, the Santa Claus Killer (Jeffrey Pardo), and the Night Stalker (Richard Ramirez), among others (also covered later on).

It should be noted that this murderer archetype classificatory framework is based on the analysis of the writings, statements, and/ or drawings made by the murderers. One of the more unsettling—and yet probative—examples of a concrete statement lending credence to narrative theory was uttered by Richard Ramirez following his death sentence in November 1989 for a total of thirteen horrific, Satanic-themed, sex murders in the Los Angeles and San Francisco areas. Ramirez was subsequently linked, in 2009, to the previously unknown murder of a nine-year-old girl in San Francisco in April 1984:

Big deal. Death always went with the territory. See you in Disneyland.[54]

As the quintessential Tragedian, Ramirez was surprised to have been captured alive, ultimately making a mockery of what at the time was the longest and most costly criminal trial in US history. Could it be that specific narrative archetypes might be linked with a specific modus operandi? Consider the following statement, later transcribed to text.

If people don't have any love for themselves, that's on them. But we have love for the bees, I have love for the bees. My love for the bees, Sandy's a little bee. You know, I love that little bee, man. But not just for its honey, I love that little bee for itself. Because it has a self too, it has a life, and it loves its life, and it deserves its life. It works hard. It does good for the will of God. The will of God is what we're dealing with, we're not dealing with man's will—we already know man's will is destroying everything. We're dealing with the air we're breathing, soldier, it's the air that we breathe.[55]

These words at times seem lyrical and sage, and they could have been uttered by any modern-day poet or philosopher. In reality, they are the words of a cowardly murderer by proxy: Charles Manson. Manson is, pardon our own plain English, a scumbag. He, like many scumbags of his ilk, is a psychopath and a mentally fragile and underachieving narcissist who feels inferior to others; so, he compensated by getting others to commit serial murders for him in order to show that he was superior. An ex-convict writ large—two-thirds of his life had been spent in jails by the time he brought together his squalid and murderous "family" of hippie killers—Manson ordered the Tate-LaBianca murders in 1969 to create "helter skelter" in the world that had rebuffed his attempts to be a rock star.[56] Manson's "hit team" brutally killed screen actress Sharon Tate Polanski, along with her child in utero, at her Bel-Air home in Benedict Canyon early in the morning of August 10. Also murdered and mutilated were Tate's houseguests: coffee heiress Abigail Folger, her common-law husband, Wojiciech Frykowski; Hollywood hairstylist to the stars Jay Sebring; and delivery boy Steven Earl Parent. A day later in Los Angeles, supermarket-chain president Leno LaBianca and his wife, Rosemary, were killed as well. Manson had brainwashed his followers with drugs, sex, and pseudoreligious rhetoric, ordering them to commit the horrific murders. Curiously, Manson exhibits features of all four narrative archetypes as we understand them today. But the label that best describes him is that of self-styled cult leader hero. His words above make that abundantly clear. His overblown and unfounded ego led him to rationalize his crimes in pseudopoetic terms that reveal within them a perverted sense of leadership.

METAPHORS

The narrative mechanism produces, above any other type of discourse, figurative language and poetic images. Metaphor in particular is the linguistic means through which authors, murderers, and readers alike come to grips with the brutality of murder. Those who kill for sexual reasons describe their killing as exciting and fulfilling, not regretful or objectionable, thinking only of their own perverse sexual desires and how to satisfy them. In turn, we call them "predators" to make sense of this paradox. The following words are by serial killer Pedro Alonzo López, who was convicted of murdering eighty women, although he claims to have raped and killed more than three hundred, in Colombia, Peru, and Ecuador. He became internationally famous after being interviewed by photojournalist Ron Laytner in prison in 1980. The interview was published widely.[57] What follows is a selection of quotes from that interview:

> "At the first sign of light I would get excited. I forced the girl into sex and put my hands around her throat. When the sun rose I would strangle her."

"I walked among the markets searching for a girl with a certain look on her face, a look of innocence and beauty."

"I often put three or four girls in a single hole and talked to them."

"There is a wonderful moment, a divine moment when I have my hands around a young girl's throat."

"I look into her eyes and see a certain light, a spark, suddenly go out. Only those who kill know what I mean."

"The moment of death is enthralling and exciting. Someday, when I am released. I will feel that moment again. I will be happy to kill again. It is my mission."

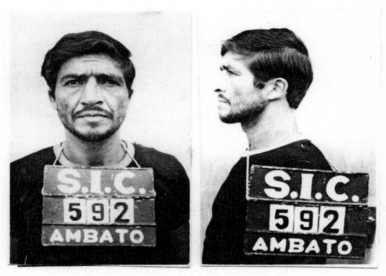

Fig. 1.4. Pedro Alonzo López.

These statements reveal the type of deranged mind that seeks to carry out rape and murder for self-satisfaction. There is no ideological cause or revenge for some betrayal here. There is just self-adulation and a complete disregard for the welfare of others, especially women. When López became sexually aroused, he would go out, like a sexual predator (a rather apt metaphor) looking for his prey, and then he would relish in the "joy" of strangulation.

Criminologists have attempted to explain Pérez's actions as

having resulted from the effects of his troubled upbringing. He was the son of a prostitute and had suffered serious abuse as a child. His own words are revelatory in this regard.

> "My mother threw me out when I was eight after she caught me touching my sister's breasts. She took me to the edge of town but I found my way home again."
>
> "Next day she took me on a bus and left me off more than 200 miles from home. There I was found by a man who took me into an abandoned building and raped me over and over again. I decided then to do the same to as many young girls as possible."[58]

But there is more to the López tale than rearing aberrancies. Indeed, López seems to be proud of his notoriety, as can be seen in his words of self-praise and his horrific characterization of his young victims, never once showing any sign of remorse.

> "I am the man of the century. No one will ever forget me."
>
> [Asked why he chose only very young girls, he explained] "It's like eating chicken. Why eat old chicken when you can have young chicken?"[59]

The role of family upbringing shows up frequently in the metaphors used by the murderers themselves. Take the well-known case of Alyssa Bustamante, who murdered a nine-year-old girl brutally. She not only stabbed her but also sliced her throat. She then put her in a shallow grave that she covered with leaves. What was Bustamante's motive? She pointed out rather glibly that she simply wanted to find out what it felt like to kill. At her trial, she said to the girl's mother, as she sat stunned in the courtroom: "I know words can never be enough and they can never adequately describe how horribly I feel for all of this. If I could give my life to get her back I would. I'm sorry."[60] But her diary entry and Twitter messages tell us something else:

"I just f—[ing] killed someone. I strangled them and slit their throat
and stabbed them now they're dead. I don't know how to feel atm
[at the moment]."

"It was ahmazing. As soon as you get over the 'ohmygawd I can't do
this' feeling, it's pretty enjoyable. I'm kinda nervous and shaky
though right now. Kay, I gotta go to church now . . . lol."

"All I want in life is a reason for all this pain."[61]

Fig. 1.5. Alyssa Bustamante.

Her words gave her away. Even though she was raised in a broken home, it nevertheless failed to deter her from seeking enjoyment by inflicting the same kind of pain on someone else. An appropriate metaphor that we could use to describe Bustamante is "murderous brat," an adolescent version of the metaphor of "monster."

Another typical metaphor in the über-tale of murder is that of "follower." The "herd instinct" may in fact be at play in some murders, a term first coined by German philosopher Friedrich Nietzsche.[62] Take the case of Anita Lorraine Cobby, a registered nurse in Australia who was kidnapped, raped, tortured, and finally killed by five men on February 2, 1986. John Travers, the self-proclaimed "leader of the pack" who was deemed to have actually murdered the young woman, had a history of violent sexual behavior and bestiality. He was the one who slit Cobby's throat, almost severing her head in the process. His statement to police revealed everything: "We were all drunk and she'd f—[ing] seen all of us . . . so I cut her."[63] The fact that everyone went along is a rather conspicuous clue that the follower instinct plays a role in some kinds of murders.

A similar classic case of a "follow-the-leader" murder is that of Steven Dean Gordon and Franc Cano, who together carried out a series of kidnappings and sexual assaults of prostitutes that began in 2013 in Orange County, California. The following dialogue between the older Gordon and his younger follower, Cano, is rather revealing in terms of what goes on in the minds of sexually-motivated murderous duos:

Gordon: I can't hurt this cat. I just can't.
Gordon: Why is the cat's phone here?
Gordon: Are you gonna answer?
Cano: Phone is power off. No worry. Your last question, if you want, you can let her go.
Gordon: Why?
Cano: Cuz you don't want to take care of it.
Gordon: I (need) that cash.
Cano: Then go get it after you take care of her . . . Or I will go get it.
Gordon: How? Walk into the hotel room?

Cano: Maybe

Gordon: What you wanna do seriously?

Cano: You're gonna get your hands dirty.

Cano: That's all

Cano: Wake up

Gordon: How?

Cano: You go down there while I watch her but first you survey the area for cams out. . . . I would park the truck on the street.

Gordon: You are forgetting what I'm wearing, huh?

Cano: So don't let that stop you. I would do it if it wasn't curfew, but if I has (my parole agent). I would go.

Gordon: Well, I'm (fearful).

Cano: Then get rid of her.

Gordon: How?

Cano: Happy hand

Gordon: Can you do it?

Cano: I thought the next one, you were going to go at it.

Gordon: I can't. Cat is beautiful.

Gordon: This is the best one yet.

Gordon: Bye-bye, Kitty

Cano: No time for that. Either Kitty walks or goes to sleep . . . I am not gonna sit here (all) night and text.

Gordon: Kitty goes to sleep. Can I sleep till 2 a.m.?

Cano: Then get some water so that cat can take a hot shower since it might walk with seven lives.

Gordon: She can't leave.[64]

This dialogue, which took place via text messages a few hours before midnight on March 13, 2013, shows how the ruthless killers debated about whether to kill prostitute Jarrae Estepp, a twenty-one-year-old mother from Oklahoma whom the two creeps had dubbed metaphorically the "Cat" and "Kitty." The timid Gordon argues that he was incapable of killing Estepp. As he put it, he couldn't do it because she was "beautiful." But the callous Cano takes a leadership role, throwing Gordon into a corner, much like bullies do in a schoolyard scrum, ordering him to "get rid of her." Cano had a curfew, and a parole agent was monitoring his whereabouts at the time, so he could not do it himself since he was under observation. Moreover, as Cano reminded him: "I thought the next one, you were going to go at it. Either Kitty walks or goes to sleep." Feeling the pressure, Gordon replies: "Bye-bye, Kitty . . . Kitty goes to sleep." The next day, workers at an Anaheim recycling facility found the body of the poor woman on a trash conveyer belt.

What strikes us most is the senselessness of these murders. As the great detective-fiction writer Raymond Chandler so aptly put it: "It is not funny that a man should be killed, but it is sometimes funny that he should be killed for so little, and that his death should be the coin of what we call civilization."[65] The subtext inherent in these words is something we will revisit in subsequent chapters.

MURDER IN THE NAME OF HONOR

The vendetta murder born from Sicilian Mafia tradition captures the essence of the biblical "eye for an eye" metaphor. It is a form of retributive justice in some cultures that endures to this day; it serves to redress crimes wherever the state and its justice system are greatly distrusted or where and whenever societies discriminate against a certain race or group. In places where a blood feud may have developed, the clan of the murdered individual must seek vengeance on the murderer or on his or her family. As mentioned, this kind of murder in the name of honor is found throughout time and across the world. Today, it is particularly common among criminal organizations. The Mafia has always portrayed itself as an "honorable society" that lives by a code called *omertà* (code of manly honor). With this code, murder becomes a justifiable act of retribution; without it, murder would just be gutless homicide. Avenging some dishonor through murder not only gives justification to a brutal act but may also be the main reason why police crusades against the Mafia have proven largely ineffectual in defeating it. The code is what allows the gangsters to see in murder a means toward some warped mission that the gang aims to achieve. Vendetta, silence, and honor all converge in the code of *omertà*, imbuing it with great emotional resonance. Such codes are themselves based on the narrative mechanism that produces symbolic artifacts and rituals that allow criminals to justify or rationalize their murderous actions.

Take the case of Giovanni Brusca, known as Lo Scannacristiani, which literally means "he who cuts the throats of Christians," with the latter term, *cristiano*, generally meaning "any good person" in Italian. Brusca was a hit man for one of the most brutal Mafia capi of all time, Totò Riina, whose murderous rampage peaked in the early 1990s with the killing of the famous anti-Mafia judge Giovanni Falcone. Riina had ordered Brusca to murder the son of gang member, Santino Di Matteo, who had turned state's witness. Brusca kidnapped and held the child, Giuseppe, in a basement for twenty-six months. He then strangled the boy and dissolved his corpse in acid. There is little doubt that he did this in part because of the code of *omertà*, but in larger part because his hit man role was well compensated. In fact, the ruthless Brusca lived in luxury. The police officers who arrested him in May 1996 found a wardrobe filled with designer clothes, cell phones, Cartier watches, jewelry, and other accoutrements of the affluent lifestyle he so obviously enjoyed. While in jail, he confessed to having murdered more than one hundred people, in the name of *omertà*. Mafia analyst John Dickie elaborates as follows:

> The terrifying thing about the Sicilian Mafia is that men like "Lo Scannacristiani" are not deranged. Nor are their actions incompatible with the code of honor or, indeed, with being a husband or father in Cosa Nostra's view. Until the day he decided to turn state's evidence and tell his story, nothing that Brusca did, including murdering a child not much older than his own, was considered by Mafiosi to be inherently dishonorable.[66]

Not all Mafiosi are like Brusca, of course, and, by and large, the murder of women and children is discouraged and even punished by most clans. But obeying and abiding by the code of honor takes precedence over anything else. This is madness, of course, but not of the superior kind, such as that of an Othello or a Hamlet. It is the kind of "wise guy" madness that comes from a perverted herd instinct. Murder in criminal groups is, in a phrase, a Machiavellian act; it is hardly seen as a breach of some form of morality. It hollers out self-interestedness. The words of political commentator George Will are rather appropriate with regard to this point: "Machiavelli and Hobbes and other modern political philosophers defined man as a lump of matter whose most politically relevant attribute is a form of energy called self-interestedness. This was not a portrait of man warts and all. It was all wart."[67]

MURDER ON SOCIAL MEDIA

In a fascinating 2015 article titled, plainly enough, "10 Chilling Social Media Confessions to Murder," published on *Listverse*, Robert Grimminck reports on people who have committed murders and then either bragged about them on social media or else attempted expiation through them.[68] These constitute interesting data for substantiating the narrative model described above. Social media have become modern psychoanalyst couches where everyone can confess or brag about his or her sins and seek either reprobation or approval from the denizens of the global village. A few cases noticed by Grimminck will suffice. We will return to this topic subsequently.

In March 2015, twenty-seven-year-old Jacob Rogers murdered his roommate (also twenty-seven years old) in Racine County, Wisconsin, shooting him several times after waking him up from a deep sleep. Rogers walked away and then came back and shot his victim a few more times to make sure he was dead. As the police searched for Rogers, the latter went on Facebook and posted the following:

> That's the truth. I DID IT. Stole money and threatened the wrong person. I'll surrender when they find me.[69]

Seeing himself as a Revenger, Rogers believed that his roommate had stolen money from him. While the motive may be an old one, the announcement—as much attention-seeking proclamation as it is confession—of the murder on Facebook is new. Social media are, apparently, where people now live, and perhaps even die, as Identification Discovery's program called *Web of Lies* now makes rather obvious. Both the program and Rogers's message suggest, in their own ways, that we may have become immune to the ravages of murder, conditioned by contemporary cultural factors, including the many tales of murder that have now become part of everyday narratives on social media and elsewhere. This may explain the banality of murder today—an act people perpetrate for commonplace or senseless reasons with no qualms of conscience. The matter-of-fact way in which Jacobs admitted to murdering his roommate for having wronged him, even pleading innocent despite the evidence, is an abysmal reminder that the era of Shakespearean tragedy may well be long over. Jacobs committed the murder for self-interestedness, to use George Will's rather apt term.

The murder of thirteen-year-old Lamonee Johnson-Chisolm in November 2012 in Newport News, Virginia, is yet another conspicuous example of killing for the sake of it. Lamonee and a friend were standing outside a store when someone opened fire on them, killing him and wounding his friend. The fifteen-year-old shooter, Kashawn Hines, soon after posted an apparent heartfelt apology on Facebook:

> I ain't know I was going to kill you. I swear to God I didn't mean to kill you. What I'm trying to say is that I'm sorry.[70]

Lamonee's mother found the message on the Internet a few days later and informed the police about it. However, after Hines was arrested, he recanted his confession, claiming that he was simply joking around when he admitted to the murder.

"Familiarity breeds contempt" is no longer a simple cliché today. It can lead, and often does lead, to senseless murder. Take the case

of forty-year-old Rosemarie Farid and her sixty-four-year-old roommate, Donald Gavagni, in 2014 in Sunrise, Florida. Farid saw many
of Gavagni's habits as irritants—he played guitar too loudly, they
were constantly fighting over the dog, and so on. These soon became
burdens, leading her to beat Gavagni's head against the floor, where
he slowly died from his injuries. Obviously relieved that she got rid
of the source of her contempt, she uploaded video to her Facebook
page in which she stated:

> Donny was driving me so insane that I was like delirious from the
> fighting. I couldn't take it anymore. I was having fantasies about
> stabbing him in the neck with a very sharp little knife—I knew I
> had to get out.[71]

She encouraged her friends to watch it and was openly proud
of her video. Retribution and the settling of emotional scores taste
sweet, reflecting an aberrant form of narcissism and entitlement that
social media now allow for almost on a daily basis. Murder is a
means to solve problems of a truly meaningless nature in everyday
life, not a Sophoclean or Shakespearean act of tragic grandeur.

Matricide (killing one's mother) was once a momentous and
calamitous act, as the ancient tragedies and legends tell us. But in
today's social-media world, it seems to constitute nothing more than
another act of personal problem solving. On June 14, 2015, Gypsy
Blancharde from Springfield, Missouri, had her boyfriend, Nicholas
Godejohn, stab her mother to death, after which she gave the following status update on her Facebook page:

> That Bitch is Dead![72]

Gypsy seemingly suffered from leukemia and was confined to
a wheelchair from, again seemingly, muscular dystrophy. After the
murder, she left with Godejohn to his place in Big Bend, Wisconsin.
The police found her by tracking the locale of her Facebook posts.
After arresting the ersatz Bonnie-and-Clyde duo, investigators

discovered that Gypsy was twenty-three, not nineteen (as she had claimed), and that she could walk and did not suffer from leukemia. She had faked everything to profit from fraud.

In Greek tragedy, those who killed their mothers were tormented by the avenging Furies. After Orestes and Electra (in Sophocles's play Electra) had murdered their mother to avenge her participation in the death of their father, Agamemnon, the Furies pursued Orestes, driving him out of his mind. Gypsy Blancharde was hardly tormented by anything, let alone the Furies. All she feared was getting caught. Gypsy was as heartless as any street thug killing someone who is simply in his way. Today, however, these same tragic portrayals of murder have become farcical and trivialized, though the basic narrative conventions remain more or less intact.

The question of why those who kill choose to expose themselves on social media and electronically disseminate their manifestos, memoirs, or other written content is a perplexing one. Social media have evolved, it seems, to become modern venues for expressing rudimentary human needs—the need to present oneself in a favorable light to others, the need to confess in public, the need to gossip, the need to stay connected to institutions or ideologies, and so on. The great communications theorist Marshall McLuhan argued that our technologies shaped the ways in which we evolved.[73] Social-media and its culture of vapidity and vanity have certainly changed the rules of human evolution, at least in part. After growing up in this type of culture, many people may feel it is the only option available to them, as they are unable to imagine any other channel for self-expression. The triumph of social media therefore lies in their promise to allow human needs to be expressed individualistically, even though most users quickly realize that all these platforms do is instill compulsive attachments and establish new codes of conformity. Social media are antidotes to boredom, but they do not cure it.

Consider the case of Bart Heller of Fort Wayne, Indiana, who had been dating nineteen-year-old Erin Jehl, who in 2011 was nearly twenty years his junior. The couple broke up in December of that year. Jehl and a friend went to Heller's house to retrieve some of her belongings, including her pet. After catching both girls inside the home, Heller shot the two to death. Before later turning the gun on himself, Heller posted the following on his Facebook page:

> someone call 911. three dead bodies at 3229 lima road fort wayne indiana. I've killed ryann, erin, and myself. people were warned not to f—[ing] play me and ruin me. they didn't listen. sorry about your luck.[74]

Again, there is no tragic remorse here. There are no Furies to chase Heller in the afterlife. He is extinct, having left just a miniscule mark of himself in cyberspace.

IS THERE TRULY A TALE OF MURDER?

The senselessness and banality of the types of murder discussed previously may have always existed, and one can argue that it is because of ecclesiastical and classical literary traditions that we have mythologized murder, rather than face a horrific fact—that murder might be simply a tool of self-interestedness, a knee-jerk response to anger and hate. There is no Sophoclean or Shakespearean tragedy in this act; the words of murderers every day on Facebook or some other social network clearly bring us back down to earth—into the darkened recesses of the human condition.

There are, however, recurring story tropes to every murder—a human tale of vengeance, vendetta, hatred, envy, greed, and even boredom—that might tell us a lot about who we really are as a species. The classic tales of murder certainly narrativized this, and the plain words of contemporary killers show that there is no one theory or overall tale of murder, but, rather, many such tales. From Cain and Abel to Charles Manson, both the motives and motivations for murder are disparate and complex. They put forth a portrait of the human species as having two sides—both of which are engaged in a proverbial tug-of-war. Only sporadically do we kill for survival; most of the time, our motives are hardly biological. They involve both emotionally volatile and yet strangely subconscious forces. We will return to this topic in the final chapter, where our own über-tale, as we have named it, will come to a conclusion.

Bear in mind that some murders are still seen as morally, historically, and culturally significant, not senseless and trite acts, all of which recall the tragic conventions of ancient plays. The public funerals following the murders of Abraham Lincoln and John F. Kennedy, to mention but two, were communal rituals enacted for fallen heroes—it was not coincidental that the second movement of Beethoven's *Eroica* symphony, a powerful funeral march, was played constantly at JFK's funeral. Beethoven had composed the symphony originally for Napoleon, later changing his dedication. As René Girard notes in his study of the social rites of death from antiquity to the present, the murder of heroic figures necessitates collective mourning, which is part of the maintenance of the sacred and, thus, the sustainability of civilization.[75]

Our selective overview in this chapter of the über-tale of murder reveals that there is more to murder than a single theory can ever explain. We kill because we hate, because we are offended, because we want something, and even because we are bored. When we do notice a murder publicly, there is some connection to ideals or myths. We seldom if ever read about the death of plebeians, slaves, or vassals. We read of the murders of kings, queens, saints, and others who stand out from the hoi polloi. Today, there may be *too many* tales of murder such that a more populist narrative—the murders of everyday people—prevails as the dominant trend. We are especially intrigued by the everyday murders in suburbia—a comparatively recent method of organizing populations and establishing social codes and cultures—as suggested by the popularity of films, cable series, and other media texts that strip the veneer of safety and sterility from these places. Beginning arguably with John Carpenter's 1978 film *Halloween*, which was the first to overtly challenge the perceived safety of the suburbs while also serving as a progenitor to the deluge of serial-killer films that followed in the 1980s, middle-class, "family-friendly" America has since emerged as the dominant setting for murder stories, both factual and fictional. Using an amalgam of images, interviews, unpublished documents, and other materials related to the murder in question, and generally conforming to Poe's template, programs such as the ABC network's magazine series *48 Hours* and its accumulating crime-themed spinoffs, *48 Hours Mystery*, *48 Hours Investigates*, and *48 Hours: Live to Tell*, are supplemented by acclaimed and epochal films such as *Gone Girl* (2014) based on the Gillian Flynn novel of the same name, and the even darker *Prisoners* (2013) to simultaneously indulge our engagement with the myth of suburbia and cathartic need for stories of murder, tragedy, and mayhem—the twenty-first-century version of prurient Victorianism.

A recent well-known example is the case of Laci Peterson, a pregnant young woman who was murdered in 2002. The national and even international media attention her case received was so emotionally compelling that some women were said to have faked their own kidnapping in order to garner interest in their otherwise loveless lives. Laci's disappearance over the holiday season was particularly captivating. She was pretty and pregnant, a typical suburban housewife who lived far from the squalor of inner-city ghettos where a great deal of crime occurs but rarely makes it to the airwaves. The media also saw fit to mention and even stress the fetus in nearly every news report, alluding to the larger debate on abortion in the United States and the definition of "unborn child." Once it was discovered that Laci's husband, Scott Peterson, had a secret girlfriend on the side, the story became a veritable über-tale of murder in the making. The case led to a made-for-TV film—a bygone tradition known as the "movie of the week"—as well as a full-length book, both of which possess all the elements of a Greek tragedy by revolving around what Aristotle called *pathos*, or the technique of evoking pity or sadness through the text.[76]

Fig. 1.6. Convicted murderer Scott Peterson. Image
from the California Department of Corrections

As this case and many others like it come to demonstrate, in
order for a case to become a national media sensation, the murder
must have certain underlying properties—narrative prerequisites.
These are the same properties that are found in pulp fiction and
tabloid stories of crime. If it revolves around the tantalizing mixture
of sex and violence, and especially if the characters involved are
celebrities or famous people, it is a candidate for coverage. Cold
and calculating murders of young women are also typically deemed
newsworthy. The hot-blooded and impulsive murders of spouses
by men or women, especially rich and powerful ones, are more
interesting than murders in lower-class contexts (as can be seen in
television programs such as *Dateline*). There are some exceptions to
this pattern, of course; for example, A&E's *The First 48* deals with
murders in all communities, including inner-city ones.

So why do we murder, and why are we so attracted to tales of
murder? We will attempt an answer to this in due course. Using data
from brain-imaging studies, Barbara A. Oakley, a systems engineer,

put together a persuasive case suggesting that infamous killers, such as war criminal Slobodan Milošević, have some form of antisocial personality disorder with which they were born.[77] Many killers hardly appear to be monsters physically; they are charming on the surface but harbor evil thoughts that she attributes to a pathological form of narcissism combined with emotional disturbances, a dyad that leads them to believe they are actually altruistic. Looking at murder across cultures and across time, it is obvious to us that murder cannot be explained easily without taking cultural, social, and historical factors into account. There are nasty people, and there have always been mean people around. But nastiness does not necessarily translate into murder.

As Freud maintained, there seem to be "unconscious mental acts" that we do not comprehend, and these might, purportedly, lead a Charles Manson, Dennis Rader, Pedro Alonzo López, or even a Gypsy Blancharde, to do what they did. Freud claimed that there is a continual struggle going on in our minds between the id, the ego, and the superego, as already mentioned. It is relevant to revisit his description of the id here:

> We can come nearer to the Id with images, and call it chaos, a cauldron of seething excitement. We suppose that it is somewhere in direct contact with somatic processes, and takes over from them instinctual needs and gives them mental expression. These instincts fill it with energy but it has no organization and no unified will, only an impulsion to obtain satisfaction for the instinctual needs, in accordance with the pleasure-principle.[78]

The id does indeed seem to be an unconscious factor in bringing about murder. But this is one among many possible explanations for murder. As we have seen already in this chapter, there is no one "tale," fictional, forensic, or psychiatric, that can account for every act of murder (including our supposed über-tale). The natural-born-killer theory maintains that some people are hardwired from birth to be killers. The upbringing theory ascertains, on the other hand, that killers are made, not born. This includes those killers who seek fame through serial murder, living in a maniacal celebrity culture.[79] Both sides of the debate present solid evidence for their stance, but there really is no way to decide which one is correct. Any theory is a tale; so, we should read theories as narratives of sorts. As we shall see, there might be an overall motive for murder, located somewhere in the human DNA. By studying the narrative mechanism that attempts to rationalize it, we might be able to penetrate it.

For now, it is sufficient to say that any search for an all-encompassing theory of murder might reveal an unconscious need to understand who we are through murder itself. This is a theme in Michelangelo Antonioni's marvelous thriller film *Blow-Up* (1966), in which a successful fashion photographer in the city London, whose daily life revolves around jazz, marijuana, and easy sex, starts to realize that his life is actually rather boring and devoid of meaning. He then meets a beautiful, young, and mysterious woman, whom he photographs in all kinds of poses and states of dress. One day, he notices something frightfully suspicious in the background of one of the photographs he took of her in a park. After examining the blow-up of the photo, he notices details that suggest that a murder had taken place—that he had caught on film. He goes back to the crime scene, but the body had since disappeared. Bewildered, he searches for the body or at least an explanation of why it is not there. Neither comes. So, at the end, he watches a tennis match (likely in a dream) with the players playing the game with nonexistent, imaginary balls. The image slowly fades, leaving only the grass (where the body was photographed). The unsolved murder leaves the protagonist and the viewer in a state of moral suspension. The subtext is obvious—when we end up not knowing the truth behind a murder, we tend to experience a type of existential angst, one which leaves us in a state of uncertainty.

It is by examining the content of the murderers' texts and words, looking for patterns if there are any, that perhaps we can solve the mystery behind Antonioni's metaphor. Murder for gain, revenge, vendetta, lust, jealousy, envy, hatred, anger, or any other emotional motive is fairly easy to explain as a consequence of the limbic system's operations, as we will subsequently discuss. Other murders, such as thrill murders, are not so easy to understand. Death is something we all face as being "natural;" bringing death about through murder is something we perceive instead as "unnatural," and this is why we seek explanations for it. King David murdered Uriah the Hittite to claim Bathsheba, and he escaped punishment. New Englanders in Salem, Massachusetts, hanged women as witches and would today be themselves tried for murder. The killing of infants, invalids, and the aged was accepted homicide among various peoples of the past, probably because food was scarce, and the right to life was only for those who could earn their keep. Killing is murder only in a context—historical, social, and emotional. In the 1965 movie *The 10th Victim*, this theme surfaces loud and clear. The film tells of a future society that has evolved past wars to keep the population manageable, and utilizes instead a televised murder show titled the *Big Hunt*. However, romantic feelings between the combatants start to complicate the hunt, thus emphasizing the fact that there is a moral-ethical side to murder that inhibits the formulation of any overriding theory. The narrative theory proposed here is just one possible theory—a view that narrative reveals why murderers do what they do. It is theoretical only in the sense that it provides a particular key to unlocking the reasons for murder. There are many others.

It is fitting to end this overview chapter with the words of French philosopher Joseph de Maistre, who actually summarizes the reasons for murder rather insightfully:

> There is no instant of time when one creature is not being devoured by another. Over all these numerous races of animals man is placed, and his destructive hand spares nothing that lives. He kills to obtain food and he kills to clothe himself; he kills to adorn himself; he kills in order to attack and he kills to defend himself; he kills to instruct himself and he kills to amuse himself; he kills to kill. Proud and terrible king, he wants everything and nothing resists nothing.[80]

Chapter 2

THIS IS THE ZODIAC SPEAKING

"For the writer, the serial killer is, abstractly, an analogue of the imagination's caprices and amorality."
—Joyce Carol Oates, "Where Are You Going, Where Have You Been?" *Epoch Magazine* (Fall 1966), p. 12

"If the blue meanies are going to get me they'd better get off their asses and do something."[1]

These words, written by the mysterious Zodiac Killer, were meant to goad the police (the "blue meanies") into trying to catch him. The Zodiac, like many other serial killers, enjoyed playing a cat-and-mouse game with the police, seeing himself as part of the aristoi, and seeing everyone else as the hoi polloi; that is, as meaningless pawns that he could use to satisfy his own desires, urges, and self-interests.

The Zodiac was a remarkably organized and narrative-focused serial killer who carried out his twisted crimes in Northern California in the late 1960s and on into the early 1970s, and whose identity remains officially unknown to this day.[2] Widely speculated to be disgraced elementary-school teacher and child molester Arthur Leigh Allen, the killer was the one who dubbed himself the "Zodiac" in a series of lurid communiqués and manifestos that he composed to taunt the local Bay Area press, whom he apparently considered to be as gullible and predictable as the police. These letters included four cryptograms of which only one has ever been fully decoded. The letter that follows was sent by the Zodiac Killer on August 1,

1969, to three newspapers: the *San Francisco Examiner*, the *San Francisco Chronicle*, and the *Vallejo Times-Herald*. This consistent use of a basic substitution cipher was his "calling card," as much as one can exist for a serial offender. More technically, it was his criminal signature, rather than a modus operandi, which is more instrumental and variable in nature. The letter was in some sense a proof of concept for his self-styled Zodiac narrative, indicating to the newspapers that he knew details about the murders of two teenagers that only the killer himself and a handful of detectives would know. This is known as "holdback evidence" (details withheld from the media to preserve the integrity of the case), and it included the type of weapon used and the position of the corpses left at the scene by the killer. The Zodiac made the demand that if the newspapers did not publish his letter on the front page, he would go on a "kill rampage." He also tantalized the newspapers, indicating that his identity could be determined by decoding his ciphers. This manifesto achieved its apparent purpose—it caught everyone's attention, and the "legend of the Zodiac" entered the realm of modern-day criminal folklore.

Dear Editor:

This is the murderer of the 2 teenagers last Christmass at Lake Herman & the girl on the 4th of July near the golf course in Vallejo. To prove I killed them I shall state some facts which only I & the police know. Christmas 1. Brand name of ammo Super X. 2. 10 shots were fired. 3. The boy was on his back with his feet to the car 4. The girl was on her right side feet to the west.

4th of July 1. Girl was wearing paterned slacks. 2. The boy was also shot in the knee 3. Brand name of ammo was western. Here is part of a cipher the other 2 parts of this cipher are being mailed to the editors of the Vallejo times & SF Examiner. I want you to print this cipher on the front page of your paper. In this cipher is my identity. If you do not print this cipher by the afternoon of Fry 1st of Aug 69, I will go on a kill rampage Fry night. I will cruise around all weekend killing lone people in the night then move on to kill again, until I end up with a dozen people over the weekend.[3]

The overall tenor of the letter, abrupt and aggressive in its tone, suggests that the writer was a control freak, a megalomaniac, and a malignant narcissist anxious to stake his grisly claim to fame. This assessment is reinforced by the fact that he played gruesomely with the minds of the police and the journalists by employing cryptography and what appear to be intentional misspellings, presumably to trip up forensic linguists who would compare his style to a known or quasi-known model—a mode of unraveling identity through the analysis of linguistic mannerisms that, as we saw with the Unabomber manifesto (discussed in the previous chapter), can help identify the author. The Zodiac stopped killing a few years later, leaving everyone in the dark about his identity, which seems to have been a clever strategy itself in a larger plan to protract his fame and future-proof his own legend by remaining anonymous. He clearly enjoyed his verbal duels with those in authority, suggesting that he was likely a loner who hated people, or perhaps someone—like a number of the killers discussed in this chapter—who falls somewhere on the scale of schizoid personality disorder, as evidenced by the explicit threat: "I will cruise around all weekend killing lone people in the night then move on to kill again, until I end up with a dozen people over the weekend." A similarly detailed threat about destroying a school bus and killing school children later followed.

The writings and confessions of serial killers allow us to penetrate their minds and, more generally, to seek answers to the phenomenon of serial murder itself—a type of murder that is, by way of comparison, an only recently identified phenomenon and still not entirely understood. It is defined as multiple spaced killings of at least two in number that are planned and driven by some impulse, and in most cases linked to a disordered sex drive, whether or not the murder is explicitly a sexual homicide by definition. This sexual motivation is rooted in a paraphilia—a bizarre, destructive, and dysfunctional erotic fixation not only on certain types of victims but also on specific objects, situations, actions, sights, sounds, or thoughts. Whether consciously or not, the serial killer seeks to express his motives through the narrative mechanism, as can be seen in the Zodiac's letter. In fact, all serial killer narratives allude in some sense to other narratives of murder, texts crafted by both fiction writers and other murderers. The serial killer is one part murderer, one part self-styled literary author—a morbid dramatist who loves to enact his own performances. This narrative-dramatic element may also explain the cinematic and telegenic nature of serial-killer stories, and why the media and public are mutually obsessed with their crimes and accompanying motives and narratives. The serial killer is a dark celebrity, or what crime historian and cultural theorist David Schmid has dubbed an "idol of destruction," operating in a society irrationally enamored with fame, however dubious.[4]

Among the films inspired by the case of the Zodiac, we mention the iconoclastic 1971 *Dirty Harry* and David Fincher's 2007 *Zodiac* as the two most clearly based on or inspired by his crimes. In the first film, a serial murderer displaying a range of motives named Scorpio (a sign of the Zodiac) is killed by hard-nosed cop "Dirty" Harry Callahan (played by Clint Eastwood) in a final showdown—one reminiscent of the frontier justice seen in Eastwood's earlier film career as an actor in spaghetti Westerns. The message of the film is rather transparent. To snare a serial killer, you have to play his own ruthless game—an eye for an eye. While the Zodiac was never identified, thereby escaping justice, through the cinematic medium, society at the time was given the opportunity to experience an ersatz form of catharsis—if the real killer cannot be brought to justice, at least we can get him on screen. The second film, David Fincher's *Zodiac*, which is based on the 1986 Robert Graysmith book of the same name, tapped into the fear of the unknowable that the real Zodiac evoked in his heyday. It is a remarkably accurate period piece that follows the exploits of a cartoonist (Graysmith himself) and a newspaper reporter at the *Chronicle* (named Paul Avery) who had both become mutually obsessed with tracking down—and identifying—the Zodiac. The film is essentially a procedural and thus, unlike its forerunner, *Dirty Harry*, dissects the actual murder investigation by focusing on the most renowned and puzzling feature of the Zodiac's craft—his cryptic messages.

These two films, focusing on a single offender and produced separately over a period of thirty-five years, combine to underscore the grip that the specter of the serial-killer persona has on modern society, blurring the lines between fiction and reality. Actually, it was Alfred Hitchcock's silent 1926 masterpiece, *The Lodger*, that introduced the serial killer as not only a staple on-screen character but also as a new genre of film altogether. The film, one of Hitchcock's lesser-known titles in America, also predates Fritz Lang's 1931 German film, *M*—a fictionalized biopic about serial killer Peter Kürten, which, while worthy of great acclaim, is often erroneously cited as the first serial-killer film. Within the subsequent fifty years, the serial killer would go on to become not only a motion-picture staple but also an über-narrative based on the Shadow archetype. As Carl Jung, who developed the theory of archetypes that inhabit the collective unconscious of all people, once wrote, "everyone carries a shadow and the less it is embodied in the individual's conscious life, the blacker and denser it is. . . . In spite of its function as a reservoir for human darkness—or perhaps because of this—the Shadow is the seat of creativity."[5] Serial killers evoke the Shadow archetype, and its dark form of creativity, constituting modern-day Gothic monsters.

This chapter will look at how the words of serial killers themselves, like those of the Zodiac, enable the creation of a serial-killer corpus—a type of literary data set and body of texts—for examining the reasons behind serial murder, including why we are so fascinated by it. We will also attempt our own tentative explanation of serial murder, although we will leave our overall interpretation of murder to the last chapter. We believe that one effective way to properly address serial murder is to treat it like an ongoing mystery story written by the killers themselves as a type of collected anthology.

Like the Zodiac's cryptograms, this anthologized story is cryptic in nature, the killers contributing to it, challenging us to decode their work. But first, some background facts and figures to provide some context to this story's plot.

SOME STATISTICS

The operating definition of serial murder since 2006 is the murder of two or more victims in separate incidents over a certain period of time (revised from the previous definition of three victims over a thirty-day period), and where there are concrete forensic linkages among the victims that can be established.[6] Many serial killers elude authorities for so long because their existence and the connections between their crimes often go unnoticed (because of so-called linkage blindness, which means that a common criminal signature or a connecting pattern has not been noticed by investigators). Consider the case of Milwaukee's North Side Strangler, Walter Ellis, who claimed the lives of at least seven prostitutes between 1986 and 2007. As Ellis carried out his murders, the police failed to realize that the sex slayings were the work of the same individual. Under pressure to stop the killings, not one but three men were subsequently charged with murder, with the murders committed by Ellis being broken up into groups of three and then attributed to each innocent man by the police and district attorney. Remarkably, all three were later convicted on flimsy circumstantial evidence at their trials before ultimately being cleared by DNA evidence, but only after Ellis was finally arrested and linked to all of the murders.

Overall, the statistics do not substantiate the common impression of serial killers perpetrated by the media—namely, that they are highly intelligent, cunning, unstoppable, and lurking around every corner. In the United States, where the phenomenon is most prominent, the statistics reveal that this is not the case:

Between 1900 and the 1950s, the highest number of cases of serial murder per decade was 51.

During the1960s, the number of cases rose dramatically to 174.

The rate peaked in the 1970s (534 cases), the 1980s (692 cases), and the 1990s (614 cases).

In the first decade of the 2000s, the numbers dropped significantly (337 cases).

Since 2010 there have been only 93 cases (up to 2015), despite the "serial" threshold having been lowered in 2006. This drop in incidents, in spite of the adoption of a more liberal definition of serial murder, indicates a notable decline in its occurrence.[7] However, given that the number of *unsolved* murders in America is actually increasing, a counterargument might be that there are just as many serial killers today as in the past—perhaps more—and that, once again, proper linkages between crimes simply aren't being made as they should be.[8]

There is no question that despite the statistics, serial murder continues to exist one way or another. Yet it no longer seems to own the media spotlight as it once did, having conceded its place to a new maniacal trend; namely, the mass-shooter epidemic that has dominated the United States since 2010 in particular, and which we discuss in detail further on. Also, while statistics confirm that the majority of serial killers are white males, experts now agree that the phenomenon of intra-ethnic serial murder within the African American community has been woefully overlooked, representing a huge gap in both the related research and in law-enforcement operational priorities.[9] As seen in the case of the Grim Sleeper, Lonnie Franklin Jr., who killed with impunity in Los Angeles for over thirty years, many inner-city murders, including sexual homicides, fall victim to linkage blindness or are wrongfully written off as gang crime by police. There is little question that serial killers preying on African American women have been operating, and remain at large as Franklin did for so long, in Cleveland, Atlanta, and Kansas City, based on the available data, and where clusters of over fifty stranglings (the leading modus operandi and a preferred method of killing among sexual murderers) in each city remain unsolved and have yet to be acknowledged as connected by police.[10] Regardless of locale or ethnicity, based on the details gleaned from police investigations, confessions, and criminological meta-analysis, the following motives for serial murder have been more or less established (all percentages are approximate):

enjoyment (thrill, lust, power): around 40 percent
financial gain (hit men and other professional killers): nearly 30 percent
anger: 15 percent
gang-related: 5 percent
avoiding arrest for other crimes: under 2 percent
cult-related: around 1 percent
multiple motives: around 7 percent

Consider also, in terms of self-narrative and storytelling context, how serial killers navigate their daily world with respect to employment—how their jobs define their lives between their murders and help form their identities. Consider also how certain occupations might allow them to stoke their violent fantasies and cultivate their paraphilias, to find meaning in their crimes, or merely leave their minds to wander or become idle—the devil's workshop, as they say. For instance, a curious correlation between repetitive machine work and necrophilia has been established, as well as a nexus between occupations requiring solitary travel and sexual sadism. Consider also how some of these same occupations might actually be used as covers by serial killers to stalk their prey under the guise of legitimate travel or the need to approach and engage strangers. Most important, with respect to our analysis here, consider the role of writing in some occupations—the role of exposition as a storytelling format used in daily logs, incident reports, and other records to account for one's actions during the workday or to document events and observations. Consider then the role of either writing, or of working with one's hands in any capacity, in most of the jobs that seem to be overrepresented among serial killers, some of which seem odd at first blush. The most commonly recurring occupations held by male serial killers either immediately before or during the commission of their crimes, itemized by category, are:

Skilled: (1) Aircraft assembler, (2) Shoemaker, (3) Automobile upholsterer

Semiskilled: (1) Woodsman/forestry worker, (2) Truck driver, (3) Warehouse employee

Unskilled: (1) General laborer (mover, landscaper, etc.), (2) Hotel porter, (3) Gas-station attendant

Professional: (1) Security guard, (2) Military personnel, (3) Religious official[11]

This portrait of leading serial-killer occupations is far from definitive. The vast majority of people holding these occupations are not deranged sexual murderers and are in fact law-abiding citizens who go to work, take pride in their jobs, and pay their taxes. But this same portrait is one that poses a timeless question pondered by all social scientists of causation versus correlation—of chicken versus egg. Are people, men specifically, with existing paraphilias, personality disorders, and even psychopathic traits drawn to these occupations for some reason? Or, conversely, do these same occupations, either by virtue of their solitary, repetitive, or mundane nature—or the fact that a few hold some degree of perceived authority and power—bring something to the surface in people with underlying dark fantasies but who might not otherwise pose any real threat? In other words, could certain occupations enable serial murder?

There is no obvious answer. However, the fact that serial murder is a ticket to a thrill ride for some (perhaps most) deranged individuals supports one of the hypotheses about murder from the previous chapter—namely, that boredom and professional and/or financial underachievement combined with disordered fantasy development may be triggers in some people. This is also substantiated by some of the texts we will examine in this chapter. In many of the cases we analyze here, it is easy to discern the narrative mechanism at work—the mechanism that generates the Hero, the Professional, the Revenger, and the Tragedian archetypes in the minds of killers, as well as metaphorical constructions discussed previously, such as the predator and the follower. Intelligence factors have often been cited in a bid to explain serial murderers, but these factors are not as crucial as some analysts have historically led us to believe. By and large, serial killers demonstrate normal intelligence on the IQ curve and are neither low-functioning loners nor criminal geniuses in the vein of Hannibal Lecter. They all, however, have one thing in common—the majority of their victims are women (over 50 percent), mainly white (nearly 70 percent), and relatively young (average age of 33). These figures correspond to the fact that, while African American serial killers are being increasingly identified within criminological research, white heterosexual males are overrepresented in this category of murder. Also, with rare exception, serial killers do not or will not murder outside their own race or ethnicity; so, it stands to reason that white females will therefore constitute the largest victim group. Clearly, there are sexual, racial, and psychological issues buried in these statistics. But what stands out for us are three factors: boredom, pathological narcissism, and a sense of grandiosity, as the words of serial killers themselves reveal.

WHO ARE SERIAL KILLERS?

In November 1888, the front page of the *London Daily Post* was emblazoned with the following shock headline: "Jack the Ripper Claims Fifth Victim." The headline heralded the emergence of a new type of murderer—the modern serial killer. The crimes attributed to the elusive Ripper were indeed gruesome, but not any more so than the countless butcheries that had occurred throughout history until that point. There was, however, a difference. The killer or killers who inherited the moniker Jack the Ripper had a recurring preferred victimology—downtrodden prostitutes in London's impoverished and pestilent Whitechapel district. Although there is no question that the heinous murders and mutilations attributed to the Ripper actually occurred, the problem with the emerging fable was, as we discussed in the prologue, that it had no real narrative precedent on which to spin itself. Five prostitutes—the canonical five, as they're still known—were killed in the same horrific fashion, and with the same modus operandi. From these murders a basic storyline emerged—they were all murdered by a doctor or aristocrat in a top hat who wrote taunting letters to the local press. But, as we argued previously, the story simply doesn't wash. As mentioned, Scotland Yard still has a total of eleven victims—not five—in its unsolved Whitechapel murders file. The additional six victims have been largely forgotten because the equally gruesome details of those murders inconveniently do not square with Ripper mythology.

Officially there never was any mention of a single killer. As we saw, the killer's name and the theory of a single murderer were the concoctions of journalist Thomas Bulling, who likely cooked up the Ripper tale to sell newspapers. There were four Ripper letters, not three, as the myth prefers to tell it.[12] In the end, none of these details matter. With the Ripper tale, brutal sexually motivated serial murders were trivialized and monetized as part of a fledgling crime-tourist industry while the real killer or killers walked free. The age of mass hysteria and of the serial killer as media celebrity was born.

The image of the serial killer as a shadowy and terrifying figure who commits murders as a result of being compelled by some inner dark force (the Shadow) emerged with the Ripper legend, riding in the slipstream of the contemporaneous Gothic genre and the detective stories of Poe, Dickens, and Doyle. After the Ripper, tales of serial murderers—true, untrue, or otherwise embellished—merged into an overarching master narrative that became a metaphor for understanding the raison d'être of murder. The term "serial murder," as we know it today, was actually coined by a senior police detective in interwar Germany's Weimar Republic who used *sirienmörder* ("series murder" in German) to describe the inexpiable crimes of Peter Kürten, the so-called Vampire of Düsseldorf mentioned previously.

To this day, the Ripper story, more so than any other serial-killer narrative, has become a media mythology all its own, evolving—or perhaps devolving—into its self-styled school of study known as "Ripperology," cultivated by amateur armchair detectives, hobby-ists, and murder enthusiasts who feed a gullible public. The Ripper case, over a century later, continues to sustain a protracted, world-wide media frenzy. The dramatic murders of prostitutes in the midst of a changing urbanizing world caught everyone's attention, with many seeing the murders as a symptom of modernity and its loss of moral values. The British media's obsession with the Ripper, as less a person than as a metaphorical construct, soon surfaced in America, where journalists became mesmerized by the case of Howard Henry (H. H.) Holmes, who killed at least twenty-seven, and as many as two hundred, people at his ghastly Chicago "Murder Castle" in the early 1890s. From the sensationalistic coverage of the case, the serial-killer saga spread throughout the United States, where it was appropriated by pulp fiction and dime novel writers, particularly after Holmes became the first killer to sell his own story to a major media outlet, rational-izing his murders in his own words. Sometimes cited as America's Jack the Ripper, Holmes established the blueprint for the serial killer as raconteur—self-styled storyteller, dramatist, and narrator, exposing himself autobiographically to the world.[13] It is now an expectation that undergirds our perception of real and fictitious serial murderers alike.

So, who is the serial killer? Who are the people behind the atroci-ties and the accompanying stories that they and the media produce in tandem? There are so many theories about *him* (and as the statistics above show, it is mainly a *he*) that it would be useless to even try to extrapolate from them a general psychological profile. It is perhaps for this reason that so-called criminal profiling (known as the actu-arial method in the United States) is only accurate about 4 percent of the time, which, ironically, is the equivalent of luck.[14] Most theories portray the serial killer as a psychopath, sociopath, or psychotic with no empathy for others or control over his impulses. But although the serial killer is indeed clinically insane, he certainly knows how to enact his insanity in a methodical and meticulous way.

So, what is going on in his mind? Perhaps many things are going on simultaneously. Certainly, many of the best fictional works about serial killers understand this, portraying him not only as a psychopath but more significantly as a Gothic monster who is motivated by a deep hatred of the world and the compulsion to control it on his own terms. A classic example of the killer as controller is Charles Perrault's fairytale "Bluebeard." The story details the misadventures of an evil aristocrat who, with a distinctively repugnant blue beard, murders each of his wives for disobeying his order to not look into a locked room, a room that contained the bodies of his previous wives. Nobody really knows why Bluebeard became a serial murderer. In fact, no one seems to care. But there is little doubt that obsessive control of women was a primary motivating factor. In the end, his young new wife exposes him; and it is her brothers who finally slay Bluebeard, putting an end to the mayhem. Today, a controlling husband who murders his wife, or a series of wives—often with a financial or other extrinsic motivation—is known as a Bluebeard killer. True to form, the legend tells us something about reality—if only in the text.

THE ZODIAC—SENIOR AND JUNIOR

One of the more prominent aspects of the original Zodiac case was, as we saw, the killer's use of cryptography to write his letters and manifestos. One of his encrypted texts, consisting of 408 symbols, was cracked by a husband-and-wife team; but in it the killer had not included his name as he had mendaciously promised. In November 1969, he sent a letter constructed with a 340-character code to the media that has never been deciphered. It is reproduced below. At the bottom it includes the killer's telltale symbol—a circle with a cross overlay—that he had, by this point, adopted as his criminal signature. To call it a trademark would be to state the obvious given that, like much of his writing, the Zodiac Killer appears to be a plagiarist who purloined the emblem from—not surprisingly—the Zodiac wristwatch company, today owned by Fossil, Inc.

Fig. 2.1. A 1969 cryptogram sent to the San Francisco–area media by the Zodiac Killer, and the first such cryptogram to feature his distinctive emblem as a signature at bottom center.

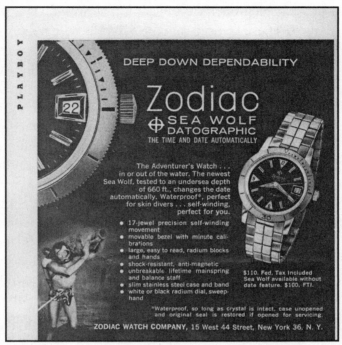

Fig. 2.2. A contemporaneous late-1960s magazine advertisement for the Swiss wristwatch company Zodiac, bearing an identical brand logo to the Zodiac signature. While the twelve signs of the Zodiac do use a celestial cross, the stylized interpretation of that cross by the watch company is sufficiently proprietary that its concurrent—and identical—reprinting by the Zodiac Killer cannot be dismissed as coincidence. Image from Zodiac™ Watch Company.

The mystery, incitement, and widespread paranoia that this likely unsolvable cipher evokes to this day all attest to the Zodiac's main intention for composing and sending it—to intentionally obfuscate his identity and to revel in the stupidity that he attributed to the police. The Zodiac's writing can thus be seen to be part of a nefarious and pretentious strategy. There is little doubt that he was a spiteful narcissist bent on showing his superiority as an aristoi to the world of the hoi polloi. The individuals he killed were nothing more than pawns in this plan. By 1969, the Zodiac's writing had become increasingly paraphiliac and as compulsive as the murders themselves—the tail had started wagging the dog. Since the preceding letter has never been properly decoded, it may well be that it cannot be deciphered because he used random symbols with no key or code behind them, doing so to intentionally stymie efforts to decode it and frustrate those in authority. But simply writing and posting the letter might also have proven sufficiently satisfying for the Zodiac, perhaps evidence of an understudied and still-misunderstood disorder known as *coprographia*, a compulsion that—whether on its own or in concert with acts of violence—impels individuals to use words to hurt, terrify, or humiliate while sexually and murderously fulfilling their needs and desires. In effect, the serial killer feels an urge to murder and communicate with his audience in tandem.

The combination of the two—murder and communication—definitively links violence, fantasy, and writing within the same disordered wheelhouse. The first officially documented case of this murder-narrative disorder that took the form of what we today recognize as coprographia was child killer and cannibal Albert Fish. Dubbed the Werewolf of Wysteria and Brooklyn Vampire by the period media, Fish sent sadistically bizarre and taunting letters to the families of at least nine victims he murdered between 1924 and 1932, up to the time he was sentenced to die in the electric chair at the infamous Sing Sing prison in 1936. By the time of his death, it is speculated that Fish had begun substituting the thrill of murder for the thrill of writing autobiographical letters detailing his murders. Writing had become, as it did clearly with the Zodiac, an end in itself—a more effective and less risky mechanism for instilling terror and pain. What few experts had bothered to assess was how—much less why—writing, versus other actions, was a logical offshoot of actual serial murder. The murderer-as-author appears as a common pattern, as we have seen with both the Zodiac and Fish. But while Fish signed his letters with his own name, the Zodiac preferred anonymity. The meaning of the Zodiac's circle-cross symbol has been a matter of debate—there are websites devoted to speculating about what it signifies, apart from the obvious parallel with the Zodiac watch manufacturer. The watch logo aside, the circle has ancient origins as an astrological symbol, and the Zodiac's simultaneous use of cryptography and astrological symbolism suggests that he was reveling in his own self-styled mythology—he was the apotheosis of the Hero criminal archetype.

While the Zodiac did indeed manage to elude capture through his furtive writing and killing methods, his overall style would inspire an heir apparent to his legend, one who would, however, eventually be caught. The Zodiac "junior" was a similarly disordered serial killer who not only adopted the original Zodiac's symbol but who also clearly wanted to finish the mission his idol had left unfinished. Beginning in 1990, Heriberto "Eddie" Seda—a comparatively less organized offender—embarked on a three-year reign of terror, not in the California Bay Area, but nearly three thousand miles away in New York City. Before being caught on June 18, 1996, Seda had killed three people and critically wounded four others. Upon arrest, and as was already speculated given his emulation of the earlier Zodiac letters and emblem, Seda admitted that he idolized the original Zodiac Killer and wished to protract his crimes as a type of East Coast emissary. At the time, he lived with his mother and half sister in East New York; he did not work and kept largely to himself.

On November 17, 1989, the NYPD's 17th Precinct began receiving letters marked with the heading: "This is the Zodiac," an obvious allusion to the letter and accompanying salutation sent to the *San Francisco Examiner* twenty years earlier (August 4, 1969), constituting a narrative "retake" of the original (senior) Zodiac's correspondence with the California media. The first of the letters contained a menacing warning of twelve murders yet to come, one for each sign of the Zodiac. It also claimed that one murder had already taken place; but with no supporting evidence or knowledge of holdback evidence deducible from the letter, the police dismissed it as a hoax. The manifesto also contained a drawing of a circle divided into a pie configuration consisting of twelve sections with oblique lines, each pie slice representing an astrological sign of the Zodiac. As he had threatened to do, the author soon went on a killing spree to carry out his diabolical plan—a plan intended to complete the unfinished handiwork of Zodiac senior.

Given that few, if any, copycat killers—a rare and contested phenomenon in its own right—are such gushy fan boys, the question emerges: What was going on in Seda's mind? As Kieran Crowley has observed in his book about Zodiac junior, *Sleep My Little Dead: The True Story of the Zodiac Killer*, Seda may have been abused as a child, both physically and mentally, like a great number of other serial killers.[15] While childhood abuse is not necessarily deterministic and not all abused children go on to become predators, there appears to be a strong correlation between childhood trauma and propensity for both sexual violence and serial murder. Given that Seda did not replicate the modus operandi and especially the symbolism of the original Zodiac Killer's crimes (Seda committed run-by shootings with a homemade zip gun), his motivation appears to have been his adoption of the legend of the original Zodiac to obfuscate his sexual sadism. On the other hand, Seda may have believed, in his twisted imagination, that the work of the Zodiac needed to be completed, perhaps to restore within his own mind a sense of harmony from the disorder he felt. In the end, his words reveal rather bluntly that his adoption of the Zodiac persona was really to get vengeance for not having been able to satisfy his lustful desires. During his confession, Seda admitted that he killed in order to satisfy his sexual whims, not to emulate the original Zodiac as a kind of deranged disciple. As his sister reported him saying: "I'm going to start killing. I'm going to start killing because I'm not getting no sex."[16] Adopting the Zodiac's story—and writing style—was therefore little more than a tactic to conceal his base libidinous motives. Through a type of Zodiac redux, he sought to hide the pathetic nature of his perversions and his willingness to supplant sex acts with murderous violence. In the end, Seda tried to pull off his ultimately unconvincing ruse by writing a few letters in the style of the Zodiac, and the public and media were hooked. It was nothing more than pageantry and fakery.

SELF-IMPORTANCE

There is something inherently egomaniacal about all serial killers, something in their writing and storytelling that blurts out a perverted and inflated sense of self-importance. To put it more directly, serial killers are malignant narcissists who kill to satisfy some deviant urge, seeing themselves as superior in many cases despite having no real corresponding achievements. At the very least, they see their urges as trumping the rights—and even the lives—of others. These urges are typically sexual in nature, but they can also be driven by a superiority complex as a type of auto-eroticism. In *Crime and Punishment* (explored in chapter 1), Raskolnikov is motivated to kill because he sees others as unreflective automatons whom he feels compelled to save from their humdrum existence; he displays a particular form of narcissism or self-importance that can be called simply intellectual. The same type of intellectual self-importance is seen in the case of the Unabomber, also discussed in the previous chapter. Kaczynski was a modern-day Raskolnikov—an ideological aristoi who committed murder to teach the world what he saw as a self-styled moral lesson, by targeting those whom he thought were destroying it. The difference of course is that Raskolnikov's murders were recounted by Dostoevsky as novelist whereas the Unabomber wrote his own manifesto to explicate his mission while he was still at large. The letters of the Zodiac junior were intellectual charlatanism—the writings by Kaczynski were not. Kaczynski holds a doctorate in mathematics and was a professor at UC Berkeley, and he used his intellectual skills to compose a treatise on the state of the world that still raises many important points today—points rendered irrelevant, mind you, by his murderous actions.

A motivated killer like Kaczynski is more the exception than the rule. Serial killers are hardly intellectual aristoi, like Raskolnikov, Hannibal Lecter, or Professor Moriarty. They are, generally speaking, low-functioning creeps and cowards who continuously lie and fly false flags to conceal their failings. Take, for instance, the Green River Killer, Gary Ridgway, whose methods and motives varied greatly from those of Kaczynski. Ridgway murdered prostitutes rather than university or airline experts, drawing on a lexicon that highlights an inherent brand of cowardice and vileness.

> "I picked prostitutes as victims because they were easy to pick up, without being noticed. I knew they would not be reported missing right away, and might never be reported missing."
>
> "I liked to drive by the clusters around the county and think about the women I placed there."
>
> "I'm a murderer, not a rapist."
>
> "I always wondered what it would be like to kill someone."[17]

These statements constitute a perfect textbook page for a literary criminological analysis of the serial-killer mind. The first citation is a rather clear acknowledgement of his own cowardice; Ridgway victimized those who were most vulnerable and thus the easiest to kill and dispose of. In the second statement, he evinces an inflated sense of self-importance, indicative of the Hero narrative archetype—delusions of unrequited romance and grandeur through which he fantasized about his horrific and necrophiliac crimes as amounting to works of art. This is also evident when he qualifies his craft as murder and not as rape. The last statement reveals that Ridgway was also a thrill seeker who, again in line with the Hero typology, saw murder as a calling—an area of curiosity and a Quixotic journey of self-exploration to be pursued at all costs. In other words, his destiny.

Ridgway eventually pleaded guilty to forty-eight charges of murder, but he is suspected of killing upward of one hundred women. His hatred of prostitutes is saliently obvious in his words, but he also extends his visceral aversion to the human race and beyond.

> "I hate most prostitutes. I didn't want to pay them for sex."
>
> "I don't believe in man, God nor Devil. I hate the whole damned human race, including myself. . . . I preyed upon the weak, the harmless and the unsuspecting. This lesson I was taught by others: Might makes right."[18]

Ridgway's endemic hatred of not only women but the whole of humanity is central to his delusion of self-importance, a state of mind that propelled his particular narrative mechanism—manifesting itself in both oral and written form. As such, it reveals how a Hero killer internally rationalizes and even mythologizes his crimes.

Take, as another example, the case of Carl Panzram, an early-twentieth-century serial killer who confessed, in his autobiography, to having committed twenty-one murders, along with over one thousand rapes of young men. He was executed in 1930 for the murder of a prison employee at Leavenworth Federal Penitentiary. In his autobiography, he describes himself as "rage personified," a rage that comes to the surface through his own words (needing no further commentary).

> "I'll kill the first man that bothers me."
> "I have no desire whatsoever to reform myself. My only desire is to reform people who try to reform me, and I believe the only way to reform people is to kill them. My motto is: Rob 'em all, rape 'em all, and kill 'em all."
> "Hurry it up, I could hang a dozen men while you're fooling around." [His last words before being executed.][19]

Some serial killers take their disordered and inflated sense of superiority and compulsion to create myths about themselves a step further, into a deliberate barbaric quest for celebrity status. This is arguably the characteristic that most separates serial killers from other offenders who kill under different circumstances or for different motives (discussed in the previous chapter). The serial killer's reflexivity of action, or his autobiographical self-awareness as an ersatz public figure, suggests that fame and celebrity are two of the chief driving forces in his cliché-laden mind. In the digital age, celebrities emerge out of nowhere even when they offer no demonstrable talents or noteworthy achievements other than simply being online. They are what we call para-celebrities, for the most part charlatans who are to genuine public figures what the paranormal is to the normal—that is, they operate alongside the real thing but lack authentic verisimilitude. They spring from the most vapid of formats—reality television, gossip forums, social media—and their accomplishments, if any, are quickly forgotten. The serial killer's sense of self-importance fits in with this bizarre demimonde created by cyberspace. He is hardly a monster in the Gothic tradition; he is a pathetic celebrity seeker who thrives on unfounded braggadocio, forcing his perceived self-importance upon the world.

This curious phenomenon appears to have begun, or at least gained significant momentum, during the decadent 1980s when to be wealthy or notorious, in the absence of any qualities or accomplishments, was grounds for celebrity status. As corporate raiders, televangelists, stock swindlers, and real-estate tycoons flaunted their garish possessions and lifestyles in the public eye, the entire culture of celebrity underwent a reengineering. Suddenly, it seemed that anyone could be famous for any reason; and, if wealth or genuine talent were out of reach, more depraved steps could be taken to ensure notoriety. One of these was serial murder, as the rise in statistics for murder during that era (as cited at the outset of this chapter) aptly demonstrate. While the gangsters of the public-enemy era, such as John Dillinger and "Machine Gun Kelly" (George Francis Barnes Jr.) earned some degree of romanticized outlaw celebrity, by the 1980s, the rise of the para-celebrity serial killer convinced the FBI and Congress that serial murder was a major domestic threat facing America, since the usual motives for murder (revenge, jealousy, betrayal, and so on) no longer applied. It was a whole new ball game—one that made serial murder a particularly cold-blooded and nefarious form of killing without precedent.[20]

Take the case of the BTK Killer, Dennis Rader. As discussed briefly in the previous chapter, Rader claimed that it was a "monster" inside of himself that compelled him to commit his murders; however, he also admitted in virtually the same breath that he enjoyed reading about his sadistic crimes—targeting entire families for execution in some cases—in the local, state, and national media. Like both Zodiac

Killers, senior and junior, Rader also wrote letters to taunt authorities and torment the residents of the city of Wichita, Kansas. And
like Albert Fish, Rader demonstrated a penchant for coprographia,
especially during the respites, or "cooling-off periods," between his
murders. He even went so far as to reveal to an intended victim that he
had been hiding inside her home, waiting for her to come, one night
in 1979 after stalking her and learning her nightly routine. On the date
that Rader had selected to ambush, torture, and kill her; however, she
had other plans and did not arrive home as planned, thereby saving
her own life unwittingly. Rader, thwarted in his desire to murder her,
obtained sadistic gratification by instead composing and later mailing
a macabre poem, written in free verse, to the would-be victim, making
her aware of how close she had come to a horrific end that night. The
poem, titled "Oh, Anna Why Didn't You Appear?" is a bloated attempt
at poetry, one in which he admonishes his victim for not appearing to
satisfy his whims and indulge in a kind of rapturous fear.[21]

Rader killed to provide a sense of worth to his otherwise useless
life, coming to see himself as being above the rules of morality,
beyond good and evil—a kind of Nietzschean superman. In the end,
he turned out to be a creepy little man, with absolutely no worth
to his life. His attempts at poetic writing were equally as awful, as
anyone can see for himself or herself.[22]

The murderous Nietzschean figure is actually defined insightfully, and ironically, by convicted murderer Albert Loeb: "A
superman is, on account of certain superior qualities inherent in him,
exempted from the ordinary laws which govern men. He is not liable
for anything he may do."[23] The case of Nathan Leopold and Albert
Loeb, wealthy students at the University of Chicago, is a relevant
one, since they espoused Nietzsche's construct of the superman, or
Übermensch ("overman"), as an intellectual Hero figure. They kidnapped and murdered schoolboy Robert ("Bobby") Franks in May
1924 simply to demonstrate that they could do it, in exemplifica-
tion of their purported intellectual superiority. Their arrogance, in
keeping with the Hero mind-set, spurred them on to play their self-

styled Nietzschean role—carrying out the perfect crime—thus ful-filling their envisaged destiny. The Franks murder by two otherwise law-abiding and intelligent individuals with a shared delusion later inspired the 1929 British stage play and eventually the 1948 Alfred Hitchcock film, *Rope*, starring Jimmy Stewart.

This same sense of immunity from the laws of common people may be the reason why serial killers have no fear of punishment. The words of the Railway Killer, Angel Maturino Reséndiz, the itinerant hobo responsible for up to fifteen murders across the United States and Mexico in the 1990s near railroads, bear this out concretely. Shortly after arriving on death row, he made the following statement:

> I don't believe in death. I know the body is going to go to waste. But me, as a person, I'm eternal. I'm going to be alive forever.[24]

In ancient myths, this kind of attitude was called *hubris*—excessive pride or self-confidence leading to self-destruction. Whatever we call it, it demonstrates that some, perhaps all, serial killers are narcissists who are prepared to reject what the rest of society accepts as moral behavior. A classic example of such hubris, as we have already seen, is Charles Manson (see chapter 1), who ordered murders for no other reason than to carry out his personal supercilious vendetta against society and, as was presented at his trial by the late famous prosecutor Vincent Bugliosi, to initiate a race war between whites and blacks, inspired by the song "Helter Skelter" on the White Album by the Beatles. The helter skelter mind-set was a mainstay at Manson's cult compound in Death Valley. Manson is believed to have seen his prophesized race war as his path to eventual world domination, becoming the leader of the new world order after the blacks inevitably destroyed the whites but would ultimately desire, as he theorized, a white leader in the aftermath.

> "I've killed no one. I've ordered no one to be killed. These children who come to you with their knives, they're your children. I didn't teach them, you did."

"Total paranoia is just total awareness."

"Believe me, if I started murdering people there'd be none of ya left."

"You know, if I wanted to kill somebody, I'd take this book and beat you to death with it. And I wouldn't feel a thing. It'd be just like walking to the drug store."[25]

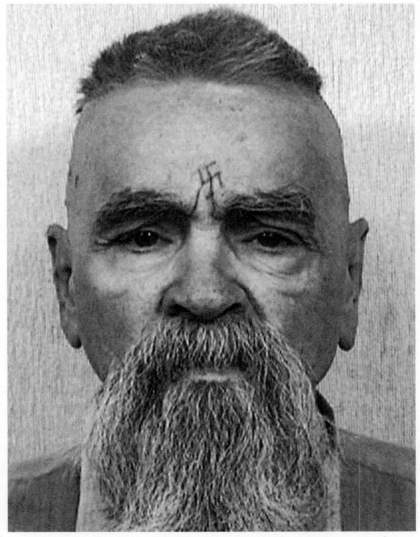

Fig. 2.3. Charles Manson in 2012. Image from the California Department of Corrections.

"I've killed 20 people, man. I love all that blood."

"Even psychopaths have emotions, then again, maybe not."

"We've all got the power in our hands to kill, but most people are afraid to use it. The ones who aren't afraid, control life itself."

"You maggots make me sick, I will be avenged. Lucifer dwells within us all."[26]

Fearlessness not only of punishment but even of death is, in fact, a recurrent theme in serial-killer tales. Consider again the words of Albert Fish, who has become a case study in both coprographia and other related paraphilias, including both pedophilia and necrophilia. Fish's manifestos went beyond providing gory recitations of his crimes and transcripts of his murderous fantasies. Fish instead shows an outright indifference toward death, and emphasizes his satisfaction in inflicting pain on others.

"Going to the electric chair will be the supreme thrill of my life."

"I have no particular desire to live. I have no particular desire to be killed. It is a matter of indifference to me. I do not think I am altogether right."

"I always had the desire to inflict pain on others and to have others inflict pain on me. I always seemed to enjoy everything that hurt. The desire to inflict pain, that is all that is uppermost."

"I saw so many boys whipped, it took root in my head."

"I like children, they are tasty."[27]

Many epithets were devised to describe Fish. He was known not only as the Werewolf of Wysteria and Brooklyn Vampire (as mentioned) but also as the Gray Man, the Moon Maniac, and the Bogey Man—all appropriate metaphors that reflect the horror of his monstrous and sadistic crimes that included sexual torture and cannibalism. Between his crimes, in addition to writing letters about the murders and sending them to his victims' grieving families, he also inflicted pain and mutilation on himself—over a dozen needles were found in his scrotum by doctors examining his body after he was executed.[28] Fish's crimes were so ghastly at the time that they defied any definitive clinical or forensic categorization, hence the litany of Gothic metaphors assigned to him by the public, the press, and even the police of the period. Today, in addition to his specific paraphilias, we recognize in his own words (reproduced above) an allusion of his murders to vampirism and especially its intrinsic use of blood symbolism.

A more recent example of such symbolism is the case of Welsh teenager Mathew Hardman. Arrested in 2002 for stabbing a ninety-year-old woman to death, Hardman had positioned her body post-mortem with her legs splayed on a stool, with two candlesticks placed on her corpse, and with a third candlestick placed on a nearby mantelpiece. He had thus simultaneously posed the body and choreo-graphed the entire room to suit a specific narrative of the vampire ritual that was to follow. Hardman then carved out the victim's heart and drained the blood from her leg, drinking it as part of a vam-piristic rite, believing that these symbolic actions would render him immortal. When the police searched Hardman's bedroom, they dis-covered books and Internet materials on vampirism. Hardman came to be known, rather aptly, as the Vampire Boy Killer.

MONSTERS

H. H. Holmes, mentioned several times already, built a notorious "Murder Castle," as it came to be known, where he hid his victims, living in his own made-up Gothic story world, complete with mon-sters and vampires. Here's what he said:

> I was born with the devil in me. I could not help the fact that I was a murderer, no more than the poet can help the inspiration to sing. . . . I was born with the evil one standing as my sponsor beside the bed where I was ushered into the world, and he has been with me since.[29]

The murderer-as-monster is a theme that we have been pursuing in some detail in this book, since it unites two main aspects of literary criminology—the motives for murder and their explication through narrative and its attendant symbolism. Monsters have been around in literature, myth, and pseudoscience since humanity's beginnings, of course. They prowl at night and seek victims relentlessly. Sounds like the inner-narratives, interviews, and manuscripts created by many of the serial killers discussed here, doesn't it? To paraphrase Holmes, they were born with the devil inside them. And the devil often appears in the guise of a monster—an aberrant and grotesque figure. But sometimes the devil can appear harmless, even handsome and charming; and even witty and droll. Sometimes the devil is less the Jungian Shadow than he is another one of Jung's archetypes—the Trickster. A case in point is the monster known as John Wayne Gacy.[30]

Gacy was not looking for his fifteen minutes of fame. He was looking to satisfy his gruesome libidinous urges, with no consideration whatsoever for his victims. He raped and killed at least thirty-three adolescent males between 1972 and 1978. Following his arrest in December 1978, he was quickly dubbed the Killer Clown because he also worked as a clown at children's gatherings, thus conforming with not only Jung's Trickster but also the historical mythology in many cultures that clowns are secret folk devils—jokers hiding evil intentions and machinations behind a jocund mask. It's a foundational mythology that cross-cuts time and space, and which is at the heart of the ongoing and bizarrely postmodern killer-clown craze, or "Great Clown Scare of 2016," that was rooted in the universally sinister iconography of the creepy clown. It's an iconography that, once paired with social media, essentially created a new form of social panic.[31]

The evil-clown figure has become a fixture in the modern collective imagination, epitomized by Stephen King's 1986 novel *It*, which has many subtle allusions to the Gacy case. Gacy lured his victims to his home, where he would sexually assault and strangle them after first plying them with liquor. Once his victims had their inhibitions diminished by alcohol, he would goad the young men into trying a "handcuff trick" that he used as a contrivance for producing steel handcuffs that would minimize resistance, placing them on his victims in order to restrain them before then attacking and killing them. He interred twenty-six of these victims in the crawlspace under his home, three others on his property, and four in a nearby river. The glut of maggots found everywhere in Gacy's house became a symbol of the hideousness of his crimes. Forensically, maggots allow the investigator to estimate the time elapsed since death. But in this case they also served a symbolic purpose—they represented destructive forces within Gacy's mind, recalling Pink Floyd's marvelous concept album *The Wall*, where maggots are insects of moral destruction.

Fig. 2.4. John Wayne Gacy. Image from the Des Plaines, Illinois, Police Department.

After twenty-eight corpses were dug up from beneath his home, Gacy made the following casual-sounding and self-pitying statements:

"I should never have been convicted of anything more serious than
   running a cemetery without a license."
"They were just a bunch of worthless little queers and punks."
"I see myself more as a victim rather than a perpetrator. . . . I was
   cheated out of my childhood."
"You can kiss my ass." [Uttered just before being executed.][32]

Gacy's dismissal of his victims as "worthless little queers and
punks" reveals his supercilious and manipulative view of his victims
as irrelevant pieces of meat. He also refers to being "cheated out
of" his childhood, thus completing his own criminal profile with
elements of both a superiority complex and a troubled childhood—a
lethal combination indeed.

The case of Jeffrey Dahmer presents us with a similar breed of
monster. Unlike Gacy, however, Dahmer admitted his guilt from the
start. There are also a number of mitigating factors in the Dahmer
story, which may have shaped him into the monster that he ultimately became. Like Gacy, Dahmer kept the remains of his victims
in his home. The remains of a total of thirteen dismembered males
were found in his apartment; he also confessed that he had saved the
frozen body parts to eat later.

Dahmer was raised in a broken family, and he was sexually
abused at the age of eight by a man in his neighborhood. In his
youth, he decapitated and dismembered a dog and mounted its head
on a stick next to a wooden cross—a symbolic act that speaks of
ritualistically expressed anger against the events in his life that kept
him from growing up normally. An early indicator that Dahmer was
undergoing a deep internal struggle was at age seven, when he gave
a bowl of tadpoles to a teacher as a twisted sign of affection. When
the teacher gave away the bowl to one of Dahmer's friends, he killed
the tadpoles in revenge. By the age of thirteen, he had become an
alcoholic; and while in high school, he confessed to having sexual
fantasies about corpses, a complex and particularly aberrant paraphilia known as necrophilia. At the age of eighteen, he killed his
first victim the year his parents divorced, 1978, suggesting that the

breakup of his family was a key factor—a psychological trigger known as decompensation, that is, a trigger for sexually motivated violence—ultimately shaping him into the monster he would become. Addressing the court at his sentencing, Dahmer revealed his inner turmoil by claiming, "I knew I was sick or evil or both."[33] If Dahmer had been raised by an intact or more vigilant family able to take notice of his deranged behavior and substance abuse, and more importantly had he not been sexually molested, would he have gone on to become that same monster? In this case, the discourse-based evidence is rather revealing. Read his words:

> "I carried it too far, that's for sure."
> "My consuming lust was to experience their bodies. I viewed them as objects, as strangers. It is hard for me to believe a human being could have done what I've done."
> "I couldn't find any meaning for my life when I was out there, I'm sure as hell not going to find it in here. This is the grand finale of a life poorly spent and the end result is just overwhelmingly depressing. . . . It's just a sick, pathetic, wretched, miserable life story, that's all it is. How it can help anyone, I've no idea."[34]

The theme of the excerpt can be seen in the part that reads: "I couldn't find any meaning in my life." There is a sense of self-pity here, describing his "life story" as "sick, wretched, and miserable." Did this turn him into a ritualistic monster whose "consuming lust was to experience their bodies"? Dahmer engaged in twisted hierophantic ritual, showing a desire for transcendence through desecration of the body. The souvenirs he took of his victims were mementos of this desire.

Gacy and Dahmer were pegged as monsters by others, mainly the media. But as we have seen, some serial killers actually describe themselves as monsters, feeding an obvious need to frame their psychopathic self-awareness in narrative-mythical terms. Let's take another look at, once again, the words of the BTK Killer, Dennis Rader:

"When this monster entered my brain, I will never know, but it is here to stay. How does one cure himself? I can't stop it, the monster goes on, and hurts me as well as society. Maybe you can stop him. I can't."

"I actually think I may be possessed with demons, I was dropped on my head as a kid."[35]

Fig. 2.5. Jeffrey Dahmer, following his arrest in Milwaukee in July 1991. Image from the Milwaukee Police Department.

Like other serial killers, BTK would describe his "possession" by demons as being the result of some childhood event—that he was dropped on his head as a kid. This is exculpatory narrative at its best, with the subtext being "it's not my fault." It is what in conventional criminology is known as a neutralization strategy, more specifically what is known as the denial of responsibility—one of the five leadings strategies used by offenders to neutralize and minimize their wrongdoing.[36] Serial killers seem to be particularly effective at this, serving as their own self-styled psychoanalysts, or more accurately, their own narrative therapists. But, as BTK's words suggest, the narrative mechanism is, in his hands, a device for manipulation, deception, and confabulation. Serial killers are inveterate liars. They love to play the part of the evil or uncanny monster who terrorizes the villagers, bringing to reality an archetypal narrative through their twisted minds. But they also like to hide behind our offender-centric and adversarial justice system once they're caught. It's hypocrisy; it's cowardice. Their "explanations" are thus part of an expeditious rationalization mechanism, allowing them to enjoy their role as a fearsome monster but also a pitiable victim of a failed upbringing.

The monster subtext comes out not only in the lexicon used by the killers, as we have seen here, but also in the actual style of their handwriting. Consider the following note left by David Berkowitz, the Son of Sam, which was found in his car upon his arrest on August 10, 1977:

The leftward slant of the letters, all capitals, is a common font used in horror movies and pulp-fiction magazines to suggest creepiness and convey a scream. We can actually hear in our heads the monster shouting at us through the font itself. But he is a gutless monster. Berkowitz wanted to attend his victims' funerals but avoided doing so because of police surveillance. He was completely invested and involved in every aspect of his crimes, indicating that he was not really out of touch with reality—certainly not to the extent of being considered insane. His use of a horror film calligraphy underscores his willful intent to frighten readers. There is insanity in the writing style and contents of the letter, of course. But there is also a great deal of cleverness, plotting, pageantry, and self-gratification. To be able to plan, commit, and keep a tally of each murder, Berkowitz showed calculating lucidity amidst his contrived madness. As investigators eventually discovered, he was abandoned as an infant, then adopted by Pearl and Nathan Berkowitz. Pearl died when he was sixteen, which greatly anguished him. He researched his birth parents, portraying his victimization as follows: "I was an accident, unwanted. My birth was either out of spite or by accident."[37] He lived, like many documented killers, in isolation, was sexually incompetent, and was "prone to fabricate elaborate lies about his bedroom prowess, all the while intent upon revenge against the women who habitually rejected him."[38]

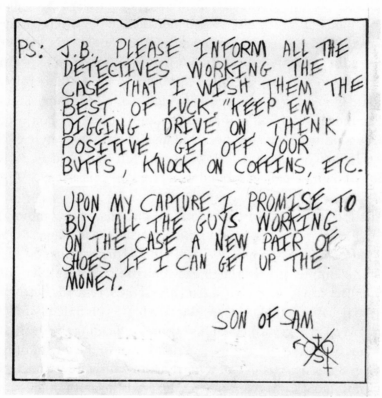

Fig. 2.6. Son of Sam Letter, August 10, 1977.

The following letter was left near the bodies of two of his victims in August 1977 and was addressed to NYPD detective Joseph Borelli. In this letter, Berkowitz introduces his self-made nickname, the Son of Sam, for the first time.[39]

I am deeply hurt by your calling me a wemon hater! I am not. But I am a monster. I am the "Son of Sam." I am a little brat. When father Sam gets drunk he gets mean. He beats his family.

Sometimes he ties me up to the back of the house. Other times he locks me in the garage. Sam loves to drink blood. "Go out and kill," commands father Sam. Behind our house some rest. Mostly young—raped and slaughtered—their blood drained—just bones now. Papa Sam keeps me locked in the attic too. I can't get out but I look out the attic window and watch the world go by. I feel like an outsider. I am on a different wavelength then everybody else—programmed too kill. However, to stop me you must kill me. Attention all police: Shoot me first—shoot to kill or else keep out of my way or you will die! Papa Sam is old now. He needs some blood to preserve his youth. He has had too many heart attacks. "Ugh, me hoot, it hurts, sonny boy." I miss my pretty princess most of all. She's resting in our ladies house. But I'll see her soon. I am the "Monster"—"Beelzebub"—the chubby behemouth. I love to hunt. Prowling the streets looking for fair game—tasty meat. The wemon of Queens are prettyist of all. It must be the water they drink. I live for the hunt—my life. Blood for papa. Mr. Borrelli, sir, I don't want to kill anymore. No sur, no more but I must, 'honor thy father.' I want to make love to the world. I love people. I don't belong on earth. Return me to yahoos. To the people of Queens, I love you. And I want to wish all of you a happy Easter. May God bless you in this life and in the next. And for now I say goodbye and goodnight. Police: Let me haunt you with these words: I'll be back! I'll be back! To be interpreted as—bang bang bang, bank, bang—ugh!! Yours in murder, Mr. Monster

A feature that instantly stands out is the misspelling of words, especially those associated with emotionally charged content, such as "wemon" (*women*). This implies a fixation that is projected onto the written word, where it reveals its warped form (literally). As in the words above, Berkowitz also circuitously and astutely provides a snapshot of his upbringing, identifying it indirectly as the source of his criminal behavior. What is especially noticeable is his own self-analysis as someone who is "programmed" to kill because of Sam—constituting a self-styled Gothic description of his inner turmoil, including allusions to vampirism ("he needs some blood to preserve his youth"), Satanism ("Beelzebub"), and caricature monstrosity ("chubby behemouth"). The metaphor of the hunt is also part of his underlying narrative and is an especially revealing one, tying his motives to a feral sense of female hunting, given his inability to attract women in a socially acceptable way. Ironically, he claims to love the world and does not want to kill anymore, but taunts the police with "I'll be back." As we have seen, this is a perverted way for the killer to reach out to his audience, hoping to tug their emotional strings of pity.

Other features to note are the following, all of which are intended to be exculpatory in nature:

He claims that his childhood memories haunt him.

Berkowitz blames "Sam" who commands him to "Go out and kill," thus attempting to exonerate himself as a victim. So, he warns: "To stop me you must kill me. Attention all police: Shoot me first—shoot to kill or else keep out of my way or you will die!"

His hatred of people comes out in cynical, mocking form, as he tells people he loves them at the same time that he designates them "yahoos": "I want to make love to the world. I love people. I don't belong on earth. Return me to yahoos."

In the following sentence he reveals his true mind–set, claiming that he, a narrative Hero, is above everyone else: "I feel like an outsider. I am on a different wavelength then everybody else—programmed too kill."

Berkowitz shows his engagement with the dark side of fantasy, provoked, so he claims, by his repressed upbringing.

And he provides an enticement for the authorities to enter into a sinister dialogue with him, since they are part of the reason that spurred him to do what he has done.

The writing is disorganized and rambling, perhaps revealing the disorientation and chaos Berkowitz was experiencing inside himself. As his follow-up letters demonstrate, the repetition of images, people, objects (e.g., blood, dogs, urine), and symbols allow him to objectify his murders, thus dissociating himself from blame, deflecting it onto "Sam," who "beats his family." Once again, we see how a serial killer's written accounts are designed both to frighten yet also to neutralize—to cultivate the denial of responsibility. In the end, of course, it was Sam who exhorted him to "go out and kill." As author Chris McNab writes: "Most of the evidence seemed to point to Berkowitz being a sufferer of paranoid schizophrenia," but this was a scheming hater of women, who used horror-story autobiography to rationalize his actions to the world. The court judge did not buy the insanity story and ruled Berkowitz to be sane and fully aware of his actions and their consequences during the murders.[40] In the end, like Rader, Berkowitz was a pathetic man whose only purpose in life was to seek revenge on women for not paying attention to him. As discussed, hate—hate rooted in the id and arising out of disordered sexual thoughts—is nearly always the underlying compulsion to murder, whether with or without an obvious sexual component to the crimes themselves.

VAMPIRES

Serial killers such as Dahmer, Rader, and Berkowitz are self-described monsters who present themselves as victims while at the same time indulging in twisted displays of power over others through murder. They repel us at the same time that we desire to know all about them, in much the same way that we want to grasp the essence of the evil and ugly personages of Gothic and monster fiction. They are ugly in every sense. The metaphor shifts, though, when the physical appearance of the killer changes. This is why we tend to refer to those serial killers who are more physically attractive as vampires, recalling the myth of Dracula, the alluring predator who attracts young women and transforms them with his bite. An example of a modern-day serial-killer vampire is Ted Bundy, who may have murdered as many as fifty women, and who became a media sex symbol after he was shown on television defending himself in court and hamming it up for the cameras. While in jail, he received hundreds of romantic proposals from smitten females afflicted with the only paraphilia more common among females than males: hybristophilia, which is defined as a sexual attraction to a person who is either known or suspected to have murdered, raped, or engaged in similarly horrible crimes.[41] Bundy's pen pals, like all hybristophiliacs, were also potentially dangerous themselves as accessories and minions willing to do his bidding. The vampire's spell can indeed be alluring.

Bundy was described in childhood as a "great kid." He was a Boy Scout, ran a paper route, was on the school track team, and had his own lawn-mowing business. He even served as a chairman at the Seattle 1968 presidential convention for Nelson Rockefeller. He earned a degree in psychology in 1972, entered law school shortly thereafter, and worked as a night janitor to pay the bills. Bundy even wrote a rape-prevention pamphlet for a Seattle crime-watch group and volunteered at a suicide-prevention hotline. On the surface, he was a regular guy who was very handsome and hardworking. But the vampire within him made Bundy one of the most heinous serial killers of history before he was finally caught and convicted, later being executed in Florida's electric chair on January 24, 1989—a date that local Florida businesses proclaimed as "Fry Day," a macabre pun used to offer execution-day sales.[42] Bundy apparently hailed from a crime-free and supportive family. But not all was perfect in his upbringing—there was trouble brewing behind closed doors. Every house, as they say, has a toilet.

A more detailed look at Bundy's formative years suggests that the elaborate façade he spent years building—the academic, professional, and athletic achievements—were in fact acts of compensation. They were used to stave off the period of decomposition—the psychological unraveling that prompts sadists, sexual deviants, psychopaths, and other breeds of serial offenders to indulge their paraphilias—that ultimately led to his series of murders that eventually came to include acts of necrophilia. To begin with, Bundy's twenty-two-year-old unmarried mother lived with her parents, and

Bundy grew up thinking that his mother was actually his sister. His grandfather—whom he thought was his father—was abusive and racist. Consequently, as McNab writes, "Ted expressed himself with violent tempers, and even terrorized relatives by placing kitchen knives under their bed clothes."[43] Bundy was also bullied at school and, when threatened, he concealed his violent personality through cunning adaptation; he constructed a convincing surface charm and air of confidence—a "mask of sanity"—that has since become one of the telltale indicators of the high-functioning psychopathic personality.[44] Bundy's own words in this respect are truly revelatory. His release for his suppressed and perverted sexual fantasies was, so he says, through pornography, where he could ignore the actress as a human being and see her as an object for whom he did not have to experience empathy:

> "So what's one less? What's one less person on the face of the planet?"
> "I didn't know what made things tick. I didn't know what made people want to be friends. I didn't know what made people attractive to one another. I didn't know what underlay social interactions."
> "From time to time, we would come across books of a harder nature. More graphic. This also included detective magazines, etc., and I want to emphasize this. The most damaging kind of pornography, and I'm talking from hard, real, personal experience, is that that involves violence and sexual violence. The wedding of those two forces, as I know only too well, brings about behavior that is too terrible to describe."[45]

Here we can see that his need to combine sex and violence in a pathological way was the trigger that set off his aberrant urges. This was truly clever of Bundy—he blamed pornography, thus deflecting the blame away from himself onto the exploitive mass culture in which he lived. In some ways, the words of serial killers are pseudo-psychoanalytic narratives, stories through which they are attempting to rationalize what they have done so that others can "understand" them and take pity on them, rather than condemn them. These are cowards who seek social validation and acceptance for who they are—no more, no less. It is relevant to reproduce here an edited and reduced version of Bundy's final interview with James C. Dobson (JCD), an evangelical Christian author and activist who was clearly drawn to the Bundy case as a way to, ostensibly, expose the inherent evils of pornography to society:

Fig. 2.7. Ted Bundy in 1977, from the FBI's "Ten Most Wanted Fugitives during the 1970s."

JCD: Walk me through that. What was going on in your mind at that time?

Ted: Before we go any further, it is important to me that people believe what I'm saying. I'm not blaming pornography. I'm not saying it caused me to go out and do certain things. I take full responsibility for all the things that I've done. That's not the question here. The issue is how this kind of literature contributed and helped mold and shape the kinds of violent behavior . . . I can only liken it to (and I don't want to overdramatize it) being possessed by something so awful and alien, and the next morning waking up and remembering what happened and realizing that in the eyes of the law, and certainly in the eyes of God, you're responsible. To wake up in the morning and realize what I had done with a clear mind, with all my essential moral and ethical feelings intact, absolutely horrified me.

JCD: You hadn't known you were capable of that before?

Ted: There is no way to describe the brutal urge to do that, and once it has been satisfied, or spent, and that energy level recedes, I became myself again. Basically, I was a normal person.

. . .

Ted: I wasn't some guy hanging out in bars, or a bum. I wasn't a pervert in the sense that people look at somebody and say, "I know there's something wrong with him." I was a normal person. I had good friends. I led a normal life, except for this one, small but very potent and destructive segment that I kept very secret and close to myself. Those of us who have been so influenced by violence in the media, particularly pornographic violence, are not some kind of inherent monsters. We are your sons and husbands. We grew up in regular families. Pornography can reach in and snatch a kid out of any house today. It snatched me out of my home 20 or 30 years ago. As diligent as my parents were, and they were diligent in protecting their children, and as good a Christian home as we had, there is no protection against the kinds of influences that are loose in a society that tolerates.

. . .

JCD: Outside these walls, there are several hundred reporters that wanted to talk to you, and you asked me to come because you had something you wanted to say. You feel that hardcore pornography, and the door to it, softcore pornography, is doing untold damage to other people and causing other women to be abused and killed the way you did.

Ted: I'm no social scientist, and I don't pretend to believe what John Q. Citizen thinks about this, but I've lived in prison for a long time now, and I've met a lot of men who were motivated to commit violence. Without exception, every one of them was deeply involved in pornography, deeply consumed by the addiction. The F.B.I.'s own study on serial homicide shows that the most common interest among serial killers is pornography. It's true.

JCD: What would your life have been like without that influence?

Ted: I know it would have been far better, not just for me, but for a lot of other people—victims and families. There's no question that it would have been a better life. I'm absolutely certain it would not have involved this kind of violence.

JCD: There is tremendous cynicism about you on the outside, I suppose, for good reason. I'm not sure there's anything you could say that people would believe, yet you told me (and I have heard this through our mutual friend, John Tanner) that you have accepted the forgiveness of Jesus Christ and are a follower and believer in Him. Do you draw strength from that as you approach these final hours?

Ted: I do. I can't say that being in the Valley of the Shadow of Death is something I've become all that accustomed to, and that I'm strong and nothing's bothering me. It's no fun. It gets kind of lonely, yet I have to remind myself that every one of us will go through this someday in one way or another.

JCD: It's appointed unto man.

Ted: Countless millions who have walked this earth before us have gone through this, so this is just an experience we all share.[46]

The pseudo-religious psychobabble that Bundy spouts out here is disingenuous and self-serving. He expiates himself with the last statement, saying that "countless millions" have gone through what he has experienced. He claims to have walked on the dark side, like a vampire, but, by implication, he is now in the light, seeing the folly of his ways and—conveniently enough—blaming the pornographic images as the stimuli that ruined him. Yet, at the same time, he patronizes the interviewer and the audience by suggesting that he is *not* blaming pornography. It's yet another of the countless contradictions that defined Bundy's life—and death.

Acclaimed musician turned cultural pundit and author Gary Lachman sees an intrinsic connection between vampiristic mythology, with its characters in dark costumes, and serial murders.[47] He describes the 1999 Columbine high school massacre, discussed in greater detail in the next chapter, as follows: "Dressed in black raincoats, the two casually slaughtered their classmates, before turning their guns on themselves. It later turned out that they had devised a plan for even greater destruction, including hijacking a plane and crashing it into a major city."[48]

It should come as no surprise that some serial killers actually use the vampire epithet to describe their crimes, as if they were recounting a horror story of which they are the author. A few examples will suffice here. Known as the Vampire of Hanover, Fritz Haarman was one the first cases of a vampiristic serial killer on record. Starting in 1918, he killed as many as twenty-seven youths (from ten to twenty-two years of age), by biting their throats. After killing as many as nineteen victims, women and children, in the 1990s, Philip Oyancha confessed to Kenyan police that he drank their blood as part of some vampiristic ritual which he learned about in school—or so he claimed. Perhaps the best-known vampire serial killer was Andrei Chikatilo, who, starting in 1978, killed fifty-two victims, mutilating their eyes and sexual organs and often drinking their blood. During his trial, he blurted out the following statement: "I am a mistake of nature, a mad beast."[49] Last, but not least, starting in 1977, Richard Chase—known as the Dracula Killer and the Sacramento Vampire—murdered six people in the city of Sacramento, cannibalizing their dead bodies and drinking their blood. His perverted thirst for blood was a motivating impulse in the killings.[50] One wonders about the relation between fantasy literature and real life when it comes to serial murder. If there had been no monsters or vampires delivered into the world through the mythic and narrative channel, would such killers ever have been able to glean inspiration for their actions? And in the absence of such literary archetypes, would they have gone on to commit murder to reify the archetype into a real-life behavior? Does art imitate life—Aristotle's mimesis view—or does life imitate art? This is not just a rhetorical question for the reader to ponder. It is the cornerstone question of literary criminology, and we will return to it subsequently.

Over the course of history it has been assumed by a number of criminal courts, psychologists, and the public at large that serial killers were criminally "insane" (a largely obsolete term) at the time of their crimes. In some ways, this is an apt metaphor, meaning, literally, "not sane." However, there is a distinctly paraphiliac sexual element present in nearly every case of serial murder, at least those committed by males, thus revealing a twisted form of the id at work here that seeks expression through imaginary constructs, such as vampirism. Richard Chase, for instance, stated that he drank the blood of his victims because he feared that, by not doing so, his own blood would turn to dust. If true, such a delusion would indeed furnish evidence that he suffered from some form of psychosis, perhaps paranoid schizophrenia. However, the fact that Chase also collected newspaper clippings detailing the murders of the contemporaneous Hillside Stranglers in the nearby Los Angeles area, coupled with the fact that he was so aroused by the violence he inflicted on his victims and the huge amount of blood at his crime scenes—a paraphilia known as hematolagnia—that he ended up raping at least one of his victims suggests he was very much aware of what he was doing. That is, he was not only aware but very much enjoyed it as well. Chase, like other hematolagniacs, or vampire killers, carried out his grisly crimes in a manner that defies conventional psychological or psychoanalytic explanation. Insanity, after all, as Freud and Jung certainly understood, has deep roots in a worldview and its supporting social substratum.

PREDATORS

As humans, we were, once upon a time, hunters, killing animals for subsistence and survival. Some evolutionary psychologists claim that the hunting instinct may have carried forward in all of us as a primordial trait that is, like the sex drive, rooted in our ancient hard-wiring. If this is even partly true, it might explain why we call some serial killers *predators* (as discussed in the previous chapter). This is the subtext in the book *Hunting Humans*, by Michael Newton, not be confused with the identically named text by famed Canadian criminologist Elliott Leyton.[51] We are, of course, aware that the predator category is a metaphor, just like the monster and vampire. But it is through metaphor that we come to understand reality, as we discussed previously. Indeed, the four murder narrative archetypes of Hero, Professional, Revenger, and Tragedian are essentially metaphors that have become narrative figures and can thus be used to characterize the psychology of murderers.[52] Take once again the case of Richard Ramirez, the serial killer known as the Night Stalker who killed in the Los Angeles and San Francisco areas in the mid-1980s. He was not only a monster and a vampire, but also a predator—a hunter—who saw death as part of living and took a gruesome satisfaction in seeing people die. He showed no attempt at remorse and instead bragged to his cellmates and to the authorities:

> "I've killed 20 people. Man, I love all that blood."[53]
> "I love to kill people. I love watching them die. I would shoot them in the head and they would wiggle and squirm all over the place, and then just stop. Or I would cut them with a knife and watch their faces turn real white. I love all that blood. I told one lady to give me all her money. She said no. So I cut her and pulled her eyes out."[54]

Words and phrases such as "shoot in the head" and seeing his victims "wiggle and squirm all over the place" are applicable to predatory hunting, where some hunters—some but not necessarily all—kill for sport and take pleasure in doing so. Like the Zodiac in his quoting—actually plagiarizing—Richard Connell's *The Most Dangerous Game*, Ramirez chose to hunt the most dangerous animal: humans. In so doing, he took gratuitous pleasure in the blood he spilled, inflicting pain, as he described it, so he could "watch their faces turn real white." Brutality is meant to bring pleasure here, including acts such as pulling out the eyes of a victim. A predator killer is a beast, figuratively and in actual behavior. He is brutal, bloodthirsty, and cold-blooded. The difference between a human and an animal predator is that the latter does it as part of its survival instincts; the former does it for egomaniacal, self-serving reasons.

Predatory serial murder is not restricted to the male gender. Female serial murder is comparatively rare, with only sixty-four offenders having been identified in the United States since 1826 to the time of writing this book.[55] As criminologist and author Peter Vronsky asserts, there has been an unexpected number of female predators around the globe over the course of modern and early-modern history.[56] The case of Hungarian noblewoman Elizabeth (Erzebet) Báthory is a well-known one and its merits discussing briefly here, as she tortured and killed over six hundred young women in the early 1600s. She was labeled a vampire, a witch, and a cannibal, as a rhetorical means of trying to psychologically and socially understand her horrific crimes. Báthory murdered only peasant girls until 1609, which allowed her to go undetected, or at least unpunished, because the families could not press charges against a member of the nobility, especially one belonging to the richest family in Hungary and to whom the king owed stacks of money. Not unlike contemporary offenders like Gary Ridgway, who hunted down helpless and deserted prostitutes, Báthory also knew that many peasant girls' disappearances and deaths would go unnoticed—what we today refer to as the missing missing. The torture of peasants and servants for minor offences or indiscretions was common at the time, being made possible by a culture of indifference toward violence and a slippery moral slope that enabled Báthory's eventual massacres. As a young girl, Báthory actually witnessed her own father torturing a servant by sewing him up alive inside a dying horse, and her fiancé publicly castrated a servant with whom Báthory had an affair, throwing him to a pack of wild dogs.[57]

It was only when Báthory started murdering upper-class girls that she was arrested, testifying to the double standard in victimology based on class in her era—one that arguably persists even today in a more surreptitious way. The king later sent his palatine to investigate Báthory, and while several of her accomplices were sentenced to death for their part in the crimes, Báthory herself could not be executed, because of her social position. She was instead sentenced to imprisonment in her castle—a rather comfortable house arrest.

In television series like *Women Who Kill*, the Báthory narrative is updated to depict murderous women who belong to all social classes. The focus is again on gender, since female serial killers are rare. And when one does surface, the media take instant notice. Take the case of Aileen Wuornos, who murdered seven men in Florida between 1989 and 1990. Throughout her consecutive trials, Wuornos maintained that the murders she committed were all acts of self-defense against men who had raped and brutalized her, or whom she believed would be capable of such actions. But her testimony turned out to be convoluted and dubious—a deflective neutralization strategy not unlike Ted Bundy's convenient vilification of pornography. Wuornos's final murder, in fact, was of a Good Samaritan who was attempting to offer her help, wanting nothing in return. She killed him, it seems, for no reason at all—other than perhaps for the pleasure of it. Wuornos was a lesbian who was in an intimate relationship with a woman named Tyria Moore, who later became an informer and testified against Wuornos. In the end, Wuornos was a cold-blooded predator who exploited the presumption of the "gentler sex" in her bid to elicit public sympathy. In reality, she murdered men as a matter of personal satisfaction—once again, a product of the disordered id and ubiquitous sense of hatred. Consider her words, as spoken aloud following her first murder trial in 1992:

"May your wife and children get raped, right in the ass." [Spoken to the jurors who convicted her.]

"To me, this world is nothing but evil, and my own evil just happened to come out 'cause of the circumstances of what I was doing."[58]

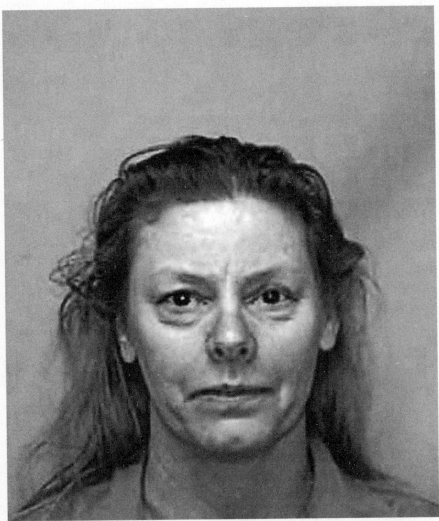

Fig. 2.8. Aileen Wuornos. Image from the Florida Department of Corrections.

Note how she verbally attacked the male jurors spitefully, cursing them perversely, implying that she had suffered at the hands of men and wishing that they underwent similar suffering: "May your wife and children get raped." And if that deflection was not enough, then the blame is to be put on "evil," she claims, rationalizing her actions as part of the intrinsic evil that exists in the world, not as anything unique. The subtext is obvious—anyone is capable of evil, no matter how sanctimonious he or she might claim to be. It is the essence of the human condition.

Predators enjoy the hunt and then relish in defiling or otherwise performing indignities to the bodies of their victims. Arthur Shaw-cross, the Genesee River Killer, claimed to have eaten the vaginas of three of his eleven known female victims, describing his atrocities as follows:

> "I took the right leg of that woman's body, from the knee to the hip took the fat off and ate it. . . . When I bit into it she just urinated right there."
>
> "She was giving me oral sex, and she got carried away. . . . So I choked her."[59]

Shawcross's mutilation of the victim's body is evocative of the kind of mutilation that many animal predators carry out on prey. The difference may be that the animal predator is designed by biology to do so instinctively; the serial killer does so intentionally, taking pleasure in mangling, maiming, disfiguring, butchering, or dismembering the bodies of his human prey. What is especially appalling to us is the intention behind the brutality.

The best known case of a mutilator predator is Andrei Chikatilo, mentioned briefly above. His words are truly disturbing and frightening, and they reveal that he was motivated by a sexual dysfunction dating back to his childhood. What is more disturbing is that he was aware of his actions, and that he was able to articulate the source rationally. Unlike the other serial killers mentioned above, however, he did not deflect the blame to someone or something else. He took full responsibility, perhaps as a strategy of expressive therapy:

"I felt a kind of madness and ungovernablity in perverted sexual acts. I couldn't control my actions, because from childhood I was unable to realise myself as a real man and a complete human being."

"My inconsistent behavior should not be misconstrued as an attempt to avoid responsibility for any acts I have committed. One could argue that even after my arrest, I was not fully aware of their dangerous and serious nature. My case is peculiar to me alone. It is not fear of responsibility that makes me act this way, but my inner psychic and nervous tension. I am prepared to give testimony about the crimes, but please do not torment me with their details, for my psyche would not be able to bear it. It never entered my mind to conceal anything from the investigation. Everything which I have done makes me shudder. I only feel gratitude to the investigating bodies for having captured me."[60]

Chikatilo was sexually aroused by violence and the desecration of his victims' bodies, a practice in the spectrum of necrophilia known as necromutilimania. He did not kill his victims in the same way each time, alternately stabbing, strangling, or beating them to death. But in all murders there was some element of mutilation and even cannibalism for sexual gratification. Chikatilo admitted that he could only become sexually aroused by committing violent acts. As crime author McNab points out, "he would eat external and internal body parts, expressing a particular fondness for consuming the uterus of female victims."[61] As McNab goes on accurately to say, "The attacks were crazed, monstrous affairs."[62] During his trial, Chikatilo himself showed that he was aware of his monstrosity, admitting, "I am a freak of nature, a mad beast."[63]

THE OEDIPUS COMPLEX

The term *Oedipus complex* was coined by Freud, as is well known, to explain the relation of children to the parent of the opposite sex and the problems that this can create if the bond is too strong and unnatural. Freud believed that children harbor an innate hostility toward the parent of the same sex and an attraction to the parent of the opposite sex; this attraction eventually manifests itself in a proclivity to engage in neurotic (sexual) behavior that is attenuated through socialization.

Some (perhaps many) serial killers may be reliving their Oedipal sexual fantasies in a warped and perverted way. The cases of Berkowitz and Bundy could certainly be elucidated in these terms. For Berkowitz, Sam was his imaginary enemy—an external tormentor who, in the tradition of Gothic literature, was a catalyst for his descent into madness—perhaps blocking his need to engage in sexual normalcy as a father figure. For Bundy, the fact that he did not really know who his real mother was, until later in life, may also have negative Oedipal overtones. But the classic case of a serial killer impelled by the dysfunction of the Oedipus complex within him is Ed Gein of Wisconsin, the inspiration for the novels and later the films *Psycho*, and *The Silence of the Lambs*, as well as *The Texas Chain Saw Massacre* franchise, among others. The deranged killer became a grave robber and murderer after the death of his possessive mother. He kept her corpse and snatched other corpses from graves in order to give her mother "companions" in his decaying and dilapidated farmhouse. After police found body parts that in many cases had been fashioned into furniture and clothing items, Gein confessed to two murders.[64]

As investigators soon after discovered, Gein's religiously fanatical mother had convinced him to avoid women as he was growing up because they were sources of sin and disease. As a repressed sexual being, it comes as no surprise that he had a compulsion to do what he did, as he admitted to a sawmill owner named Elmo Ueeck:

> "She isn't missing. She's at the farm right now." [Referring to his dead mother.]
> "I had a compulsion to do it."
> "They smelled bad."[65]

Another well-known case that has homicidal Oedipal nuances is that of Edmund Kemper, also known as the Co-ed Killer, a ruthless serial murderer who abducted, raped, and killed women, mostly college-age hitchhikers, in and around Santa Cruz in the 1970s. His first victims, however, were his paternal grandparents and his own mother because, as he later explained: "Even when she was dead, she was still bitching at me. I couldn't get her to shut up!"[66] As for the murder of his grandmother, he had this to say: "I just wondered how it would feel to shoot Grandma."[67] From this he goes on to murder his first girl, gloating morbidly in the mutilation that he will wreak. He elaborates as follows.

> "The first good-looking girl I see tonight is going to die."
> "I remember there was actually a sexual thrill . . . you hear that little pop and pull their heads off and hold their heads up by the hair. Whipping their heads off, their body sitting there. That'd get me off."
> "With a girl, there's a lot left in the girl's body without a head. Of course, the personality is gone."[68]

The compulsion to desecrate the female body seems to have its roots in the hatred of significant female figures in Kemper's life—especially his mother. Clearly, contrary to the original notion of the Oedipus complex, where the desire is to murder the father, this twisted form seems to induce the individual to kill not only his mother but also the female gender through the disfigurement of female bodies. The fact that someone like Kemper felt the need to articulate this feeling is arguably a twisted form of self-analysis or therapy. Certainly, serial killers, for the most part, can never be accused of leading an unexamined life. As Kemper's bizarre autobiographical narrative demonstrates, serial killers, perhaps even more than the general population, consistently demonstrate a detailed if not deluded self-awareness of events and people, a view that reflects at least one of the four main dramatic modes of tragedy, comedy, romance, and satire.

A final example of an Oedipal killer is Henry Lee Lucas, another self-described victim of a troubled upbringing with a warped fixation on the mother figure. In 1960, Lucas was, in fact, convicted of the murder of his mother. Like Kemper, he began his serial killer career by first dispatching his tormenting matriarch. He was later arrested in 1983 for the murder of two women; eventually he was convicted of the murders of eleven women. He would later confess with great braggadocio of killing hundreds of women while serving as part of a secret cult he claimed was called the Hand of Death. These claims resulted in the creation of a federal initiative known as the Lucas Task Force dedicated to corroborating—and in some cases—inducing—his confessions to murder. Read his words:

> "I hated all my life. I hated everybody. When I first grew up and can remember, I was dressed as a girl by mother. And I stayed that way for two or three years. And after that was treated like what I call the dog of the family. I was beaten. I was made to do things that no human bein' would want to do."
> "Sex is one of my downfalls. I get sex any way I can get it. If I have to force somebody to do it, I do . . . I rape them; I've done that. I've killed animals to have sex with them, and I've had sex while they're alive."[69]

As mentioned throughout this book, hatred is a toxin produced by the id—hatred of either a specific person or type of person, including just nondescript hatred in general; it is a leading motive for murder across all types of homicide. Hatred of the mother seems to be a particularly vicious form that ends up impelling individuals like Lucas to take out their inner turmoil not only on their mothers but also on women in general. It is a kind of projection of hate from the particular to the general. This has obvious sociological implications with regard to the role of the family in human life, implications that are beyond the scope of the present book. Suffice it to say that murder always has an emotional source, and hatred seems to crop up regularly as the *main* source.

We all are subject to the Oedipus complex; yet, few of us become murderers because of it. Thus, there is something else going on in killers like Gein and Lucas. Murder is a mystery, and we will deal with this in the final chapter.

BACK TO THE TOP

We began this chapter by asking, who is the serial killer? Our trek through selected serial-killer writings, statements, and manifestos has led us through a veritable quagmire of evil motives and desires that allows us to construct a complex narrative profile. In this profile, the idea that stands out most is the sense of the mythical and the archetypal in the murderer's mind, as can be seen especially through the dark images that are found in most of the statements. We have, in doing this taken a detour to hell, to recall the address of the third letter purportedly authored by Jack the Ripper.

Serial murder is a modern-day engagement in death as opposed to life, the dark as opposed to the light, evil as opposed to good. The tension between such contrasting forces is within us all, but in the deranged mind they often gain expression through murder. Serial killers are fundamentally haters of women (and in some cases men) who live in a world constructed by their own disordered thinking, sexual attachments, and violent fantasies where victims are to be desecrated and defiled. They are totally enwrapped in self-interestedness, justifying their brutal murders through the creation of narratives that are replete with mythic images of monsters, vampires, and predators—Gothic entities behind which they hide their cowardice. They live by a different game and set of rules—of their own convenient making.

The persona of the modern serial killer is where the real and the imaginary merge, as in all myths. Indeed, this is perhaps why we find it irrelevant to distinguish between a Ted Bundy (a real serial killer) and a Hannibal Lecter (an imaginary one) in any conceptualization or understanding of who (or what) the serial killer is. Attempts by criminology and forensic psychology to create a profile of the serial killer are interesting, of course, but they tell us little about the human mind's implantation in unconscious mythical worlds, which are very real in the serial-killer mind.

Serial murder is far less of a threat to the well-being of society than other forms of crime, and is still a statistically rare phenomenon. It is, however, the perception of the monstrosity of the crime involved that atrophies us spiritually—that leads us into believing that it is an everyday occurrence of our contemporary paradigm. The dominant narrative also leads us to believe that the actual deaths are less important than the perceived "unfairness" of those deaths. A young woman who falls down and dies tragically will never make the evening news; one who is kidnapped and brutally murdered by a serial killer does. The former is seen as part of destiny; the latter is seen as going against some inherent basic principle of human actions.

But maybe we, through our engagement with murder fiction, have come to believe in the myth of the serial killer ourselves. In his in-depth study *Criminal Shadows*, forensic psychologist David Canter examined both fictional and real serial killers, finding little difference between the two in public perception, even though real-life serial killers are quite unlike their fictional counterparts.[70] The real ones are lucky, rather than clever; they are banal, rather than interesting; and they seldom play mind games with the police. But the fact that they are perceived as identical is evidence that there is a powerful synergy between fiction and reality. We have produced a "serial-killer culture," as criminologist Peter Vronsky aptly calls it.[71] Also, the location of serial murders is critical to our perceptions. As we mentioned in the opening chapter, context is everything when it comes to interpreting murder.

The cultural construction of Jack the Ripper, like Bigfoot, the Loch Ness monster, and other staples of cryptozoology, has produced a modern-day legendary figure—an immortalized figure who few seem to care was never really a single person, much less the person depicted in the myth. On the other hand, other very real killers, such as the Atlanta Ripper, who in 1911 claimed twenty victims but was never caught or identified, go essentially unnoticed by comparison. The primary difference is that London was the center of a huge newspaper industry while Atlanta was not. The story of Jack the Ripper was retold and quickly recirculated in popular legend and literature while the Atlanta Ripper quickly faded from public consciousness. Serial murder "epidemics" are as much about the mythic imagination as they are about killing, or what true-crime historian Mark Seltzer calls the "modern compulsion [of] observation."[72]

We end this chapter by returning again to the film *Se7en*, which is truly a modern essay on serial murder. The serial killer could be anyone and everyone; and indeed he is called "John Doe" in the movie. As the film also suggests, the serial killer has become a kind of twisted voice of conscience in the communal imagination. To this end, John Doe issues the audience a dire warning in which he laments the pervasiveness of deadly sins in every aspect of modern life. He claims that he is setting the example for rejecting the tolerance of these sins, and that people will forever study him and his actions—suggesting, in a twisted moralistic sense, that his crimes are ultimately meant to improve society at large.[73] As we will see, this is precisely the theory to which many killers subscribe—and transcribe.

Chapter 3

DARK ODYSSEYS

"In our country, a great many crimes are committed to gratify public expectation . . . to satisfy the demands of public opinion . . . [crimes] instigated by half-witted journalists, who first goad the offender to his crime, and, the next day, rate him soundly for his commission."

—William Gilmore Simms,
***Homicide in American Fiction*, 1957**

"This is the story of my entire life. It is a dark story of sadness, anger and hatred."[1]

A disillusioned and deranged young man named Elliot Rodger began his manifesto in part with the above statement; it was a rambling monograph constituting a disclaimer of sorts about the details of his macabre and grisly actions to follow. The manifesto, appropriately titled *My Twisted World*, was e-mailed to over thirty people; Rodger also uploaded a video to the Internet that served as his last will and testament immediately before he went on a killing spree in the California coastal town of Isla Vista, a suburb of Santa Barbara, in May 2014. A textbook Revenger in terms of the corresponding narrative protagonist typology, Rodger's autobiographical and self-analytical manifesto, along with the accompanying video titled "Elliot Rodger's Retribution," were replete with condemnations of young women—specifically attractive women—whom he saw as the antagonists in his life story. He saw young and attractive co-eds as thwarting his sexual destiny not only because he could not possess them but also because others could. He expressed rage toward his female peers at the University of California–Santa Barbara for rejecting him, while he also wished death upon the "sexually active men" whose virility and successes in courtship matters Rodger enviously saw as an affront to his own manhood. Repeatedly citing that he was a virgin and that his involuntary celibacy had left him socially alienated, Rodger vowed revenge on those he saw as being his tormentors. Shortly after e-mailing his manifesto and recording his final monologue, Rodger began his murder spree by first stabbing his three roommates to death while they slept. He later went on a shooting rampage outside a UC–Santa Barbara sorority house whose female members were representative of the types of attractive women whom he felt had rebuffed him over his lifetime. As he put it in his own self-analytical, self-pitying words:

> I'm 22 years old and I'm still a virgin. I've never even kissed a girl. I've been through college for two and a half years, more than that actually, and I'm still a virgin. It has been very torturous. College is the time when everyone experiences those things such as sex and fun and pleasure. Within those years, I've had to rot in loneliness. It's not fair. You girls have never been attracted to me. I don't know why you girls aren't attracted to me, but I will punish you all for it. It's an injustice, a crime, because . . . I don't know what you don't see in me. I'm the perfect guy and yet you throw yourselves at these obnoxious men instead of me, the supreme gentleman.[2]

Following the murder of his roommates, Rodger went on to shoot a total of ten people at random, also running down several victims with his car. After killing three female victims and injuring scores more, Rodger collided with a parked car while driving erratically. When the collision rendered his BMW inoperable, he then elected to take his own life with one of the several handguns he had with him, before police arrived.

After the massacre near the manicured college campus, Rodger's manifesto and videos—including several earlier monologues uploaded to YouTube while the rampage was still in the planning stages—were the subject of tremendous scrutiny and analysis across the media, criminological circles, and several academic venues. His pathologically self-pitying and misogynistic rage formed the basis for many of these preparatory communications, and it became clear that sex—or more accurately the lack thereof—dominated his worldview and impelled his inner narrative. Rodger actually retreaded many of the same themes previously published to a website by forty-eight-year-old George Sodini, a socially and sexually alienated systems analyst who had uploaded his "exit plan" to the Internet before committing a massacre at a women's aerobics class in a suburb of Pittsburgh, Pennsylvania, in the summer of 2009. At the scene of his rampage, which left four women dead and nearly a dozen injured, Sodini left a handwritten note that served as an addendum to his website manifesto. In it, he condemned the "desirable women" who shunned him. Like Rodger, Sodini committed suicide at the scene of his massacre.[3]

Fig. 3.1. A screenshot of a smug and sneering Elliot Rodger's final video outlining his bizarre and vengeful motives for an impending shooting rampage in Isla Vista, California, in May 2014.

Rodger's manifesto was a facsimile of sorts—a recitation of the same deranged, disaffected, and maudlin themes expressed by Sodini before him—but it proved to be far more detailed, providing an exhaustive disquisition of his upbringing and family problems. In it, Rodger also revealed his disdain for specific ethnic groups and his pseudo-Nietzschean sense of superiority over people generally, retreading, in this case, Leopold and Loeb. The racist and ideologically charged nature of Rodger's writing, including his stated disgust with interracial couples, actually suggests that the dominant theme of sexual deprivation in his writing was little more than a convenient narrative he constructed to rationalize a more generalized rage—a larger pattern of disordered thinking that had led him to perceive everyone else as being inherently inferior. In fact, Rodger, a *post-millennial* (a contested demographic, but generally defined as those born after 1992), was part of an atypical group that is thought to be the most sexually inexperienced generation in modern history,[4] a theory that, if true, suggests that Rodger's twisted feelings are not unique among his peer group. His sense of entitlement, however, is analogous, generally speaking, to that felt by serial killers, as we saw in the previous chapter. This entitlement led Rodger to believe that he was an aristoi and thus that his rage was justified—that his exceptions of special or preferential treatment were somehow above the law. Again, like Leopold and Loeb, his writing, like his verbal riffing in his online videos, suggested that he was somehow not subject to man-made law. In fact, the autobiographical details in Rodger's manifesto and the narcissistic manner with which he engineered the narrative surrounding his crimes provide key insights and meaningful context for analyzing similar writings and their relation to media coverage of mass murderers. Unlike Sodini and Rodger, those who commit mass murder (defined as the slaying of four or more victims in a single or multievent incident) are mostly school shooters. Like Sodini and Rodger, however, they are also typically cowardly killers who justify their crimes through selective narrative frames based on the theme (and plot) of revenge before ultimately taking their own lives, and who typically leave behind some form of writing as their dying declaration.

As our narrative method implies (see chapter 1), this is a key but often overlooked aspect of homicidal modeling and analysis. The connection between the murderer's actions and his writings is a significant one, since the latter is really a kind of externalization of the inner emotional turmoil that murderers experience and grapple with before ultimately rationalizing their actions. This connection might allow us to better understand what the American Psychiatric Association defines as schizoid personality disorder. Unlike many serial-killers narratives, where the creation of associated documents, diaries, and communiqués can have a paraphiliac purpose—as seen in the cases of Albert Fish, Dennis Rader, and both Zodiac Killers, among others—the narrative mechanism and autobiographical impulse of mass murderers allows us to detect their reasoning for murderer that is functional to the process of actually planning an attack. In other words, their writing transcends mere fantasy to become a window into both their motive and even their modus operandi.

MASS MURDER

Distinct from serial killers, mass murderers, who are also sometimes called "mass shooters" because of the dominant weapon of choice (firearms), typically lack a paraphiliac drive and often demonstrate little concern with evading capture or even surviving their attacks. By definition, a mass murderer is an offender who kills at least four people in a single incident or series of consecutive incidents, with the now-outmoded term "spree killer" deemed redundant, given that it historically described the same phenomenon but with murders occurring in different locations. Today, it is recognized that whether a shooter walks or drives between targets or attack locations, and whether the incidents are measured in minutes or hours, "mass" and "spree" essentially describe the same phenomenon and associated set of motivations and methods. As such, by the late 1990s, the consolidated terminology allowed a comprehensive taxonomy of ten mass-murderer types.[5] These are listed below.

> *The Family Annihilator*: someone who murders his or her own family in its entirety before later typically committing suicide.
>
> *The Profit Murderer:* someone who murders multiple people in one or a series of incidents in order to gain some material profit, often insurance money or ransom. An example would be Jack Gilbert Graham, who blew up a United Airlines flight with a suitcase bomb in November 1955, killing all forty-four passengers on board. The motive? One of the passengers was Graham's mother, for whom he had taken out a life-insurance policy worth $37,500 immediately before the flight. He framed and carried out the murder as a terrorist incident to hide the true reason, with dozens of others killed as collateral victims.

Fig. 3.2. Jack Gilbert Graham. FBI photo.

The Sex Murderer: a rare mass murderer type given that there tends
to be little or no paraphiliac drive behind acts of mass murder.
This category more accurately describes crimes committed during
wartime, including situations where small villages or neighbor-
hoods are overrun by ground forces, where the women are raped,
and everyone is subjected to mass execution. This category is one
of two that links mass murder with crimes against humanity and
genocide rather than rampage murders committed by one or more
lone attackers for some personal reason.

The Pseudo-Commando: perhaps the most commonly depicted in the
media and the one most readily associated with the recent spate of
public shootings, it describes an attacker (typically a male) who
meticulously plans his murders as a type of military operation with
military-grade weaponry and attire. The offender will, in many
cases, have an abiding fascination with the military, whether or not
he actually served in the armed forces. In most cases, he hasn't.

The Set-and-Run Killer: someone who puts time and distance between
his mass murder and himself, typically through some time-delay
strategy that will allow him to preemptively escape. Examples
include killers who use bombs or other explosives set with fuses or
timers, or who set fires in concealed locations with delay devices,
or else who tamper with products or consumable goods by poisoning them. Examples range from Timothy McVeigh's bombing
of the Alfred P. Murrah Federal Building in 1995, which killed
168 people, to the still-unsolved Chicago Tylenol mass poisoning,
which claimed seven lives in 1982.

Fig. 3.3. The aftermath of the bombing of the Alfred P. Murrah Federal Building in Oklahoma City on May 23, 1995. The building was selected by former US Marine Timothy McVeigh as a symbolic target for his personal war on the government, in retaliation for earlier enforcement actions against extremists at Waco and Ruby Ridge. A set-and-run killer like McVeigh is a notable exception to most mass murderers in that his modus operandi rules out the use of firearms in the attack. Image from US Department of Defense.

The Psychotic Killer: a mass murderer who is suffering from psychosis at the time of the attack, revealed by the fact that it is spontaneous and typically ill-planned, a response to some hallucination or other acute mentally deranged condition. This category can exist simultaneously with any of the others tabled here.

The Disgruntled Employee: a workplace attacker, typically a shooter, who seeks revenge on supervisors or colleagues for past wrongs, whether real or perceived, including disciplinary action, termination of employment, or some other form of mistreatment. The term "going postal" emerged in the 1980s and 1990s following a series of mass murders at US Postal Service facilities, when several postal employees reportedly "snapped," a term that aptly describes the state of mind of the murderer in this category.

The Disciple: a killer who carries out murders on the instructions of a charismatic leader or deadly mentor. This category describes a somewhat rare type of killer; an example of one such massacre would be the shooting deaths of US congressman Leo Ryan, his delegation, and the accompanying news reporters at the Port Kaituma Airstrip in Guyana in 1978. The attack, ordered by Peoples Temple cult leader Jim Jones, left five people dead and prefaced Jones's subsequent "suicide massacre" of over nine hundred people with cyanide-laced Flavor Aid (wrongly cited as Kool-Aid) at the cult's nearby compound.

The Ideological Mass Murderer: a killer who carries out his murders as part of some grand scheme, usually delusional in nature, that is, to fulfill some larger philosophical, religious, or cultural agenda. An example would be any mass shooting carried out in service to a terrorist organization or extremist group.

The Institutional Mass Murderer: similar to the previous category of murderer, the killer is motivated both ideologically and politically, supporting the cause of a particular institution, organization, or faction. This category is typically used to describe political despots and war criminals who order ethnic cleansings or the genocide of identifiable groups, with examples being Adolf Hitler, Pol Pot, Slobodan Milošević, and Joseph Stalin.

Note that each of these categories complements, to varying degrees, the four narrative typologies of the Hero, Professional, Revenger, and Tragedian. We see, in fact, a direct overlap of the Revenger with both the Pseudo-Commando and the Disgruntled Employee. More specifically, we see a common intersection of the Revenger, the Pseudo-Commando, the use of detailed writings, schizoid personality disorder, and attacks on public institutions such as schools and theaters that, until now, has never been examined in detail. Similar intersections can be envisaged between the other mass-murder types and the four narrative protagonist archetypes adopted by serial murderers.

Going back to some of the earliest and most noteworthy cases of mass murder, we find that a number of dominant trends with respect to writing style, narrative orientation, and intended delivery method emerge; these would all prefigure future trends linking writing and mass killing that are demonstrably different from how and why serial killers choose to create documents and other materials chronicling their work. For instance, whereas serial killers who are driven by psychopathic or sociopathic sexual compulsions seem to be drawn to acts of writing as a means of prolonging the rush of their crimes or the arousal associated with eliciting fear in victims and society at large, mass murderers compose manifestos that convey a straightforward rationalization to justify their murders, so that readers can understand their feelings—they intend at some level to elicit pathos for their actions. Serial killers tend to create texts for their own reflection, mental rehearsal, or fantasy development, and choose to spread them in a bid to taunt, torment, or pursue reader acknowledgment and thus cultivate a dark celebrity status—they are living documents. By contrast, mass murderers, almost without exception, leave their writings to be discovered in the aftermath of their crimes—they are postmortem attestations.

Given that only a few of the ten categories of mass murderers consist of killers who plan on surviving their crimes, with most intending to either commit suicide or be killed by responding law-enforcement officials at the scene (known as suicide by cop), the texts of mass murderers are as much confessions and suicide letters as they are manifestos in the criminal sense used in this book. As such, these multipurpose writings contain a number of features common to conventional suicide notes, including "insider" language that reflects a constrained perspective on life, whereby the author "is in a war situation, holed up in a bunker completely alone, unable to communicate their situation except through [the] note."[6] As preeminent forensic linguist John Olsson notes in his collection and analysis of suicide letters recovered or otherwise obtained by the British Transport Police—the agency tasked with investigating all railway-related suicides in the United Kingdom, such as when a person jumps from a railway line in front of a moving train—the authors of such documents are very clear about their intentions, referring to their own deaths quite explicitly, seeing no other way out. Such findings are in line with the research on the recurring word choices (or keywords) found in the notes comprising what is known as the Shneidman-Farberow corpus, the definitive catalogue of suicide notes in the English-speaking world.[7] This macabre collection of writings was first compiled by noted suicidologists Shneidman and Farberow back in the 1950s. Together with Olsson's own corpus, or collection, of railway-related suicide notes from the early 2000s onward, several common themes between both sets of texts emerge, all of which revolve around a sense of inevitability, anger, despair, and a willingness to accept death. The question, then, is why some people write these notes and then take only their own lives while others compose remarkably similar documents and then kill others en masse. The answer may lie in clues left in the writings themselves. These may show what is going on in the mass murderer's mind and, perhaps, how it got there.

MALIGNANT NARCISSISM

In contrast to suicide notes, the most outstanding feature of mass-murder communiqués is that they tend to be overwhelmingly ego-centric. The writings of serial killers, as we have seen, are similarly implanted in self-interestedness, but they also reveal a victim-centric component—that is, the serial killer has a certain victim type in mind; the mass murderer does not. He or she wants either to get even for some perceived wrong, or else wants to enact murder to communicate his or her anguished state of mind. The mass murderer sees himself or herself as both protagonist and narrator in a life scheme gone awry. Consider the following statements left behind by one of America's earliest mass murderers, whose crimes would in some tragic sense serve as progenitors for the gun violence that characterized not only the early twenty-first-century tale of murder, but the larger story as it exists today:

> "I do not quite understand what it is that compels me to type this letter. Perhaps it is to leave some vague reason for the actions I have recently performed. I do not really understand myself these days. I am supposed to be an average reasonable and intelligent young man. However, lately (I cannot recall when it started) I have been a victim of many unusual and irrational thoughts."

> "To Whom It May Concern: I have just taken my mother's life. I am very upset over having done it. However, I feel that if there is a heaven she is definitely there now [. . .] I am truly sorry [. . .] Let there be no doubt in your mind that I loved this woman with all my heart."

> "I imagine it appears that I brutally killed both of my loved ones. I was only trying to do a quick thorough job [. . .] If my life insurance policy is valid please pay off my debts [. . .] donate the rest anonymously to a mental health foundation. Maybe research can prevent further tragedies of this type [. . .] Give our dog to my in-laws. Tell them Kathy loved "Schocie" very much [. . .] If you can find in yourselves to grant my last wish, cremate me after the autopsy."[8]

These passages, taken from a series of notes left at various murder scenes before the killer enacted his public massacre in earnest, were written by Charles Whitman, the Texas Tower Sniper, who, after killing his wife and mother in their homes in August 1966, proceeded to go to the University of Texas–Austin, where he was an engineering student at the time. After first killing a number of employees in the tower, he climbed up to the observation deck and spent the next ninety minutes indiscriminately shooting at random human targets below, ultimately killing fourteen people and injuring over thirty before being shot and killed by an assortment of police and armed civilians. Whitman's motives remain somewhat puzzling today, but in reading his written confessions, along with the frustrated entries made in a ledger he began in 1963, titled "Daily Record of C. J. Whitman," we see his own awareness of a disturbed state of mind and that, as a consequence, he sought to eliminate it by projecting his ire and generalized need for revenge on people in general, doing so in pseudo-commando style. This was the salvo of a trend that would come to typify the next generation of mass shooters following in Whitman's wake.

Let's turn our attention to one of the "descendants" of the Whitman legacy, the mass murder committed by George Hennard on October 1991 at a restaurant known as Luby's Cafeteria in Killeen, Texas, a massacre that curiously remains understudied and little known despite being one of the largest mass murders in American history. Like Whitman, Hennard was a pseudo-commando mass murderer; he arrived at the scene with an arsenal of weapons, along with selected attire and accessories, and, after significant preplanning, deployed a blitz-style attack on the restaurant. After ramming his Ford pickup truck through the front plate-glass entrance, effectively blocking the main exit, Hennard alarmed patrons and staff who were initially uncertain if the collision was an accident. He used this diversionary tactic and the ensuing confusion to exit from his truck and, while armed with two guns, methodically began stalking, targeting, and executing the patrons inside. He ended up slaying a total of twenty-three people and shooting and injuring another twenty-seven. After the rampage, like Whitman, Hennard was shot and killed by responding officers in a surrogate suicide rather than killing himself per se—suicide by cop. Hennard, unlike Whitman, did not leave behind any written rationale for the shootings—no narrative window into his madness. But he did pen a letter to two neighboring girls in the days and weeks leading up to the attack, a document that has since provided some insight into his mind-set at the time. The letter was a forewarning of events to come, a harbinger of mass murder whose full meaning was not available until after his own death:

"Please give me the satisfaction of some day laughing in the face of all those mostly white treacherous female vipers from those two towns who tried to destroy me and my family."

"I'm truly flattered knowing I have two teenage groupie fans."[9]

Like Rodger, Hennard was a misogynist who felt that women were inferior beings and sexual objects who, he thought, owed him their full attention. He was also an obdurate racist, blaming both women and minority groups as the source of his frustrations.

Now, in the statements and texts of all three mass murderers (Whitman, Hennard, and Rodger), who hailed from different generations and geographic regions, and who also displayed markedly different writing styles, a common theme can be detected—they all aimed to rationalize their actions in a self-styled form of autobiographical storytelling. In this case, the mass murderer's narrative mechanism is used to express fury at the perceived wrongs that he has suffered at the hands of someone (usually women) and to show that the human condition is to blame for it; hence, he feels a need to take out his frustrations on everyone—the surrogate victims, to quote René Girard in *Violence and the Sacred*, first cited in chapter 1. The manifesto is therefore a means of providing philosophical justification for the murders. This frame of mind is pervasively common in dozens of writings composed by mass murders. It is, in our view, also a feature that can help us distinguish their otherwise puzzling motives since, unlike serial killers, mass murderers seem to be in control of their mental lives and not at the mercy of a sadistic inner sexual impulse that warps otherwise rational thought patterns.

Interestingly, in all the documents written by Whitman, Hennard, and Rodger, there is the recurring use of the first person pronoun ("I" and "my"), in contrast to serial-killer manifestos, where the emphasis is instead on events or other people, usually the victims. This clearly suggests that the mass murderer is fixated on his own situation as a key one—his letdowns, frustrations, and so on—referencing himself either by name or by first-person pronoun forms in his rambling screeds. However, like the serial killer, the mass murderer's writing evinces a specific sense of entitlement that puts his own needs on a higher level than the needs and even the lives of others, manifesting a disordered pattern of thinking that the American Psychiatric Association has called (as we have seen) *narcissistic personality disorder*, which is a twisted form of narcissism that can only be described as a disorder. Above all else, it interferes with daily social and occupational functioning, and is thus invariably toxic and dangerous, consuming the perpetrator to the point that he explodes emotionally and feels the need to eliminate anyone who stands in his way in order to right his perceived wrongs.

American psychologist Theodore Millon, in his pioneering work on personality disorders, identified the most extreme form of narcissistic personality disorder—malignant narcissism—as one of five subtypes of pathological self-love. It describes a rare and inevitably cancerous version of egoism that induces a person to develop his own misplaced and unfounded sense of grandiosity and entitlement—but with no supporting achievements—which is capable of generating both homicidal and suicidal feelings.[10] Consider then how the malignant narcissist squares with, for example, the other aberrant narcissist subtypes tabled by Millon, each associated, incidentally, with distinct narrative frameworks—ones in which the narcissist sees himself or herself as a leading (yet suffering) character in a world he or she perceives as a stage, and the people around him or her as spiteful audience members—or simply bit players to be killed off to suit the story. All five of Millon's subtypes fall within the spectrum of narcissistic personality disorder, and are commonly coupled with psychopathy and other mental aberrations—often referred to as comorbidities—that generally cannot be treated with any known form of therapy.

> *The Unprincipled Narcissist*: Disloyal, erratic, and arrogant, this type is inclined to criminal activity, risk taking, and vindictive behavior. A typical unprincipled narcissist is the stock swindler, embezzler, or sleazy and unscrupulous lawyer.

The Amorous Narcissist: A superficial charmer, glib smooth talker, and cocky, hedonistic indulger whose own pleasure and need to be lusted after always comes first, even at the expense of others if necessary. Examples of this type are the slimy playboy, the bar star, the "mean girl" harlot, or even the "selfie" addict.

The Compensatory Narcissist: Generally plagued by feelings of insecurity and low self-esteem, this narcissist will feign expertise and project a false bravado or veneer of superiority to protect himself or herself from meaningful relationships for fear of criticism or failure. Anyone who is overbearing, micromanaging, a charlatan, or a heavy-handed authoritarian is prone to being a compensatory narcissist.

The Elitist Narcissist: Upwardly mobile and exploitative of others, generally hailing from a privileged background or otherwise having a sense of entitlement by birthright, this narcissist is typically enabled during the formative years by parents or teachers who impart to him or her a false sense of self-importance through the promotion of a bloated form of self-esteem. Among this type of narcissist is the trust-fund dilettante, country-club scoundrel, or sorority snob.

The Malignant Narcissist: Aggressive, angry, vengeful, cruel, and seeing all others as inferior or trivial, this narcissist is the one who tends to be homicidal or suicidal. Among this type of narcissist is the sexual murderer, child molester, and school shooter.

But malignant narcissism alone does not explain why some people choose to murder innocent victims by the dozen with the intention of also dying in the ensuing fracas. In fact, the idea of narcissism would seem to be at odds with the willingness to die either by one's own hand or at the hands of the police. In reality, however, malignant narcissism is dangerous not only to others but also to the narcissist himself, especially once it becomes part of a larger pattern of disordered thinking known as *schizoid personality disorder*. In looking at the common narrative themes inherent in nearly all mass murderers' writings (where available), coupled with how these writings serve as an extension of specific behaviors exhibited in the various facets of the murderer's life, we can come to a generic understanding of what makes the mass murderer tick—when and how the countdown toward his crime begins—which might be useful in helping the authorities identify and apprehend the perpetrator before the fact, interdicting the horrific tragedies before they occur. The first step, then, is to analyze the push-pull emotional dysfunction that the murderer's narcissistic and self-pitying narratives convey in words, since these may indicate a potential personality disorder that frames his or her tortured worldview.

Fig. 3.4. Caravaggio's Baroque-era oil-on-canvas painting, *Narcissus*, depicts the eponymous hunter from Greek mythology who, as the legend goes, fell in love with his own reflection and eventually turned into a flower of the same name.

THE SCHIZOID KILLER

The figure of speech "psycho," whether intended to denote psychosis or psychopathy (or both interchangeably), gets thrown around a lot in the everyday media and popular crime literature. Now, while the correct terminology will be discussed later in this chapter, there is a seldom-discussed disorder that an analysis of homicidal texts suggests may be common to many—if not all—of the ten types of mass murderers listed earlier on. As mentioned previously, it is known as schizoid personality disorder. It is a disorder recognized by the American Psychiatric Association as characterized by behaviors, labeled "schizoid," whose defining symptoms may allow us to foretell whether an individual will actually succumb to homicidal *action*, or is limited strictly to murderous *ideation*. The disorder is often misconstrued as schizophrenia, a severe and typically chronic and clinical psychiatric disorder that, in the context of criminal offending, often leads to a classification of legal insanity. But the schizoid is not a schizophrenic, nor is he a "schizotypical" or "schizoaffective" individual, even though these terms are frequently—and erroneously—used as synonyms (again, the homicidal schizoid tends to be a *he*). While there is some variance in the severity of schizoid disorder and how experts define and diagnose it, and while in some cases genetic, physiological, or chemical factors may have a role to play, the schizoid is far from insane. On the contrary, the schizoid offender ranks among one of the most dangerous and calculating of murderers imaginable, perhaps even more so than even the criminal psychopath. He is severely mentally disturbed but not mentally ill, and in most cases he is fully aware of what he is doing and that it is wrong. He simply does not care; in fact, he may even like it. All things being equal, it's likely the closest thing to a definition of moral evil—perhaps as much as psychopathy—that exists in modern science. And yet most people have never heard of it.

As already mentioned, the disorder overwhelmingly afflicts male subjects. Its main symptoms include coldness, social withdrawal, a lack of emotional intelligence or empathy, and a general apathy toward the moral significance of life and death. The schizoid is reclusive and evasive, retreating from the real world and constructing an alternate fantasy world into which he immerses himself. Unlike the sexually motivated serial killer, the schizoid's fantasies are rarely, if ever, sexual in nature. On the contrary, they are constructed from reading, watching, or listening to fictional narratives and twisting the themes and characterizations depicted in them for egoistic purposes. The schizoid tends to substitute real-world relationships with those that he has gleaned from novels and comic books to video games. Some of these have, strangely, become what can be designated as canonical schizoid texts—recurring or preferred titles that schizoids tend to glom onto for one reason or another. An example is J. D. Salinger's 1951 novel, *The Catcher in the Rye*, which has influenced the planning and execution of at least three high-profile attacks in the twentieth-century—the murder of John Lennon, the attempted assassination of President Ronald Reagan, and the murder of actress and model Rebecca Schaeffer. These separate yet obliquely connected attacks—all linked to a single novel—were perpetrated by schizoid individuals who had constructed elaborate fantasy worlds based on the novel into which they had inserted themselves and their victims as key players. Salinger's novel deals with an antihero figure, Holden Caulfield, who rants against the hypocrisy of society, although he never takes murderous actions against it. The thematic impulse of that novel is, it would seem, highly suggestive to schizoid subjects. Several video games—and even board games such as Dungeons and Dragons going back to the 1980s—as well as films like Oliver Stone's controversial *Natural Born Killers*, previously mentioned, have also provoked schizoid murders. Such murders have been often called *copycat crimes*—they are the product of a disordered schizoid mind taking its cue from underlying narrative themes that provoke him to act horrifically. The schizoid may see himself as an extended character of that same text, constructing his imaginary identity and sense of arrogant superiority through the template of the narrative that, for one reason or another, speaks to him directly. This is ultimately what separates the schizoid from other socially aversive or awkward personalities—anger and arrogance expressed through the diegesis (the plot or storyline) of a fictional narrative.

The schizoid's ensuing "dyadic view"—fiction versus real life— is ultimately a result of an ingrained version of malignant narcissism, a mind-set made evident in the writings of mass murderers. And while not all schizoids go on to become mass murderers, it should be noted that, as increasingly confirmed by clinical and forensic studies, the disorder is present in some capacity in the vast majority of the ten mass-murderer types described in this chapter. That said, there is controversy over developing a common diagnostic criterion of the schizoid personality, as can be seen by perusing the *Diagnostic and Statistical Manual of Mental Disorders*, 5th edition (DSM-5) and the *International Classification of Diseases*, 10th edition (ICD-10), both the authoritative texts either compiled or relied on by the American Psychiatric Association and other mental-health organizations. Leading researchers in the study of the disorder have, however, developed different definitions, including diverse subcategorizations of the disorder, via a checklist of distinctive traits not unlike the one used to classify psychopaths.

Pioneering forensic psychologist Theodore Millon (mentioned earlier) proposed four schizoid subtypes: the languid schizoid, characterized by chronic laziness and a disinterest in all things; the remote schizoid, prone to seclusion, drifting, and estrangement from family; the depersonalized schizoid, showing apathy toward the well-being of both himself and others, as well as a generalized paranoia and fixation on bizarre concepts; and the affectless schizoid, inclined to emotional coldness, self-exile from relationships, and compulsive behaviors. The latter two categories would seem to correspond with what we know about most mass murderers and how their anger festers in isolation, as well as how they use elaborate fantasy scenarios to convince themselves that they are superior to those from whom they feel alienated or else who they feel have wronged them.

Some killers, such as Elliot Rodger, actually exhibit some degree of all four types. At one point, Rodger planned to murder his own mother and ten-year-old step-brother; he spent his teen years obsessing over the video game World of Warcraft; he even superimposed the narrative of the game onto his own life. At the same time, he wondered why attractive women were not swooning all over him and, lacking the social skills to approach women himself, he became fixated on the idea that other men were blocking his path to sexual success—interdicting his perceived destiny borne out of a disordered worldview and inner-narrative he developed through compulsively playing a video game. He in turn renounced all meaningful human contact, immersing himself deeper into the gaming world, completing his secondary schooling from home, and—as admitted in his own written manifesto, *My Tortured World*—performing a compulsive masturbation ritual to obviate any latent desire to seek out the companionship of real women. That is, the same young women he simultaneously lusted after and yet despised. Rodger's own words provide us with insights into the forces that shaped his murderous personality:

> "The very last day of Ninth Grade was the worst. I was having P.E. at the gym, and one of my obnoxious classmates named Jesse was bragging about having sex with his girlfriend. I defiantly told him that I didn't believe him, so he played a voice recording of what sounded like him and his girlfriend having sex. I could hear a girl saying his name over and over again while she panted frantically. He grinned at me smugly. I felt so inferior to him, and I hated him. It was at that moment that I was called to the office. When I got there, my mother was waiting for me to take me home. I cried heavily as I told her about what happened earlier. That was the last day I ever set foot in Crespi Carmelite High School."

> "The more lonely I felt, the more angry I became. The anger slowly built up inside me throughout all of the dark years. Even after the release of the new WoW expansion, I noticed that the game's ability to alleviate my sense of loneliness was starting to fade. I

began to feel lonely even while playing it, and I often broke down into tears in the middle of my WoW sessions. I began to ask myself what the point was in playing this game anymore. I spent less and less time playing it [. . .] I began to have fantasies of becoming very powerful and stopping everyone from having sex. I wanted to take their sex away from them, just like they took it away from me. I saw sex as an evil and barbaric act, all because I was unable to have it. This was the major turning point. My anger made me stronger inside."[11]

By the time Rodger graduated from UC–Santa Barbara, his parents and those around him had noted a marked personality dysfunction and sought the intervention of a counselor, to whom Rodger sent a final written manifesto before going on his vengeful rampage. However, he went largely unnoticed outside of his inner circle, because schizoids are also, in many cases, sufficiently socialized and superficially charismatic that, at least for a while, they are able to blend into conventional society and feign interest in school, social and sexual relationships, and lead a productive work life. It is this subtype of the affectless schizoid—members of which can be called the secret schizoid—that recent history has suggested is perhaps the most dangerous.

There are two case studies of secret-schizoid-motivated mass murder, occurring within a year of each other, that reflect radically different circumstances and yet are connected to each other via the same kind of narrative mechanism—one that points to the same type of twisted motivation. The murders in question were perpetrated by sad and warped secret schizoids who, like Rodger and others, were prepared, and perhaps even compelled, to commit their intentions for murder to writing ahead of time. Like the self-radicalized or home-grown terrorist whose bizarre fixations, angry preoccupations, and fantasized identity are stoked in the demimonde of the Internet or in simulated video worlds (like Rodger's immersion in World of Warcraft, a theme explored further in chapter 4), and who raise the false flag of some radical ideal to justify the act of murder, the secret schizoid is simply a ticking time bomb—an inveterate malcontent looking for an excuse to accelerate the countdown. He can be, and has often proven to be, an inherently dangerous and dysfunctional individual who sends out clear warning signs that often go unnoticed—at least until it is too late. The question is, how can the writings of this secret-schizoid killer be used as a psychological window into a demented psyche and thus as a premonition about his future plans so as to better identify and stop them? If those tasked with recognizing the warning signs and taking appropriate action—family, friends, teachers, police officers, therapists—had access to these writings earlier on, might they be able to take substantive steps to intervene? We can only hope that, in the future, the people we trust to protect us might pay closer attention to this possibility. The devil is, as they say, in the details.

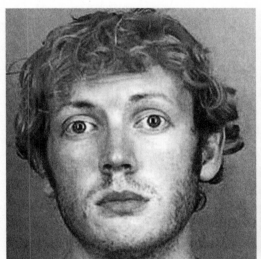 

Figs. 3.5 and 3.6. Gaunt and cowardly theater shooter James Holmes *(left)* and LA cop turned cop killer Christopher Dorner *(right)* unleashed murderous rampages in 2012 and 2013, respectively, but only after keeping detailed diaries that were found by authorities after the fact. Holmes was a failed doctoral student; and Dorner, a disgraced patrolman. Both were secret schizoids who resorted to murder, and their disordered writings revealed what they otherwise managed for so many years to conceal. Image of Holmes from the Arapahoe County Sheriff's Office.

Consider the horrific, cruel, and cowardly murders committed by James Holmes, an ostracized doctoral-program washout at the University of Colorado in July 2012. At a special midnight premiere screening of the Batman film *The Dark Knight Rises*, in Theater 9 at the Century 16 Multiplex in Aurora, Colorado, Holmes, dressed in full tactical gear, stormed the theater packed with jubilant fans after reentering through a screen-side fire exit he had previously propped open. During an opening action sequence in the film, Holmes, hiding in the darkness and knowing viewers were transfixed to the screen, lobbed a tear-gas canister into the crowd to blind the distracted Friday-night moviegoers engrossed in the movie. He then indiscriminately opened fire on the crowd with high-powered weapons. A total of twelve people were killed and seventy injured, constituting one of the highest-casualty mass murder shootings in American crime history. Among the victims was a pregnant young mother who was left paralyzed, with her child in utero, dead. Also killed was her young daughter, who had accompanied her mother to the movie theater for a family night out. Holmes was arrested at the scene by police who found him walking nonchalantly to his parked car outside. He had dyed his unkempt hair a bright red in the days before the massacre, reportedly telling the arresting officer that he was the Joker, one of Batman's arch villains. The veracity of this admission has, however, since been widely contested. Yet, in a curious act of contrition that was later entered as evidence at trial, Holmes told police that his nearby apartment, which he knew would be searched after the murders, was booby-trapped with explosives. It appears that he intended to kill law-enforcement officers and building residents as well, expecting to be killed by police at the theater rather than arrested. His qualm of conscience following his arrest thus defies any explanation.

The widely publicized investigation into the horrific theater massacre later revealed that Holmes was actually in the midst of withdrawing from his doctoral program in neuroscience at the local university ahead of being expelled—he had attempted to drop out before being officially cashiered by school administrators following a series of gaffes, including actions that revealed increasingly bizarre and high-risk behavior. However, aside from seeing a therapist for undisclosed anxieties, no one—including that therapist—saw it necessary to alert authorities to the fact that Holmes was articulating potentially dangerous homicidal thoughts. In actual fact, he was a secret schizoid very much aware of his own descent into madness and who sought to attenuate his sense of isolation and anger by killing others rather than himself. As was revealed at his trial, at which he predictably pleaded not guilty by reason of insanity, it was Holmes's writing that ultimately gave him away.

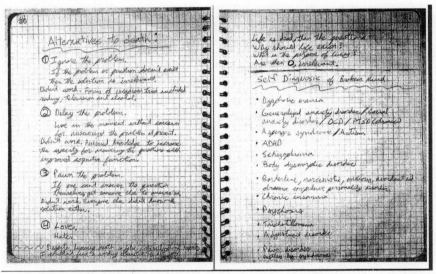

Fig. 3.7. (a) A withdrawn and self-isolated James Holmes, realizing the failure of his academic career along with other personal inadequacies and professional shortcomings, lists four alternatives to suicide that culminated in his choosing to murder innocent people in order for him to find purpose for his existence. (b) Holmes lists a series of possible self-styled clinical diagnoses for his state of mind, aware that he is mentally unstable and thus preferring to experiment with self-diagnosis rather than seek professional help. Note that schizoid personality disorder is not among the potential disorders identified by Holmes.

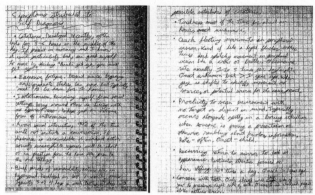

Fig. 3.8. (a) In his continued attempts to document and self-diagnose his descent into madness, Holmes begins to tabulate and describe his principal symptoms, which include "isolationism," his need to "avoid social interactions," and a sense of "invincibility." His writing reads like a textbook case of schizoid personality disorder. It should be noted that he was still a full-time doctoral student, and he was also seeing a therapist at the time, yet the gravity of his self-assessment apparently went unnoticed. (b) In this diary entry, Holmes now realizes he can and will murder multiple victims, listing the pros and cons of mass murder versus serial murder, and of different target locations and weapons.

Diary entries recovered from Holmes's apartment revealed a series of increasingly extremist ideas expressed in pseudo-therapeutic and self-diagnostic language that suggested a conscious decision to commit mass murder. In literary criminological terms, Holmes was the prototypical Tragedian as self-styled protagonist in his story, displaying and expressing an abiding sense of nihilism that spurred him on to consider murder, and the self-destruction it would bring about, as the only "rational" action to be taken in an irrational world to which he never belonged. Holmes was pragmatic enough to create a list of potential alternatives to murder, as well as a list of ideal target locations and appropriate weapons for maximizing casualties. In other words, Holmes used writing to hone his plan—a fact which makes it clear that he was far from insane. On the contrary, his manifestos reveal a clear *mens rea*—a guilty mind, a criminal intent—weeks ahead of the attack on the theater. The secret schizoid typically understands his own criminal mind-set, unlike truly insane offenders, who tend to be unaware of the gravity and wrongfulness of their actions. From both a psychological and an evidentiary perspective, the diaries are priceless. Holmes was eventually convicted on all charges and sentenced to twelve life sentences plus over 3,300 years in prison.

In addition to his diaries, which were entered as evidence at his prolonged trial after which a Colorado jury found him guilty on all charges, it was discovered that Holmes also took to the dating and casual sex website AdultFriendFinder as an unlikely writing forum on which he left cryptic warnings about his impending massacre. The following excerpts are drawn from his bizarre correspondence with users of that site:

"Will you visit me in prison?"
"Am a nice guy. Well, nice enough of a guy who does these sorts of shenanigans."[12]

It must be emphasized that these statements, along with the increasingly nihilistic dairy entries, predate Holmes's horrific attack by weeks and dovetail with efforts he put forth to mail-order weapons and tactical gear to carry out the attack in quintessentially pseudo-commando fashion. Holmes failed at attracting the interest of women online for casual sexual encounters; more importantly, not even one denizen of cyberspace noticed the significance of his ominous statements. His unusual choice of venue—a dating site—given his otherwise asexual and solitary nature, however, draws into question whether Holmes ever legitimately intended to find some hope via the website, either as a means to engage in romantic contact or as an indirect plea for help. We may never know. As will be explained in the next chapter, the things people choose to write about online are seldom self-contained or without some personal context—they are to some extent digital extensions of their disordered fantasies.

Less than a year after the Aurora theater attack, in February 2013, Los Angeles Police Department (LAPD) patrolman Christopher Dorner, a divorced former US Naval Reserve Officer hired by the LAPD and sent to the police academy in 2005, was terminated from his job on the force following several years of internal disciplinary hearings and appeals. Ultimately, a disciplinary board ruled that Dorner had made false allegations and perjured statements about an overly picky training officer he had had disagreements with years before; it was a training officer whom Dorner had also at one point accused of excessive force against an arrested subject. Like Holmes's impending removal from his doctoral program, these ominous and accusatory police board hearings focused on removing Dorner from the department triggered an emotional crisis in him that led to the crystallization of deep-seated homicidal impulses—the maturation of a worldview shaped by elaborate fantasies of revenge. Like Holmes, Dorner would emerge as the quintessential Tragedian—the schizoid's most natural narrative persona—compelled to commit his murderous plans to writing.

Beginning on February 3, 2013, once all of Dorner's appeals to save his job had been exhausted, he ambushed and murdered the daughter of the lawyer who had represented him at his police board hearings, along with her boyfriend, as they sat in a parked car. Neither had any connection to Dorner other than the fact that the twenty-eight-year-old victim he shot outside her own home was the daughter of a man whom Dorner sought to blame in part for his termination—and upon whom he wanted to inflict suffering. Then, in the following days, Dorner ambushed two pairs of uniformed police officers unrelated to his revenge plot. One pair of officers was with the LAPD; and the other, with the nearby Riverside Police Department. He killed one of the latter officers in a hail of gunfire; the others survived. On February 12, following an intense manhunt that saw several civilians being shot by jumpy officers who mistook their vehicles for Dorner's, the real killer was chased to a remote cabin near the town of Big Bear Lake in San Bernardino County, where he holed up in an abandoned hunting cabin. In an ensuing shootout with authorities, Dorner killed a detective with the San Bernardino

County Sheriff's Department before officers launched incendiary tear-gas canisters into the cabin. The exothermic canisters apparently ignited Dorner's ammunition supply and other flammable materials, and he was killed as the cabin burned to the ground with him inside.

Dorner's case is remarkable for a couple of reasons. First, despite exhibiting obvious Tragedian narrative ideation and associated behaviors, as well as some features of the Revenger personality, Dorner was also a sleeper schizoid who managed to successfully pass a police psychological test during the required background check of the LAPD's recruitment process. While the testing system used by police departments (which is generally based on the Minnesota Multiphasic Personality Inventory 2nd edition [MMPI-2- or some variant] is far from thorough and can easily be used to one's advantage,[13] it is still noteworthy that Dorner managed to pass it and successfully suppress—or at the very least conceal—his schizoid personality for so long. His LAPD training officer, as it turns out, was correct to document her concerns about Dorner's mental stability based on his inability to follow orders in the field. Like the Holmes case, however, by the time anyone took notice that something was wrong, it was already too late.

Second, Dorner produced materials to both document and rationalize his crimes well ahead of the actual murders, implying that he was aware of what he was about to carry out. On February 1, 2013, upon finally realizing that his career as a cop was over, Dorner mailed a DVD containing a video along with a bullet-riddled "challenge coin" (a symbolic talisman in police and military culture) to CNN anchor and investigative reporter Anderson Cooper. It remains unclear what, if any, action was taken by the network upon receipt of the materials; however, Dorner later followed up with a public declaration and justification of his impending rampage that was even more explicit than those posted to the Internet by Holmes. Similarly, he used multiple media platforms to frame his Tragedian narrative in secret-schizoid fashion. Note the following statements posted to Facebook as a follow-up to the package sent to CNN, and which, as part of an 11,000-word rambling screed, immediately preceded the murder of the couple connected to his lawyer and his shooting of the four police officers. The manifesto, if one can call the disjointed patchwork of verbs and nouns that, appears to represent the reality to which, like Holmes, Dorner had resigned himself, evolving into the destiny he had chosen.

"I know I will be vilified by the LAPD and the media. Unfortunately, this is a necessary evil that I do not enjoy but must partake and complete for substantial change to occur within the LAPD and reclaim my name."

"I will bring unconventional and asymmetrical warfare to those in LAPD uniform whether on or off duty. You will now live the life of the prey."

"Don't ever call me a f—[ing] bully. I want all journalist to utilize every source you have that specializes in collections for your reports. With the discovery and evidence available you will see the truth. Unfortunately, I will not be alive to see my name cleared. That's what this is about, my name. A man is nothing without his name. Below is a list of locations where I resided from childhood to adulthood.

Cerritos, CA.
Pico Rivera, CA.
La Palma, CA.
Thousand Oaks, CA.
Cedar City, UT.
Pensacola, FL.
Enid, OK.
Yorba Linda, CA.
Las Vegas, NV."[14]

Like Holmes, Dorner also furnished a detailed psychological self-portrait on Facebook, resigning himself to the inevitability of a fatal outcome—one that Holmes managed to elude. Dorner's list of the cities and towns that comprised the settings of his life story was one part neutralization strategy—a method used by offenders to psychologically let themselves off the hook for their crimes—and one part attempt to seize control of the narrative once his first two murders became public knowledge. Dorner—continuously aware of the mass media's role in contouring how history interprets such events—implored reporters via Facebook to conduct further research into his background. This was blatantly self-serving, since the vetted list of addresses, with no additional explanatory information, were concocted by Dorner to suggest a hidden "truth" of what led him down his self-destructive and murderous path—namely, the events he perceived as being engineered by the LAPD. Again, like Holmes, Dorner minimized personal responsibility and used impending life changes and comparatively minor traumas to justify extreme violence as the only remedy to his plight, which is symptomatic of the schizoid's constrained and malignantly narcissistic worldview—a view easily detected in their writing.

Identifying schizoid behavior, including high-risk escalation, is not purely a matter of clinical analysis. British psychoanalyst Harry Guntrip, who is a scholar of Freudian orientation, an esteemed fellow of the British Psychological Society, and an influential contributor to the field of study on this disorder, suggests that identifying the schizoid personality must be rooted in analyzing his relationship to people and objects during childhood. Guntrip was a proponent of Freud's object relations theory, or the idea that people's relationship to the world, what they expect from it, and what they are prepared to do it in return, is critical in the formation of personality. In the schizoid, this relationship is out of sync, leading to an odd combination of low sociability and narcissism along with withdrawal, loneliness, coldness, and emotional regression as its primary hallmarks.

Guntrip's model is based, in other words, on the idea that meaningful objects become archetypal symbols in personal narratives. The ability to respond to the realities of the world versus the expectations established in childhood partially determine the ability of a person to distinguish reality from fantasy. It is therefore interesting to note that while the serial killer easily distinguishes between the two and is prepared to kill in order to indulge his fantasies, the schizoid is either unable or unwilling to understand the difference, as his writings reveal. For some reason, schizoids—and in particular secret schizoids—see themselves as being on the verge of an impending major life change that stands to erode their fantasy world (spelled *phantasy* in object-relations theory), and they are prepared to murder randomly in order to maintain control of their self-styled narrative—to have the last word, so to speak, no matter how cruel and depraved their actions might be. Among the most cataclysmic of changes faced by schizoids still clinging to an infantilized view of the world as a stage—*their* stage—is the compulsory crossing over from the demimonde of school life to the real world and the ensuing emotional shift to a new life stage. The symbolic significance of this milestone for the schizoid mind would seem in part to explain his twisted justification for mass murder, as well as the surge in mental-health crises among college-aged students at the precipice of graduation, discussed again later.

SCHOOL SHOOTERS

School shooters present a particularly troubling snapshot of the schizoid killer personality in that, dating back to Charles Whitman, there is a dominant trend among them to leave behind narrative rationalizations of their motives and the mind-set behind their massacres. The exception—and it's a notable one among mass murderers generally—is when the school rampage is carried out not by a student at the institution but by an adult outsider. In such cases, a sexual motivation and an accompanying narrative emblematic of the Hero mind-set makes the murderous rampage more consistent with serial murder than with conventional mass-murder typologies. In the fall of 2006, several relevant incidents of this nature occurred in near succession. The most notable was the siege of a one-room Amish schoolhouse in the rural hamlet of Nickel Mines, Pennsylvania. A low-functioning milk-truck driver and pedophile named Charles Roberts IV stormed into the school and took ten small girls hostage; he was armed with two guns, bindings, and a week's worth of vital supplies, which indicated that he came prepared to keep the victims captive and barricaded for days.[15] Roberts later called his wife from the scene and admitted that he had been fantasizing about raping prepubescent girls for some time and was now prepared to act on his impulses. Even though he knew it would end in death, he claimed that he was no longer able to control himself. When police arrived sooner than he expected—before he could rape the girls— Roberts instead shot all ten captives at point-blank range, killing five of them, before taking his own life.

Another key turning point in our understanding of paraphiliac-based school shootings committed by nonstudents was the 2012 Sandy Hook Elementary School massacre in Newtown, Connecticut, the single most deadly mass murder in US history to occur at either an elementary or a secondary school. The murders were perpetrated by twenty-year-old Adam Lanza, a local wastrel who had no affiliation to the school; he killed twenty-seven children and staff members, appearing to have had a latent sexual motivation for his actions. Lanza was suffering from severe anorexia and obsessive-compulsive disorder in addition to schizoid behaviors when he first murdered his mother and destroyed his computer's hard drive to obliterate any written evidence of the motive and planning behind the attack. Unlike many mass murderers, Lanza apparently did not want his writings to become a matter of public record, in part because they might reveal him to be an inveterate hater of women and, like Charles Roberts, a secret pedophile. Lanza had apparently had sexual fantasies about children, which, once melded with his misplaced narcissism and anger, led him on a sexually motivated rampage to destroy what he was forbidden from having. A review of the documents recovered by police from Lanza's damaged computer paint a chilling portrait of a man consumed with misogynistic and pedophiliac thoughts, stoking his rage and inducing him to plan his massacre of innocents—the darkest of dark odysseys. The specific contents of these documents have not been publicly disclosed; however the titles assigned to the different texts by Lanza are revelatory in themselves[16]:

"457.full"—a written profile of a male pedophile.

"colgam01"—a spreadsheet ranking mass murderers by number of victims killed, weapons used, and target location.

"me"—an 8-page rambling document detailing Lanza's personal beliefs and bizarre views on sexuality and politics.

"selfish"—a rant written by Lanza about the inherent selfishness of all women.

"tomorrow"—an essay detailing the benefits of being thin, apparently a rationalization of Lanza's anorexic condition. Most curiously, there is also a table of keywords consisting of nouns and adjectives that Lanza compiled for unknown reasons. The full list has never been revealed.

"umm"—an essay about how marriage is a form of abuse.[17]

Lanza, as it turns out, had methodically researched the modus operandi of earlier school shooters. However, despite some evidence of copycatting in similar cases, and despite the clustering of mass murders at educational institutions in the 2000s,[18] school shootings remain statistically rare. They seem to be frequent because they are favored political props exploited by politicians and partisan groups. They are also the favored tragedies of the commercial media, given their horrific shock value and the sociological implications—and associated ratings—they engender in a dynamic and digital world. These conditions also prime—even desensitize—audiences, it would seem, to see these massacres as being commonplace occurrences in America.[19]

Studies dating back to 1999 on what were then known as "classroom avengers"[20] have documented a variety of motives among school shooters, the most common of which appears to involve either some form of trauma (real or perceived) combined with narcissism.[21] More recently, a comprehensive computer-based analysis of the writings left behind by six school shooters over fifteen years has, in fact, affirmed the recurring theme of narcissism revealed via the semantic function of their word choices. The twisted narcissism of these killers, when compared to the norm, springs almost invariably from their harboring a sense of extreme humiliation, often—though not always—developed from being bullied. Much like the schizoid's baseline characteristics, the constructed narcissism is arguably a coping mechanism—"I am better than my oppressors."[22] A combination of behavioral and communication indicators in the texts significantly support this hypothesis, since the keywords in these written records reveal that the school shooter is simply a humiliated narcissist. He is, in fact, a fragile yet malignant egoist whose own self-made fantasy world presents him with the appropriate signs, meanings, and motivations for coping with life in the short-term, including a deep-seated disdain for people—all people—in the long-term. The school shooter thus takes out his revenge not only on the bullies but also on humanity in general (or at least the community in which the bullies live), since it is the nature of humanity itself that is "at fault" in the eyes of the killer.

School shooters will sometimes commit one or more murders at primary, secondary, and even tertiary locations, so as to enact a sequence of events whose separation in time and space is perceived as chronologically significant in their minds, constituting chapters in their internalized narrative. This is perhaps why clinicians now classify these killers as either "bifurcated" or "non-bifurcated" in terms of the attack locations. The former is a killer who divides his crimes into segments or branches, killing at a preliminary location or set of locations, as Lanza did with his mother at the first crime scene (the family home) before proceeding to Sandy Hook Elementary School, which became the secondary but principal killing ground. The latter is a school shooter who is a student at the time of the rampage, for whom there appears to be no setting as an attack location other than the school itself as a general staging area. It is the setting in the self-

constructed narrative that is of symbolic importance to the Tragedian's traumatic mission, justifying, in his twisted mind, the ensuing
rampage. The writings of these particular classroom avengers therefore serve as a means of understanding the symbolic importance of
the location in mass-murder events—the importance of setting in the
narrative of mass murder.

Fig. 3.9. An ominous selfie taken by Cho prior to the Virginia Tech massacre and
sent to NBC News along with his manifesto and other materials. Cho's attire is
consistent with the pseudo-commando mass-murderer persona, which, when
coupled with a menacing pose, suggests a level of narcissism and spectacle
seldom seen even among schizoid school shooters.

Consider, for instance, the maniacal writings of Seung-Hui Cho,
the disordered undergraduate student behind the 2007 massacre at
Virginia Tech, a flagship land-grant university based in the city of
Blacksburg, Virginia, and located just over two hundred miles from
Washington, DC. As a university-level English student who had

completed several courses in poetry, creative fiction, and literary history, it is noteworthy how his education impressed upon Cho's otherwise disordered mind a need to frame the massacre as a story that, using a combination of Tragedian and Revenger themes, allowed him to depict himself as a tragic antihero and avenger committing righteous violence. On the morning of the massacre, Cho left a note in his dorm room on campus after first mailing a compendium of materials that included a more detailed manifesto, a video statement, and a series of disturbing and theatrical images to NBC News in New York.

On the morning of April 16, shortly after 7:00 a.m., Cho first shot and killed a female acquaintance and a male student in a dormitory on campus in an apparently targeted attack. Later, just after 9:45 a.m., from a post office near the campus, Cho mailed out the package containing his twisted multimedia materials, consisting of tragically farcical selfies and rambling monologues. In terms of crime-scene bifurcation, this sequence of events is remarkable and unprecedented, since by this time Cho had already murdered two people at a preliminary scene, which had yet to be discovered. Cho then embarked on the second wave of his rampage at a nearby academic building, where he barricaded the main doors to prevent either exit or entry and soon began summarily executing victims at random. Once police finally breached the locked doors to the building, Cho committed suicide by turning on himself one of the pistols he had acquired in the preceding two months.

After much deliberation, executives at NBC controversially elected to release segments of the videotape and the handwritten manifesto in its entirety:

> I didn't have to do this. I could have left. I could have fled. But no, I will no longer run. If not for me, for my children, for my brothers and sisters that you fucked; I did it for them. . . . When the time came, I did it. I had to. . . . You had a hundred billion chances and ways to have avoided today, but you decided to spill my blood. You forced me into a corner and gave me only one option. The

decision was yours. Now you have blood on your hands that will never wash off.

You sadistic snobs. I may be nothing but a piece of dogshit. You have vandalized my heart, raped my soul, and torched my conscience. You thought it was one pathetic boy's life you were extinguishing. Thanks to you, I die like Jesus Christ, to inspire generations of the weak and defenseless people.

Do you know what it feels [like] to be spit on your face and have trash shoved down your throat? Do you know what it feels like to dig your own grave? Do you know what it feels like to have your throat slashed from ear to ear? Do you know what it feels like to be torched alive? Do you know what it feels like to be humiliated and be impaled upon on a cross? And left to bleed to death for your amusement? You have never felt a single ounce of pain your whole life. Did you want to inject as much misery in our lives as you can just because you can? You had everything you wanted. Your Mercedes wasn't enough, you brats. Your golden necklaces weren't enough, you snobs. Your trust fund wasn't enough. Your Vodka and Cognac weren't enough. All your debaucheries weren't enough. Those weren't enough to fulfill your hedonistic needs. You had everything [unclear] crucified me. You loved inducing cancer in my head, terrorizing my heart, and raping my soul all this time.

When the time came, I did it. . . . I had to.[23]

Like Elliot Rodger, Cho's warped accusations, deflecting the blame on others and especially on those nameless people immediately around him, reveals an obsessive and visceral hatred of the people whose lives he perceived as better than his own—those whose mere existence tormented him. Jealousy is the oldest motive in the book, but with the schizoid killer there is always another narrative trope—another dimension; another act to follow. In Cho's case, the suggestion that he was something of a martyr by carrying out the massacre—comparing himself to Jesus Christ—brings the internal narrative mechanism for the attack closer in line with an act of terrorism vis-à-vis religious mania (though not necessarily radicalism) than it does a schizoid school shooting. That said, Cho was the apotheosis of the secret schizoid. He was described as cold and aloof by his own parents, and as highly unnerving, much like Holmes, by faculty and students at Virginia Tech. Cho's own family recognized that something was wrong with him and sought psychiatric intervention, but Cho was diagnosed—or more correctly *mis*diagnosed—as suffering from selective mutism rather than schizoid personality disorder. In hindsight, however, despite Cho's secretive nature and subtle descent into madness that had medical professionals fooled, it was his English professors who likely missed the most significant warning signs: his early writings as a harbinger of what would come next. They were literary dress rehearsals for his massacre.

A 2002 study by the US Secret Service confirmed that, as we maintain in this book, there is a narrative impulse within the disordered mind that compels the prospective school shooter to commit his thoughts and plans to writing ahead of time.[24] The escalation in violent or angry content in written materials, whether in personal communications or in school assignments, is a conspicuous feature of school-shooter writings. In Cho's case, his manifesto represented a punctuation mark on a series of similarly themed violent and rage-filled writings that he composed for official class projects in creative writing and literary fiction. Given that Cho was required to submit numerous written assignments as part of his courses, the archive of materials he submitted to instructors during his first three years at Virginia Tech provides a textual time line of Cho's intensifying homicidal mind-set. This type of comprehensive documentation is lacking in most other school-shooter cases.

RICHARD: Honey-poo. Don't you believe me? John is just a mischievous kid who having trouble getting over his father's death. He'll get over it. He just needs time.

SUE: Really?

RICHARD: Yes. Now, why don't we go to the bedroom and do it doggy style, just the way you like it, honey-poo.

JOHN: (In his room, he smiles and throws darts on the target that is the face of Richard.)

I hate him. Must kill Dick. Must kill Dick. Dick must die. Kill Dick… Richard McBeef. What kind of name is that? What an asshole name. I don't like it. And look at his face. What an asshole face. I don't like his face at all. You don't think I can kill you, Dick? You don't think I can kill you? Gotcha. Got one eye…Got the other eye.

(He runs down to the basement by his mother's side)

That fat man murder dad. He told me so while you were asleep, mom. And he molested me.

SUE: What! Ahhh!

(She grabs a chainsaw and brandishes it at Richard. He runs out of the house and into his car. Thirty minutes later John goes out to Richard and sits on the passenger side eating a cereal bar.)

Fig. 3.10. This excerpt is from a one-act play, titled *Richard McBeef*, written by Cho for a class assignment in 2006. It is replete with profanity, references to murder, the mutilation of a man in effigy, and the brandishing of a chainsaw.

Mr. Brownstone
ACT ONE
Scene One
(They each sit in front of slot machine.)

JANE: Can't believe we got through using the fake ID.

JOHN: I've always wanted to come to the casino.

JOE: Yeah. Finally a cool place to hang out where we won't be constantly bushwhacked.

JOHN: Uh! After a long ravishing day at school, we just want to be left alone.

JANE: There is like no safe place for us to hang out. We can't hang out in front of the grocery store, we can't hang out at the park, we can't hang out in the street. The only place where we are safe from him is behind the shitty dumpster.

JOHN: Mr. Brownstone.

JOE: That old fart just won't leave us alone.

JANE: He just has to make our lives miserable.

JOHN: I'd like to kill him.

JANE: I'll be damn if he doesn't die. I wish that old fart would have a heart attack and drop dead like old people are supposed to.

Fig. 3.11. Excerpt from a second play written by Cho, titled *Mr. Brownstone*, in which a group of three students in a casino plot the murder of a mathematics teacher amidst profane references to hopelessness, rape, and misery. The expression of specific motives for murder and the reliance on angry epithets to describe people and situations are more focused in this play than in Cho's previous assignment.

A paper written by Cho for a short-fiction class, completed in the spring term of 2006, roughly a year before the shootings, is the most symptomatic of his writings, virtually predicting his impending attack in astonishing detail. The assignment enabled Cho to visualize strategies that would later become intrinsic to his planning process. The essay in question is garbage in terms of its prose but is rich in terms of the intelligence it provides with respect to motive and method. The short play, ostensibly a piece of fiction, details a gunman's plans to carry out a school shooting identical to the one later committed by Cho himself. The document has never been publicly released and remains under seal, likely having never been read by anyone but the professor who graded it and a handful of law-enforcement personnel. As such, the contents cannot be analyzed concretely; however, what is clear is that the assignment, like so many homicidal writings, was an example of a roman à clef—a shrewdly veiled biography or autobiography—that was in some sense an equally veiled warning. No one at the time saw it for what it was; yet, in the days following the massacre it was all the university administration could talk about. This was in part because, as it turned out, the campus police had intervened as early as 2005 when Cho was accused of stalking two female students and then sent a suicidal instant message to his then roommate. Police brought Cho to see a campus psychologist, who flagged him as an imminent danger to himself and others. That was almost two years before the massacre and a year before his written class assignments began to show an escalation in violent content. Cho never sought out the additional psychological counseling offered to him, and the university was never made aware of the assessment, apparently for privacy reasons.[25] Had Cho's actions been dealt with criminally in response to both the stalking incident and the content of his manifestos, things might have ended differently, and he would have at the very least not been on campus in 2007.

Perhaps the classic school-shooting case that proffers a rich repository of written materials for understanding the mind-set of the schizoid school shooter is the Columbine High School massacre in Littleton, Colorado, in 1999. Columbine ushered in a new era of acceleration among mass murders, and it was a game changer for police response strategies and media coverage of such tragedies. Seniors Eric Harris and Dylan Klebold—who are, significantly, cited as role models by Cho in his deranged video produced after the first two murders—committed their plans to writing and video well before their attack.

In one video, the two scraggly and homicidal teens promulgate rants and angry, nihilistic confessionals. The footage would later form part of a larger collection of recordings that became known as the "basement tapes," so named because they were created in secrecy in Harris's basement. The tapes were in due course—not surprisingly—the subject of tremendous scrutiny, given that they constituted the boys' diaries and literary blueprints for mass murder, thereby allowing investigators to, in some sense, perform an autopsy of their minds and twisted imaginations postmortem.

Once I finally start my killing, keep this in mind, there are probably about 100 people max in the school alone who I dont want to die, the rest, MUST FUCKING DIE! If I didnt like you or if you pissed me off and lived through my attacks, consider yourself one lucky god damn NIGGER. Pity that a lot of the dead will be a waste in someways, like dead hot chicks who were still bitches, they could have been good fucks. oh well, too fucking bad. life isnt fair... not by a long fuckin shot when Im at the wheel, too. God I want to torch and level everything in this whole fucking area but Bombs of that size are hard to make, and plus I would need a fuckin fully loaded A-10 to get every store on wadsworth and all the buildings downtown. heh, Imagine THAT ya fuckers, picture half of denver on fire just from me and Vodka. napalm on sides of skyscrapers and car garages blowing up from exploded gas tanks.... oh man that would be beautiful. -- 10/23/98

you know what, I feel like telling about lies. I lie a lot. almost constant. and to everybody, just to keep my own ass out of the water. and by the way (side note) I dont think I am doing this for attention, as some people may think. lets see, what are some big lies I have told; "yeah I stopped smoking," "for doing it not for getting caught," "no I'm havent been making more bombs," "no I wouldn't do that," and of course, countless of other ones, and yeah I know that I hate liers and I am one myself, oh fucking well. Its ok If I am a hypocrite, but no one else. because I am higher then you people, no matter what you say if you disagree I would shoot you And I am one racist mother fucker too, fuck the niggers and spics and chinks, unless they are cool, but sometimes they are so fucking retarded they deserve to be ripped on. some people go through life begging to be shot. and white fucks are just the same. if I could nuke the world I would, because so far I hate you all. there are probly around 10 people I wouldnt want to die, but hey, who ever said life is fair should be shot like the others too. - 11/1/98

Fig. 3.12. Transcripts of entries in Eric Harris's diary, dated October 23, 1998, and November 1, 1998. The first suggested that the attack was still in the pre-contemplative stage, with a definitive target not yet selected but a vision of extreme violence already part of his scheme. The second entry is more of an anecdotal rant, complete with extreme profanity, and hate symbols—including those of the Ku Klux Klan; the Nazi swastika; and the associated Waffen-SS lightning bolts, the signature of the infamous Nazi death squad of the same name.

jesus christ that was fucking close. fucking shitheads at the gun shop almost dropped the whole project. oh well, thank god I can BS so fucking well. I went and picked up those babies today, so now I got 13 of those niggers. WOOHAH. the stereo is very nice, but having no insurance payments to worry about so I could concentrate of BOMBS would have been better. oh well, I think I'll have enough. now I just need to get Vodka another gun.

12/29/98

Months have passed. Its the first Friday night in the final month. much shit has happened. Vodka has a Tec 9, we test fired all of our babies, we have 6 time clocks ready, 39 crickets, 24 pipe bombs, and the napalm is under construction. Right now I'm trying to get fucked and trying to finish off these time bombs. NBK came quick. why the fuck cant I get any? I mean, I'm nice and considerate and all that shit, but nooooo. I think I try to hard. but I kinda need to considering NBK is closing in. The amount of dramatic irony and foreshadowing is fucking amazing. Everything I see and I hear I incorporate into NBK somehow. Either bombs, clocks, guns, napalm, killing people, any and everything finds some tie to it. feels like a Goddamn movie sometimes. I wanna try to put some mines and trip bombs around this town too maybe. Get a few extra flags on the scoreboard. I hate you people for leaving me out of so many fun things. And no don't fucking say, "well thats your fault" because it isnt, you people had my phone #, and I asked and all, but no. no no no dont let the weird looking Eric KID come along, ohh fucking nooo.

4/3/99

Fig. 3.13. Transcript of Harris's diary entry, dated December 29, 1998, and April 3, 1999. The second entry was written just weeks before the attack on the school. This latter entry, with the teens' plan for murder now fully formed, reflects a comparatively restrained form of prose, suggesting that Harris may have found a sense of inner equilibrium, knowing full well what was to come as part of his catharsis. As such, the tenor of the writing is more expository in its structure, factually recounting events, which stands in contrast to the previous entries, which were more descriptive and episodic.

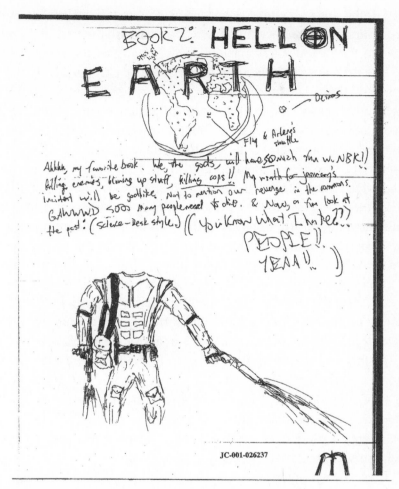

Fig. 3.14. A sketch and inscription left by Klebold in Harris's 1998 school year-book, issued in the fall of that year. Like Harris's contemporaneous diary entries, by this juncture the two were united in a mutual fantasy of mass murder and destruction but lacked a concrete plan. Note the focus, again, on violent visual schemes and cataclysmic scenarios where death on an epic scale is the primary objective. Note also the reference to NBK (*Natural Born Killers*), the 1994 Oliver Stone film, which was being used as a placeholder for their massacre. Image from columbine-online.com.

Of the two shooters, Harris was the more prolific one as a writer, and it is his diary that, once coupled with the basement tapes, became the decoder key through which many of the milestones in the killers' plans could later be identified. The comparatively private nature of these writings and their content, combined with the fact that the two boys had an assortment of earlier brushes with the law involving petty crimes—not to mention the creation and curation of the basement tapes and other media—suggests that both teens were essentially unsupervised latch-key kids. This independence likely ensured that their plan went genuinely unnoticed rather than willfully overlooked or ignored. However, as quintessentially secret schizoids with homicidal obsessions (attending senior prom, continuing their part-time jobs, and so on while still committed to carrying out the massacre-suicide), the actions of Harris and Klebold did manage to arouse the suspicion of at least one schoolmate, whose parents later called the police after reading Harris's homicidal writings posted online. As investigative reporter Dave Cullen reveals in his extraordinarily detailed and compassionate book, *Columbine*, inarguably the most definitive account of the massacre ever written, a search warrant for Harris's home was actually issued based on this tip from the concerned classmate's parents, but it was eventually shelved. Had the warrant been properly executed, the written documents would have revealed the gruesome plan, as well as a cache of weapons, thus preventing the attack.[26]

Like theater shooter James Holmes, Eric Harris meticulously compiled lists and dated his work, outlining his murderous plans in chillingly clinical detail, which makes one wonder what might have happened and what lives might have been saved if these writings had been seen for what they were: warning signs. Harris and Klebold chose not to bifurcate their acts of mass murder, other than to use explosives to maximize casualties after their own deaths. One of their post-death timed explosives was placed at a remote location in both cases, not to cause death but to act as a diversion and draw police away. Clearly, the Columbine shooters were schizoid killers who, with an impending

The Seattle Public Library
Central Library
www.spl.org

Checked Out On: 1/29/2020 17:58
XXXXXXXXX1240

Item Title	Due Date
0010091668102	2/19/2020
Mad City : the true story of the campus murders that America forgot	
0010093244191	2/19/2020
Murder in plain English : from manifestos to memes - looking at murder through the words of killers	
0010100086643	2/12/2020
Satanic panic	
0010100946093	2/19/2020
Once upon a time in Hollywood : original motion picture soundtrack.	
0010101511243	2/12/2020
47 meters down : uncaged	
0010101103678	2/12/2020
Joker	

# of Items: 6
Renew items at www.spl.org/MyAccount
or 206-386-4190
Sign up for due date reminders
at www.spl.org/notifications

Item Title	Due Date
0010009166102	2/19/2020
Mad City : the true story of the campus murders that America forgot	
0010009324497	2/19/2020
Murder in plain English : from manifestos to memes - looking at murder through the words of killers	
0010100066643	2/12/2020
Satanic panic	
0010100946093	2/19/2020
Once upon a time in Hollywood : original motion picture soundtrack	
0010101641243	2/12/2020
47 meters down : uncaged	
0010101103673	2/12/2020
Joker	

# of Items: 6

major life change in process, put a plan into action that served as a form of catharsis. The plan was essentially an asynchronous one (occurring at different times and out of sync) that would allow them to use explosives to kill additional victims in their absence, after their own expected deaths. In Holmes's case, the police managed to disarm the bombs; in the case of Harris and Klebold, their amateurish homemade propane bombs simply had design flaws that guaranteed they would never work. Harris had made them, following the online terrorist DIY guide known as *The Anarchist's Cookbook*.[27]

By using the initials NBK as a coded reference and placeholder for their planned attack at the school, it is clear that both perpetrators were influenced by the Oliver Stone film *Natural Born Killers*, discussed in detail earlier in this book. This film was no doubt their canonical text, as we have called it here before. However, the extent to which Stone's controversial film served as inspiration (versus the other media consumed by the two shooters—violent video games, heavy-metal music, graphic websites, and such—all of which were subject to intense scrutiny after the massacre) cannot be determined for certain. Copycat or "contagion" theories of school shootings and mass murders may be somewhat overstated, though there is increasing scientific merit to suggest that these murders cluster in space and time based on national news reports and social-media metrics.[28] However, there is little question that some texts become sources of influence for warped minds independent of publicity or extrinsic factors. *Natural Born Killers* and *The Catcher in the Rye* seem to appeal to schizoids disproportionately, spurring them on to murderous actions. Once such texts become coupled with ubiquitous images of violence on screens of all kinds, it is naïve to think that some killers will not be influenced by what they see, read, and hear. In brief—they are infected by this input.

Recall the Zodiac Killer. We see not only a narrative impulse in his case as we do with other serial and mass murderers but also a style of authorship, penmanship, and spectacle that suggests that he was in some twisted manner emulating not so much the crimes as the prose of others. More specifically, the Zodiac was not only a charlatan but also—in the literary sense—a plagiarist.

The Zodiac's use of cryptography is especially critical in this regard, suggesting that he may have been inspired by Edgar Allan Poe, who employed secret writing in his short stories in the mid-nineteenth century to enhance their aura of mystery, and to seduce readers, given that many of these stories were published—as a progenitor to the ongoing network television model—as episodic weekly or monthly stories to be released in installments and to favor the occasional consumer or recreational reader. Like the serial killer, the habitual reader—and later the viewer of crime stories—was thus required to defer gratification. Poe's manipulation of this emerging literary model—after pioneering the conventions of crime with the *Mystery of Marie Rogêt*—is most obviously borne out in his 1843 short story, *The Gold Bug*. Many of the facts surrounding the Zodiac story actually read like the plots in Poe's stories, and we know the Zodiac—at least the original and better-known California Zodiac— was an avid reader, tangentially quoting Richard Connell's comparatively obscure 1924 novel, *The Most Dangerous Game*, in one of his cryptograms. It is thus very likely that he was also, by extension, an aficionado of the works of Edgar Allan Poe—a forerunner in the arena of not only true crime but also commercial cryptography. Consider, for instance, that in the December 1839 issue of *Alexander's Weekly Messenger*, Poe challenged readers to write to the newspaper using a substitution cipher of their choice, and which Poe vowed he could solve. This is, in verisimilitude, precisely what the Zodiac did, as if he were sending it to Poe himself via the San Francisco press over a century later.

From *The Gold Bug* to *The Most Dangerous Game* to *The Catcher in the Rye*, the precise influence that literary and media texts have on killers is still a murky area of study and discussion. What is obvious, however, is that from schizoid killers like Elliot Rodger to psychopaths like the Zodiac Killer—perhaps *both* Zodiac Killers— narrative images and texts emerge as dominant forces in the preplanning, planning, and execution of their heinous crimes. Research on violent offenders in the United Kingdom, building on the significance of the four protagonist archetypes adopted by killers, has gone so far as to adopt what's known as the Life as a Film (LAAF) forensic interviewing technique. In essence, this method describes narrative prompts being given to incarcerated offenders to the extent where they are able to contextualize their offenses and compare their lives—and more specifically their crimes—with a specific film genre, plot, and denouement. The method is rooted in the notion that, because the criminal identity is "socially constructed through the roles people play in society," violent offenders, including serial killers and mass murderers, will inevitably relate to specific roles and iconic characters they've previously seen on the big screen.[29] The method speaks to the enormity of film as a popular medium in shaping our identities and how even the depraved and schizoid murderer is able to draw connections between his own criminal identity and the identities of specific villains in film. As such, murder is not only about story but also spectacle for the mass murderer, as was perhaps first seen during the Columbine massacre. In fact, the mass shooting transparently emulated, both in name and in scale, the atrocities depicted in Stone's 1994 film *Natural Born Killers*; but the specific garb worn by both Harris and Klebold on the day of the murders—dark trench coats, boots, and gloves—were thought to have been inspired by the contemporaneous 1999 tech-noir film, *The Matrix*. The attire, pseudo-commando in nature but with Gothic elements, became a point of fixation among the media when it was later discovered that a purported "Trenchcoat Mafia" existed as a loosely aligned group of misfits at the school.[30] Whether the killers' choice of clothing—purely theatrical and expressive and otherwise nonfunctional—was inspired by the name of this clique or the costumes used in *The Matrix* has been the subject of great conjecture; however, there is little doubt that, as the alpha of the two males—and the one whose writings left the clearest warnings signs—Eric Harris exerted great influence over his servile emissary, Dylan Klebold, and no doubt unilaterally decided on how they would dress for the massacre and their own eventual suicides. Harris was always the one who pulled the strings. Short of categorizing him as a disciple killer, it is certainly true that Klebold was conscripted by Harris as a malleable protégé he could lure into believing the message of "NBK" and thus into following Harris's lead. In fact, it might be said that Klebold was a secret and impressionable schizoid with more clearly delineated mental-health problems, whereas Harris was the Svengali—as much a controlling and manipulative psychopath as a schizoid, and the one able to turn it on and off as it suited him. In looking at the Columbine shooters as team killers, based on the dynamics of their relationship and the role that writing played in shaping their relationship and their devious plan, we find that their partnership is really not that remarkable when compared to other homicidal duos whose life stories and criminal identities were forged by film and literature.

TEAM KILLERS, SOLE AUTHORS

Rarely are killer teams comprised of any more than two offenders, with the exception being cases of disciple-based mass murder, such as the previously mentioned slayings ordered by Jim Jones in Guyana, or the massacre carried out at the Tate-Polanski mansion in 1969 by several members of the Charles Manson cult. In these rare cases, an entire troupe of killers, sometimes over a dozen in number, are deployed on orders to commit mass murder at the direction of their leader. Killer pairs similarly have one mastermind—an alpha male—who, like Harris, typically conscripts an unstable and impressionable accomplice for the purposes of carrying out his plans. With the interpersonal dynamics of team killers having been the subject of much debate over the decades, the question that prevails today is, had this pair never met, would they ever have gone on to kill independently of the other? There are no definitive answers to this question. It is a question, however, that is especially relevant in today's world where, in an age pervaded by the fear of terror attacks and random public violence, the line between mass murder and terrorism is increasingly blurred, and where terms like "wolf pack" (versus "lone wolf") are being used as common metaphors to describe the perpetration of some murders.

Going back to 1850, however, the evidence has continually suggested that the overwhelming majority of team killers end up committing serial murder, killing two or more victims over an extended period of time and frequently (though not always) with an underlying sexual motive, rather than mass murder, which describes killing four or more victims at one time and frequently (though not always) with a personal, ideological, or political motive. This historical trend toward serial murder and mutual paraphiliac drives among team killers may reflect the fact that the pair bond established between them is usually not familial in nature. They are also typically male-dominated, either with a male leader or with two males comprising the team. Exceptions to this rule are rare, to say the least, with team killers comprised of two or more females—and with a female mastermind—being limited mostly to healthcare killers, such as pairs of nurses or personal support workers who murder in tandem, or to cults like Tene Bimbo, a Gypsy clan responsible for five poisoning murders in the San Francisco area in the 1980s and 1990s.[31] The clan was first depicted in detail in author Peter Maas's 1974 novel *King of the Gypsies*, which was later made into a 1978 film that actually pre-dated the confirmed murders committed by the women, the motive in each case being financial gain. The serial murders committed by male teams, however, consistently reflect a shared set of homicidal paraphilias and preferred victim types, with the murders themselves being sexual in nature and overwhelmingly targeting adult Caucasian females for kidnapping and confinement, rape, torture, and murder—or some combination of all four. Financial gain as a motive comes in at a distant second among the motives of team killers, though a combination of motives—typically sex, money, and thrill seeking—is the most common pattern, as can be seen in roughly 60 percent of team killings committed over the last century and more.[32] The nature with which these combined motives and the associated interpersonal dynamics of the team killing relationship unfold in terms of associated writings is therefore of particular interest to the field of literary criminology.

Sexual sadists and psychopaths Lawrence Bittaker and Roy Norris, known as the Toolbox Killers, first met in prison while serving time for unrelated minor crimes. They agreed to reconnect on the outside and begin kidnapping, torturing, and murdering women for fun. After linking up as promised in 1979, they later trolled California highways in a blacked-out GMC van they named "Murder Mac," and claimed a total of five female victims. The odd origin of the name—and the rationale for naming the vehicle in the first place—was never clarified, but it's a theme later parodied in one of acclaimed crime novelist James Ellroy's lesser-known novels, *Killer on the Road*, first published in 1986. In the book, a high-functioning schizoid intent on revealing Charles Manson to be a fraud and unworthy of criminal acclaim travels the country, killing victims at random in a vehicle he dubs "Deathmobile." In the real Toolbox Killers case, the narrative created by the duo didn't end with the naming of the vehicle; they also chronicled their horrific murders—all of them committed with items normally found in a household toolbox they kept stowed in "Murder Mac"—through photo essays and audio recordings. Once finally arrested, the recordings were found to be so horrific and disturbing that the prosecutor suffered severe psychological trauma and nightmares for years afterward. The lead police investigator on the case was so profoundly haunted by the details of what he saw and heard that he committed suicide in 1987, citing the recordings in the suicide note as having destroyed him as a man. The recordings are now on file at the FBI academy, where they are used to emotionally desensitize and socially engineer new recruits.[33]

But perhaps the most probative—and disturbing—of the relevant cases with respect to homicidal narratives created by team killers is that of Leonard Lake and Charles Ng. Lake and Ng's horrific crimes went unnoticed for an extended period of time, which, if not for a lucky arrest, would have been carried out in perpetuity.³⁴ In June 1985, police in San Francisco arrested Lake for illegal possession of a handgun silencer. While in custody, he swallowed a cyanide capsule that he had concealed, and he died several days later in hospital. There was a secret, as it turned out, that Lake was prepared to take to his grave—namely, the custom-built bunker and torture chamber he had constructed next to his rented remote cabin in the idyllic California town of Wilseyville. It was there that Lake was described by neighbors as quiet and withdrawn yet strangely arrogant—textbook schizoid indicators. Lake had actually been diagnosed as suffering from schizoid personality disorder while serving with the Marine Corps in Vietnam, and he was eventually given a medical discharge. He arrived in San Francisco in the early 1970s and began to obsess over what he thought was the pending end of the world. As both a schizoid and a psychopath, Lake put a plan into motion consistent with the thrill-seeking Hero offender archetype. From the beginning, writing was central not only to how Lake would work out his gruesome serial killings but also to how he would lure both his accomplice and his victims.

After placing a classified advertisement in a local newspaper soliciting interest from men looking to become "mercenaries" (soldiers of fortune) in his employ, a petty criminal, sexual sadist, and low-functioning army washout named Charles Ng responded to the ad and met Lake at his remote cabin. By that point, now 1983, it is believed that Lake had murdered several people—including his own brother—for profit, in order to fund the construction of his soundproof torture chamber. Scouring further classified ads, Lake and Ng together found a young family privately selling video recording equipment that the two killers decided they would need to document their future murders—Ng was now completely willing to go along with Lake's plan. They soon responded to the ad and, under the pretense of being serious buyers, went to the family's address before murdering them—including their infant child—in their home and stealing the equipment. Inspired by the "success" of using classified ads to identify victims, Lake composed a series of new postings advertising jobs at the cabin, and other allurements, to entice unsuspecting victims to the remote location. The women who responded to the ads were kept as sex slaves for days and weeks in Lake's soundproof concrete dungeon, where they were repeatedly tortured and raped—with most of the atrocities being filmed. Male companions of the women or male respondents to the ads were killed quickly for their possessions.[35]

Once Lake and Ng were finished with a slave, she was strangled or shot, cut into pieces, and then incinerated along with the male victims. The remains were later scattered across the vast hillside property, which made a full recovery of victims impossible once Lake was caught. Lake's suicide ensured that the burial locations could never be identified and that he could never be convinced to confess to the exact nature of the horrors that had occurred at his cabin. By the time of Lake's death, Ng had also fled the country, and his whereabouts were for many years unknown. When police finally arrived at the cabin and found the chamber of horrors the two killers had left behind, their search led them to forty-five pounds of bone fragments believed to be from the bodies of at least eleven and as many twenty-five victims murdered over a two-year period. Their search also led them to the writings that Lake, as the only fully literate of the two killers, had kept to document his atrocities and to complement the videos, some of which depict both Lake and Ng donning robes reminiscent of those worn in satanic rituals.[36]

Lake's writings served both as planning documents and mementos through which he could relive his sadistic crimes, like Albert Fish, the Zodiac, and others, in coprographic terms. Lake even went to far as the write and post a list titled "RULES" that was found displayed on the inside of the door leading to the dungeon where the female victims were chained to a concrete slab. Written with a mechanical typewriter and in uppercase letters was a code of conduct that Lake imposed on the women he kidnapped, raped, tortured, and then killed. The women, no doubt holding out hope that compliance would provide some hope of survival or release, acquiesced to these rules as carefully tabulated by Lake, as confirmed in the horrific video recordings of the rape sessions. Like other schizoids, Lake it seems had a twisted preoccupation with preparing lists, indicating a need for organization and systematic behavior.

RULES

1. I MUST ALWAYS BE READY TO SERVICE MY MASTER. I MUST BE CLEAN, BRUSHED, AND MADE-UP WITH MY CELL NEAT.
2. I MUST NEVER SPEAK UNLESS SPOKEN TO. UNLESS IN BED, I MUST NEVER LOOK MY MASTER IN THE EYE, BUT MUST KEEP MY EYES DOWNCAST.
3. I MUST NEVER SHOW MY DISRESPECT, EITHER VERBALLY OR SILENT. I MUST NEVER CROSS MY ARMS OR LEGS IN FRONT OF MY BODY, OR CLENCH MY FISTS, AND UNLESS EATING, MUST ALWAYS KEEP MY LIPS PARTED.
4. I MUST BE OBEDIENT COMPLETELY AND IN ALL THINGS. I MUST OBEY IMMEDIATELY AND WIHTHOUT QUESTION OR COMMENT.
5. I MUST ALWAYS BE QUIET WHEN LOCKED IN MY CELL.
6. I MUST REMEMBER AND OBEY ANY ADDITIONAL RULES TOLD TO ME. I MUST UNDERSTAND THAT ANY DISOBEDIENCE, ANY PAIN, TROUBLE, OR ANNOYANCE CAUSED BY ME TO MY MASTER WILL BE GROUNDS FOR PUNISHMENT.

Fig. 3.15. A transcription of the notice of rules appended to the interior of the dungeon door inside Lake's torture chamber in Northern California. Note the regimentation of the rules that are more concerned with decorum and submissiveness than with maintaining control, with Lake as the "MASTER" (singular, therefore excluding Ng) and with "PUNISHMENT" as a euphemism for any number of horrific assaults that would be imposed if rules were violated (avoiding any overt reference to murder or rape by name).

Beyond this demented list to which his tortured captives were subjected before meeting their brutal end, Lake also committed his thoughts—including his delusions of grandeur about being a "master"—to paper as part of a narrative rationalization revealing his own self-perceived power. Like most killers in the Hero category, he relied on a specific heroic narrative—reminiscent of the Old English poem *Beowulf*—that detailed what he felt was his right to pursue adventure and to chase his destiny, but in this case through torture, rape, and murder. Like his carefully typewritten rule list, it is interesting to note that Lake always refers to himself in the singular in these writings and, like the typical schizoid mass murderer, favors the use of first-person pronouns. This suggests that he not only planned the crimes but also was acting as the leader of the pair at all times, underscoring the fact that among team killers, the mastermind does not see his collaboration with his murderous cohort as a genuine partnership or an egalitarian relationship. Rather, he uses his collaborator as a pawn, much like he uses his victims as a means of achieving his parasitic ends.

Consider the following writings by Lake, which were discovered by police once they finally located his hiding place. By this time, Ng had fled the country but was later collared for shoplifting in Calgary, Alberta, where he shot the undercover department-store floorwalker while resisting arrest in July 1985. The arresting security officer survived and, once Ng's identity was confirmed by Calgary Police, he was extradited back to California, where he was tried and convicted. He is currently languishing on death row at San Quentin State Prison—the infamous "Big Q" as it's sometimes known. Following Ng's prolonged trial, a number of courtroom observers, including jury members, were required to undergo psychiatric counseling; they were deeply traumatized by the images from the videos of the rapes and murders and by the entries in Lake's diary.[37] Out of respect for the victims, only the main portions of text from those writings have been cited here; Lake's accompanying sketches (also indicative of the Hero killer artistic style) and cartoon-bubble captions have been removed. The entries include statements made by Lake in his various video recordings, many of which mirror his handwritten diary entries:

> "I want to be able to use a woman whenever and however I want. And when I'm tired or bored or not interested, I simply want to put her away, lock her up in [her cell], get her out of my sight, out of my life."
>
> "If you love something, set it free. If it doesn't come back hunt it down and kill it."
>
> "Death is in my pocket and fantasy is my goal."
>
> "Buried Treasure." [The "treasure" in question was a map indicating where the cremated and pulverized remains of the 11–25 men, women, and children Lake murdered were buried, some with Ng and some on his own.][38]

Lake's writings at first glance appear maniacal and disordered, typical of a schizoid personality. However, the overall thrust of the narrative he creates in order to describe and rationalize his right to conquest and the inevitable fate of his existing and future victims was not created in a vacuum. He drew inspiration for his brutal murders and for his writing style from an existing canonical text, a relatively unknown novel that inspired not only Lake but also at least two other serial killers. We see from Lake's diaries that he called his heinous plot "Operation Miranda." The name is an allusion to the 1963 horror fantasy book, *The Collector*, by British author John Fowles—a book that Lake read and quickly became obsessed with. In the novel, a woman named Miranda Grey is stalked by the protagonist, a sexually disordered butterfly collector named Frederick Clegg. Realizing that the attractive young art student is out of his league, Clegg kidnaps her and confines her to his basement. There he keeps her captive until such time as she will return his affections. It would be another ten years before the term "Stockholm syndrome" was coined to describe the conflicted feelings that kidnapping victims feel toward their captors, including how they come to sympathize with them; but within the novel we see that Miranda grows to pity the pathetic Frederick. Eventually, she becomes ill and is later found dead in Frederick's cellar. After reading her diary and what she thought of him, Frederick decides to put the event behind him, and he sets out to kidnap another woman to bring back to his dungeon lair and satisfy his sadistic compulsions once again. Lake drew inspiration from the novel—he sought to emulate Frederick in much the same way that LAAF forensic interviewing today confirms that killers idolize and seek to imitate a select number of archetypal film villains through their crimes. Like the influence writers experience by reading previous literary works, so too does a schizoid killer like Lake rely on canonical texts to quite literally write himself into murderous history.

Fowles's novel was also the source of inspiration for serial killer Christopher Wilder, known as the Beauty Queen Killer, who raped and murdered at least eight women in over a dozen attacks during a crime spree across seven states in America in 1984. Once Wilder was killed by police in New Hampshire, the novel was found among his possessions. He apparently referred to the book with regularity during his murderous road trip across America. Serial killer Robert (Bob) Berdella, known as the Kansas City Butcher, who kidnapped, raped, and murdered at least six men between 1984 and 1987—video-recording his rampage, as Lake did—watched the 1965 film adaptation of *The Collector* while a teenager and later admitted that it spoke to him and ultimately altered his life.[39] Within two years of seeing the film, he began torturing small animals before later moving on to human victims. Writing is indeed a serious motivator of action—as our narrative model suggests.

Fig. 3.16. An undated photograph of the horrific dungeon cell where Lake and Ng confined, raped, tortured, video-recorded, and sketched their female victims before killing and incinerating them. The "RULES" list created by Lake was appended to the interior of the door leading to this room.

Fig. 3.17. The original cover of the debut 1963 novel of English author John Fowles, *The Collector*, which was made into a feature film in 1965. Leonard Lake is one of three serial killers known to have drawn direct inspiration for his murders from the book. Published by Little, Brown, and Co. in 1963, cover art by Tom Adams.

ONE-WAY TRIPS

The term *odyssey* has a literary source. It refers to a Greek epic poem traditionally ascribed to Homer, in which he describes the travels of Odysseus during his ten years of wandering after the fall of Troy. The hero eventually returned home to Ithaca and killed the suitors who had plagued his wife, Penelope, during his absence. We have used this term in the title to this chapter because the mass murderers whom we have discussed here are examples of mentally disturbed people who see themselves as being on an odyssey—that is, as being on their own quest to set things right in the world, to avenge themselves, as did Odysseus, for some perceived wrong. It is no coincidence, in our opinion, that deranged and depraved mass murderers like James Holmes and serial killers like Leonard Lake felt impelled to write about their quest to seek some form of perceived justice. Their dark odyssey could only come to an end with murder.

The narrative-literary framework we have used in this book is actually consistent with the theory of differential association, which alludes to the possibility that murder involves imaginary interactions—including symbolic interactions through texts and images—which serve a didactic, or learning, purpose. They allow crimes to become acts borne via a system of emulation and tutelage through some text or instruction, even if the person providing that text or instruction is unaware that his or her work will be misinterpreted or misused. Writers such as Salinger or Fowles could hardly predict that their novels would become canonical murder texts for the likes of creeps such as Holmes and Lake. All writing is in some sense didactic, but the author can hardly anticipate what it will do to the minds of schizoid individuals. The theory, first conceived in the 1930s, holds that when some individuals are exposed to certain images, behaviors, and personalities, they will become disinhibited and start experimenting with different forms of crime.[40] In essence, books like *The Collector* serve as DIY manuals for the dangerous and depraved—manuals not only for murder but for the act of writing itself. They initiate a dark odyssey—a one-way trip—in the minds of murderers.

Chapter 4

HYPERTEXT #HOMICIDE

"The medium is the message. The personal and social consequences of any medium—that is, of any extension of ourselves—result from the new scale that is introduced into our affairs by each extension of ourselves, or by any new technology."
—**Marshall McLuhan**, *Understanding Media: The Extensions of Man*, 1964

"I was thinking of tying her body onto some kind of apparatus . . . cooking her over a low heat, keep her alive as long as possible."[1]

The gruesome scenario depicted in this statement, part of a larger fantasy scenario involving the kidnapping, torturing, and cannibalizing of women that played itself out through written exchanges in an online chat room devoted to necrophilia, was composed and transmitted by one-time New York Police Department (NYPD) patrol officer Gilberto Valle. After immersing himself in necrophiliac bondage pornography, Valle—the first of several men to earn the moniker of Cannibal Cop in the 2010s—was eventually convicted in March 2013 of conspiring to kidnap, murder, and cannibalize the remains of over one hundred women. Valle's sensational case was soon followed by the arrest of a veteran police forensics investigator stationed in Dresden, Germany, who was himself later accused of killing and cannibalizing an apparently consenting victim. This second Cannibal Cop had apparently located a willing participant through a homicidal matchmaking website committed to similar perversions rooted in necrophilia, cannibalism, and an even rarer paraphilia known as vorarephilia, a disorder in which the subject fantasizes about being consumed by another person.

Such "vore" fetish sites and chat rooms—as they are called by their members—allow likeminded deviants to meet in a virtual space where macabre transcripts of their fantasies are distributed for reading, response, and commentary.[2] Remarkably, these sites and their graphically homicidal and suicidal contents, operate in plain view on the conventional Internet rather than on the non-indexed pages of the more sinister and perilous territory of the so-called Dark Web, which is generally inaccessible through conventional search engines.[3]

The very existence of these spaces and communities that now operate in plain sight raises the question, what is going on here? Has murder become a trivialized part of a larger and deranged culture of virtual spectacle and online fantasy? We will explore this possibility in this chapter. At the very least the interaction of disparate online media texts committed to fantasy enactment is a factor that needs to be investigated through the lens of literary criminology. The Internet has become one huge text—a massive anthology with millions of chapters and contributors who range from the deft and creative to the daft and cruel. The Internet—not so long ago childishly branded as the "information superhighway," as some readers might recall—is now a ubiquitous part of everyone's hyperreal world. *Hyperreal* is a term first introduced by the late philosopher Jean Baudrillard, who maintained that the permeable border between fiction and reality had at some point managed to utterly vanish, collapsing into a mind-set that he called the *simulacrum*.[4] In a world defined by two-dimensional screens and one-dimensional people, the content behind those screens is perceived by all of us today as hyperreal; that is, as more real than real—a place between space and time where reality and the simulation of reality dissolve into each other. Baudrillard used the example of Disney's Fantasyland and Magic Kingdom, which are copies of other fictional worlds. More accurately, they are copies of copies, and, yet, people appear to experience them as real. These are the "simulation machines" of our daily existence that reproduce past images to create new environments for them. Eventually, as people engage constantly with the hyperreal, everything becomes simulation. This is why, according to Baudrillard, people are easily duped by the modern media and image makers. It is little wonder that the simulated online world of what can be called "#Homicide" is more real than real; it is now an intrinsic part of how murder is being conceptualized and planned, paralleling all kinds of real-world murders perpetrated by all kinds of deranged individuals.

CYBER SCREEDS

Officer Valle's case started when he began conversing with other necrophiles and sexual sadists scattered across the globe on the interactive chat site darkfetishnet.com. He soon hatched a plan with co-conspirators to commit both necrophiliac and cannibalistic acts with women ranging from his own wife to college acquaintances, former grade-school teachers, and even adolescent strangers for whom he seemed to have a long-standing sexual-sadistic obsession. Valle was arrested before he was able to bring his murderous agenda to fruition. His intentions were discovered by his wife after she located gruesome sadomasochistic images on their home computer and thus decided to investigate further, ultimately finding on the computer the blueprint for her own murder and the sordid rituals that would follow. As the first of what are certain to be a number of cases before the courts that will explore whether online fantasies can be construed as constituting criminal intent, Valle admitted to FBI investigators that the intensity of the virtual experience ultimately obscured the line between the online and offline worlds whereby his "secret cyber life was 'bleeding' into reality."[5] Baudrillard's construct of the hyperreal is remarkably relevant in this case, with hyperreality describing Valle's relationship to murder with remarkable accuracy. In June 2014, however, a federal judge hearing Valle's appeal agreed that the fantasy, even in its detailed specificity, did not meet the legal definition of a conspiracy or contain the necessary elements to merit criminal culpability. With Valle being "guilty of nothing more than having unconventional thoughts," he walked free following eighteen months in custody.[6] Today we are left to wonder what actions may have been taken by those still unidentified co-conspirators who read and were apparently quite receptive to Valle's other online writings:

> "[She] is asleep right now, not having the slightest clue of what we
> have planned. Her days are numbered . . . she does look tasty,
> doesn't she?"
> "I would really get off knocking her out, tying up her hands and bare
> feet, and gagging her."[7]

Fig. 4.1. Former NYPD officer Gilberto Valle just prior to his being arrested and convicted for conspiracy to commit murder in 2013. That same conviction was overturned in June 2014, and he walked free after serving just eighteen months in custody on a lesser charge of misusing police databases.

The other forum users with whom Valle was corresponding, and whose own writings are as sinister as his, or even more so, remain unidentified—as do their true motives. This is the problem faced by law enforcement, lawmakers, and experts who analyze the links between criminal behavior, paraphilias, and new digital technologies. The fantasy nature of the Internet as a hyperreal world with its own subcultures and discourses makes it difficult to separate bona fide criminal intent from bizarre but otherwise innocuous role-playing. It is, however, interesting to note the descriptive specificity of some of Valle's writings with respect to his proposed female victims, including his penchant for bare feet being bound ahead of the murder, while no other bodily appendage was ever discussed in these writings—or any of his associated writings—in such detail. This element of his murderous fantasy is clearly indicative of a foot fetish that falls within the spectrum of partialism, a paraphilia that describes an erotic fixation on very specific and typically nonsexual parts of the human anatomy, including hands, ears, fingers, and toes. Such a fixation being present in Valle's case, constitutes what is known as a *preparatory paraphilia*, or gateway behavior, to other more serious *attack paraphilias*, in this case both necrophilia and cannibalism. Some notable and gruesome examples of the paraphiliac link between partialism and necrophilia in the forensic literature and annals of true crime include the stories of serial killers such as Jeffrey Dahmer, Charles Albright, and Edmund Kemper, among others (see chapter 2).

Valle did not commit real murder. He committed hyperreal murder or, more generally, what can be called a "meme murder," that is, a murderous meme that is spread through websites, where it accrues even more force and hyperreal power. Welcome to murder in cyberspace, the term coined by American novelist William Gibson in his 1984 novel *Neuromancer*, a novel that was the inspiration for the emergence of new narratives that take place typically in a bleak, dehumanized future world dominated by technology and robotic humans. Gibson's description of cyberspace is worth repeating here:

Cyberspace. A consensual hallucination experienced daily by millions of legitimate operators. A graphic representation of data abstracted from the banks of every computer in the human system. Unthinkable complexity. Lines of Light ranged in the nonspace of the mind, clusters of constellations of data. Like city lights, receding.[8]

Cyberspace now has its own communities and its own set of conventions for communicating and interacting. Movement and interaction in cyberspace are, of course, virtual. As noted urbanist and professor Mikael Benedikt notes, in cyberspace "the tablet becomes a page becomes a screen becomes a world, a virtual world. Everywhere and nowhere, a place where nothing is forgotten yet everything changes."[9] The modern human being lives in two universes, that of physical reality and that of hyperreality. What we upload online about ourselves will define us well beyond our mortal lives. In the past, only artists, writers, musicians, and other socially important individuals would have been able to leave behind their memoires for posterity through their work; now, virtually anyone can do the same thing though profiles and other social-media artifacts. Our social-media pages define us, remaining in cyberspace well beyond our physical lives. This is affecting not only how we remember and live but also how we view mortality and, as the Valle case suggests, murder and other moral aberrations.

The term *meme* is an apt one for describing how information is spread through cyberspace. Memes compete for brief but broad attention across the Internet. Some unite with others and achieve greater survival—much like genetic compounds. In other words, an individual meme that experiences a high degree of popularity does not survive unless it is felt as truly unique, whereas a meme with less distinctiveness and thus a low popularity level will thrive if used together with other memes. Cumulatively, memes create a "memetic mind space." Murder memes may very well fall into this space— they may in fact be its center. It is relevant to note that the word was first coined by British scientist Richard Dawkins in his 1976 book *The Selfish Gene*, seeking a term as a counterpart to *gene*, linguistically and conceptually, that conveyed the way in which ideas and behavior spread within a society by nongenetic means.[10] For most people today, the term refers to a piece of information spread by e-mail, blogs, and social-networking sites. It can be almost anything—a joke, a video clip, a news story—and it can also develop its own meaning code as it spreads, with users editing the content or adding comments.

For the purpose of the present discussion, it is sufficient to point out that as a propagator of memes, it is little wonder that the Internet has become a locus for murder fantasies (hence "murder memes"). In the "Twitterverse"—that large segment of cyberspace dominated by the social-media platform Twitter—a meme is identifiable by its hashtag, "#," which gives it prominence and enables enhanced circulation by theme—a type of Dewey Decimal system for cataloguing and filing ideas, topics, or discussions. The case is the same with the social-networking giant Instagram, with "hashtagging" having become so prominent as a form of digital paratext—supplemental literary information that inscribes words with additional context—that the hashtag has seeped into everyday offline texts. Even in verbal communication and everyday conversation, to preface any word or statement with "hashtag" is, in effect, to elevate it beyond its conventional meaning. It amounts to a declaration, one that makes the word more than a word—a cultural artifact. Consider then how memes enable certain ideas—from the mainstream to the taboo—to be searched and sought out with expediency. Consider, for instance, the current landscape of Internet pornographic memes, not only black-market or otherwise-illegal images but also mainstream erotica. Consider how specific images, ideas, move through the memescape and cater to a wide array of preparatory paraphilias—how they might even enable attack paraphilias. These images and narratives emanate from sites or specific vignettes produced by pornography studios devoted to themes such as bondage and simulated rape (sadism), cuckolded husbands gaining gratification by watching their wives being defiled (mixoscopia), adolescent step-daughters and babysitters being sexually initiated (blastolagnia, aka Lolita syndrome), and films generally glorifying or empowering Peeping Toms (scopophilia). Of course, like the necrophiliac and "vore" chat rooms visited by Valle, the paraphiliacs drawn to these sites will often supplement—and even intensify—their visual experience with the exchange of written materials, including summaries of fantasies, past experiences, or fictional stories. These are the sum and substance of murder-driven memetic culture—they are cyber screeds that spread quickly to feed sexually aberrant fantasies in others.

As law makers and forensic psychologists have recognized, the exchange of written materials has as important a role to play in identifying dangerous paraphiliacs as any other kind of evidence does, and perhaps even more so. This was perhaps first officially realized and legislated in Canada where, since the 1990s, written stories detailing the sexual exploitation of underage victims have been criminalized as child pornography; this stance was held up on appeal to the Supreme Court in 2001, when the link between written texts about sexualized children and actual acts of child sexual abuse became firmly entrenched in law.[11] Pedophilia ranks among the most explicitly criminalized of the over five hundred documented paraphilias, so possessing and authoring such texts or disseminating associated images via the Internet is illegal, whereas, strangely, necrophilia, cannibalism, and related high-risk attack paraphilias are not. For this reason, a defendant like Valle, until such time as his fantasies were to transition from the hyperreal to the real—from the online meme world to the offline real world and real consequences—is guilty of nothing more than, to quote his lawyer at appeal, "thought crimes."[12] The question remains, if his plans had not been uncovered by his wife and had Valle not been arrested by the FBI, would he have—like the disgraced police officer in Dresden—ultimately transformed his thoughts into actual acts of murder? The broader question is, why does the reading or writing of graphic texts lead some people to take the next step to act on their homicidal fantasies while in others it does not? As in the disordered schizoid, it might come down, again, to a sense of aberrant self-entitlement—malignant narcissism.

PSYCHOPATHY

For the sake of argument, imagine that it is the mid-1990s when the Web 2.0 and its related social media and other intuitive platforms are not yet around. In that time frame, digital cameras were, as one might recall, luxury items in many markets and not widely owned or even available. Now, imagine driving down the main drag in your home city and taking photographs—*lots* of photographs—of yourself behind the wheel with a 35mm Pentax camera. You take some photos by holding the camera in front of the windshield and others by using the rearview mirror. You then decide to stop at a local restaurant, where you rewind and remove the film and insert a new roll as you order a meal. You use your second roll to create a photographic essay of your entrée once it arrives at your table. Before leaving the restaurant, you proceed to the restroom to take additional self-portraits in the vanity mirror, just for good measure. Then, you proceed to a nearby Walmart, Walgreens, or other one-hour photo lab and obtain glossy prints of your images.

Later, you decide to distribute the pictorials of your escapade among family, friends, coworkers, casual acquaintances, old crushes, and even "frenemies," using a variety of delivery methods. You might, for example, send some via mail through the postal service. You might also photocopy snapshots and then send them out by fax machine. Within the week, there is little doubt that in that recent bygone era, a number of your family members or friends might decide to organize an intervention and arrange for you to be assessed by a psychiatrist, citing serious concerns over your mental health and grip on reality. Now, fast-forward to the present hyperreal world, where it can be easily discerned that this type of behavior, previously—and rightfully—considered deviant, is now the norm.

But while the media for making and distributing images might have changed, the truth is that it remains fundamentally abnormal behavior, psychologically speaking. All this makes fleshing out truly disordered, paraphiliac, and potentially dangerous behavior amidst a meme-based culture of vapid navel-gazing and dysfunctional attention-seeking—our golden age of narcissism—all the more difficult. With hundreds of years of cultural norms and common sense having been undone in little more than a decade, it might be argued that the online world has in fact become the murderer's new home turf. Some psychopaths are drawn to this hyperreal world where all bets are off. Others are made there from scratch.

Contrary to a popular misconception, the terms *psychopath* and *psychotic* are not and have never been synonyms. A psychotic individual is suffering from either an acute or (more likely) a chronic mental-health affliction, one typically involving either visual or auditory hallucinations. Representative psychotic maladies would include bipolar disorder, schizophrenia, or anything that requires ongoing pharmacological treatment and professional monitoring, whether in-patient or out-patient. When the psychotic individual complies with the prescribed treatments, he or she can live a well-adjusted life. For this reason, crimes associated with psychosis are often subjected to legal tests so as to determine "criminal insanity" as it has been historically defined, now recast as "not criminally responsible by way of mental disorder," or some variation of this locution. As discussed in the previous chapter, schizoid personality disorder is a common trait among school and mass shooters; it is also an example of a personality *disorder* that is not a clinically diagnosable mental *disease* per se. Psychopathy, on the other hand, might be more appropriately conceptualized as a combination of personality disorders—an alloy of conditions like borderline personality disorder, antisocial personality disorder, histrionic personality disorder, and narcissistic personality disorder—all of which constitute a dysfunctional mind that is immune to medication or traditional therapeutic intervention. The psychopath is therefore not "sick" in the conventional sense—not at least in terms of how psychosis is identified and treated. There is consequently no one way to pin down the characteristics of psychopaths. The underlying defect may be in their hardwiring, part of their neural constitution; or, it may be the result of upbringing and environmental stimulation. The best mode of detecting psychopaths, according to most experts, is, as they put it, to "trust your instincts." A psychopath cannot be cured of anything; he or she (once again, usually a *he*) cannot be dissuaded from his objective by reason; he cannot be made to regret, sympathize, or be reasonable.

Beginning with the work of German psychiatrist Emil Kraepelin in the early twentieth century, the modern concept of the psychopath as a deranged loner, a member of that unenviable one percent of society (pun intended), slowly took shape.[13] Later, it was given prominence by the seminal work of American psychiatrist Hervey Cleckley titled *The Mask of Sanity*, published for the first time in 1941. The central theme of Cleckley's characterization is that a psychopath possesses the ability to mimic a person functioning within the accepted constraints of norm-based behavior, while in reality he is actually pursuing self-centered and often outwardly destructive goals at the expense of others.[14] Cleckley's definition continues to guide both the understanding and conceptual development of the psychopathy classification in criminology and its respective constructs up to the most recent assessment criteria, traversing both clinical and forensic case studies.

Currently, the standard for measuring psychopathy is the Psychopathy Checklist-Revised, or PCL-R, developed by Robert Hare in 1970.[15] After several revisions, the current version consists of twenty items rated on a three-point scale.[16] The administrator scores each of the items as either: 0 ("aspect does not apply to the subject"); 1 ("aspect is a partial match to the subject"); or 2 ("aspect is a good or reasonably good match to the subject"). The twenty items are divided into two factors and four facets, described as follows:

Factor 1 Traits: Interpersonal/Affective Expression
Facet 1: Interpersonal
Glibness/superficial charm
Grandiose sense of self-worth expressed as pompous arrogance
Pathological/compulsive lying
Cunning and manipulative
. . .
Facet 2: Affective
Lack of remorse or guilt
Shallow affect/lack of emotional depth
Callousness or lack of empathy
Failure to accept self-responsibility
. . .
Factor 2 Traits: Social Deviance
Facet 3: Lifestyle
Need for stimulation and proneness to boredom
Parasitic lifestyle (living off others)
Lack of realistic, long-term goals
Impulsivity
Irresponsibility
. . .
Facet 4: Antisocial
Poor behavioral controls (unpredictability; never learning from
    mistakes)
Early behavioral problems
Juvenile delinquency
Revocation of conditional release
Criminal versatility
. . .
Additional Factors
Promiscuous sexual behavior
Many short-term (and typically volatile) intimate relationships

Scored out of a maximum of 40, the PCL-R is used most frequently
in forensic contexts to evaluate offenders ahead of sentencing or
in parole hearings in order to obtain a general risk indicator, with

the questions being integrated into general ones about childhood, self-image, sexual preferences, and so forth. The highest scores on record among convicted killers are said to be those obtained by Clifford Olson, the so-called Beast of British Columbia, at 38/40; and Charles Manson, who, having been assessed by proxy by several psychologists, consistently scored in the same range.[17] Any score over 30 is generally thought to indicate psychopathy, while between 25 and 30 implies strong antisocial tendencies, or what has historically been known as *sociopathy*, a term generally falling out of official use. That said, not all psychopaths, even those who score high, are necessarily homicidal or even similar to each other—one size does not fit all. As a result, American forensic psychologists Theodore Millon and Roger Davis developed ten variants of psychopathy to account for the great variation in behavioral patterns.[18] A short description of each of the ten subtypes of psychopathy is as follows:

The unprincipled psychopath is highly narcissistic, deriving satisfaction from exacting vengeance through humiliation. He exploits and abuses other people, and generally enjoys the anguish that he creates.

The disingenuous psychopath enjoys popularity and usually has a convincing social mask that he puts on to charm others in the short term. However, long-term relationships eventually suffer due to trust unreliability, intense resentment, and the tendency to plot against others. He views life as a zero-sum game and always strives to be on the winning side of the inevitable win-lose outcome.

The risk-taking psychopath lives for the rush that he or she gets when taking risks and putting lives (his own and those of others) in danger. He thrives on a lifestyle of dangerous and treacherous activities, and he is convinced that he is immune to repercussions or discipline, even that he is invincible.

The covetous psychopath is driven by an abiding sense of avarice and revenge. He is exhibitionistic and self-indulgent, relentlessly pursuing aggrandizement and believing that he has been deprived of a rightful share of love, support, and material rewards. In the process he often has little concern for the people whom he deceives and exploits to suit his selfish ends.

The spineless psychopath views himself as defenseless and weak and will therefore strike out first in a counterphobic manner to avoid or preempt the aggression of others, typically rivals, whether real or perceived. He tends to project a false bravado and is desperate for others to see him as invincible and a force to be reckoned with; it is, however, all smoke and mirrors.

The explosive psychopath is driven by deep feelings of rage that are directed against those who are innocent or vulnerable. The main difference from the other types lies in his tendency to erupt instantaneously in a sadistic and savage manner. The tantrums are unpredictable and often erupt when he feels thwarted or threatened, as a reaction to frustration or fear.

The abrasive psychopath is oppositional and surly by nature, resembling a rebellious teenager who never grows up. He is unable to build deep relationships due to enduring and defining personality traits that make him contentious and quarrelsome. The abrasive psychopath often uses insults in an indirect but intentionally antagonistic tactic, causing or magnifying incessant discord with others.

The malignant psychopath is driven by paranoid beliefs and follows power hierarchies. Compared with other types of psychopaths, he is often less effective in inflicting harm on others. He often endures terrible abuse and sees the world as a dangerous and treacherous place, thus resorting to fantasy rather than to action, inventing scenarios that project people into dark and menacing roles.

The tyrannical psychopath is stimulated by the vulnerability of others, which he exploits to sustain his cunning and calculating demeanor. He derives satisfaction from subordinating and subjugating victims, delighting in their fear and humiliation. An important distinctive feature is that he will target those whom he predicts will submit easily, while avoiding conflict with those more likely to fight back. He relives and relishes the memories of conquests and suffering, even to the point of amusement. The tyrannical psychopath is one of the most violent, cruel, and treacherous types, one who uses crude and vulgar methods to force victims to cower and submit to his whims.

The malevolent psychopath is also cold-blooded and ruthless, and perhaps the most prototypical of the types, with a blend of paranoid and sadistic features. He is intolerant and deeply suspicious of tender emotions, which he generally sees only as tools to manipulate and hurt others. He seeks and enjoys power, which he enacts in the deliberate mistreatment of others.[19]

At any given time, someone minding his or her own business online is bound to intersect with any one or more of these deviants. In fact, the Internet now offers an unprecedented opportunity for psychopaths driven by a need for power and attention to engage in their machinations with anyone, including unsuspecting users. Many of these cyberpsychos are also drawn to specific careers that offer certain perks or sustain certain lifestyles and façades of power. The most overrepresented occupations held by psychopaths are, in order: chief executive officer (CEO), lawyer, TV and/or radio personality, salesperson, journalist, police officer, religious official, chef, and managerial civil servant.[20] In our #Homicide culture, it should come as no surprise that psychopathy has migrated to online spaces, with tyrannical and malevolent psychopaths—both of whom are invariably violent and homicidal—taking up residence there. In fact, they were among the first to repurpose the early Internet for murderous schemes—and to contour their writing so as to document their crimes in cyberspace as well as lure their victims.

LONELY HEARTS

As we saw in the Lake and Ng case (previous chapter), classified want ads functioned in the pre-Internet era as a gateway for killers to enact their tyrannical or malevolent psychopathy. The ads served as carefully worded mechanisms for both luring victims and also for satisfying paraphiliac impulses of a coprographic nature. In earlier generations, a specific type of classified ad murderer, known as a "lonely hearts" killer, also emerged; he was an especially sadistic type of psychopath, with the ability to entice and charm prospective victims by posing as a suitor or courtier to single and often vulnerable women. Decades before Internet dating and hook-up mobile applications changed everything, "lonely hearts club" classified ads—a general term for any number of want ads for romantic partners—offered predators the opportunity to deploy a contrived and superficial charm to attract their prey. The lonely hearts killer is now described in the criminological literature as one who uses the craft of anonymous writing based on an alluring (and made-up) autobiography to gain the confidence of naïve and trusting victims. The first—or at least the best-known—of these killers was a sadistic and psychopathic TV repairman in the Los Angeles area, Harvey Glatman.

Between 1957 and 1958, in tawdry LA magazines, Glatman used all kinds of charm-based ruses supplemented with offers of photo modeling work to bait at least three victims to their deaths, even picking up one young woman in front of her family while posing as a doting and gentlemanly suitor.[21] The girl ultimately met the same fate as his other victims—bound and gagged, photographed while being sexually assaulted, and then strangled and dumped in the desert. Glatman was eventually caught red-handed by a California Highway Patrol officer as he was trying to force what would have been his fourth victim into his car on Halloween 1958. Glatman, also known as the Glamour Girl Slayer, was convicted and executed in San Quentin's infamous gas chamber—the green room—within less than a year.[22]

Today, psychopaths and serial murderers using Glatman's modus operandi have simply adapted it to the modern age; they've moved away from the simple offline print classified ad to various new forms of online soliciting, using the Internet's vast reach to target legions of victims with even more clever ruses. Just as social media allow highly disordered people a soapbox on which to spout their radical and deranged ideas to vast audiences, so too do they allow the motivated psychopath a platform from which he can disseminate writings in order to more easily facilitate his hunt for victims. Once again, it would seem that social media allow motivated predators not only a space to scout for victims more efficiently but also a place for them to cultivate their paraphilias. In some cases, sexual psychopaths contemplating violent acts may seek specific chat rooms to find like-minded individuals in order to discuss their respective fantasies. In some cases, they may seek out specific websites, images, or memes that reflect specific paraphilias. In other cases, they may immediately delve into experimenting with digital versions of existing paraphilias of both the preparatory and attack variety. Consider, for instance, how the authorship of threatening, insulting, and humiliating written content—cyberbullying, cybermobbing, trolling, and flaming—might itself constitute the online manifestation of existing sexual fetishes linked to violent offending. In other words, it is logical to envision how misconduct in cyberspace—most or all of which involves some degree of writing—might serve as its own preparatory paraphilia.

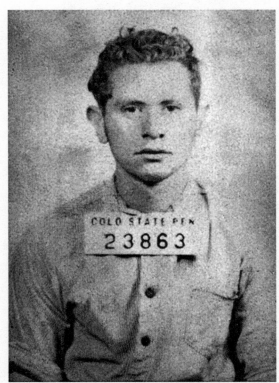

Fig. 4.2. Mug shot of TV repairman and amateur photographer Harvey Glatman, who became known as the Lonely Hearts Killer and the Glamour Girl Slayer after writing personal want ads for models in various pulp magazines in the late 1950s in order to lure his victims. Image from the Colorado State Penitentiary.

Fig. 4. 3. The chilling image of victim Judy Dull, bound and gagged and then photographed by Glatman in her helpless state before he murdered her in 1957.

As research now suggests, there is parallelism between the written content of cyberbullying messages and the linguistic structures used by obscene telephone callers (a disorder known as scatologia) and by serial killers such as Dennis Rader and Leonard Lake in terms of coprographia.[23] The cyberbully, troller, or other online deviant also exhibits in many circumstances the same form of sexual psychopathy and sadism in his writing style as do some of the serial killers who have used hypertext compositions to lure their victims, rather than simply to harass, annoy, and insult them. In the end, whether it is cyberbullying or serial murder—or both—the architecture of the Internet is one that provides psychopaths, through their writing, a channel for them to engage and indulge freely in their fetishes and paraphilias with a broad audience looking on.

Consider the case of John Edward Robinson, known as the Slave Master and who is widely touted as the Internet's first serial killer.[24] A failed priest turned X-ray technician and con artist, Robinson was paroled from prison in 1993 after serving six years for fraud convictions in both Kansas and Missouri. He was released into a world in the midst of adopting the World Wide Web and its chat-room culture that allowed people with specific shared interests—however weird and arcane—to find each other and communicate via the written word in real time. Although he was an ex-con, Robinson nonetheless managed to present the convincing persona of a sensible family man, keeping his background as an embezzler and forger concealed as he made his foray into this new world—one ideally suited for a duplicitous psychopath. Through his chat-room communiqués, he could indulge his psychopathic and paraphiliac tendencies with impunity. After adopting the screen name Slavemaster, Robinson began exploring various chat rooms reserved for members of the sadomasochistic, bondage, and sub-dom community, posing as an experienced kinky sex guru. By this point, even without the assistance of social media and the fantasy worlds and anonymity they offer, Robinson is widely believed to have killed a number of people, with at least three women disappearing and never being found. Robinson's Slavemaster online persona simply afforded him a new and expedited means to reel in new victims.

Over the next few years, Robinson wrote to various women using these same BDSM chat rooms, managing to entice several to his home in Kansas City with the promise of fetish sex and bondage or, in at least two cases, sexual slavery as part of a twisted yet consensual living relationship. All of the women he ensnared eventually vanished, while Robinson continued to access their bank accounts and cash their Social Security checks. His final suspected victim, a Polish immigrant with whom he actually filed an application for marriage, signed a lengthy 115-item "slave contract" that Robinson had prepared and which listed a number of rules and regulations she had to follow. She too later vanished without a trace, until 2000, when police searched Robinson's home and found her body dissolving in a chemical vat. In the end, Robinson was convicted of only three of the suspected eight or more murders he committed as far back as 1984. Robinson was a Web 1.0 cyberpsycho; however, only a few years after his incarceration, Web 2.0 presented others of his psychopathic ilk with an even more powerful medium for enacting sexual violence through their writing.

ONLINE ALLUREMENTS

From the outset, social media and dating apps have been used by psychopaths for their particular sinister purposes, luring countless victims into their clutches by hiding behind a keyboard or mobile device. In fact, according to author Michael Largo, deathtrap "lonely hearts" Internet dating ads have been used to commit hundreds of documented murders in America alone, starting as far back as the mid-1990s.[25] This would seem to correspond with the fact that there has been a spike in serial killers in recent years—since roughly the shift from the first-generation to the second-generation Internet and the ensuing explosion of social-media sites—than in previous pre-Internet years.[26]

Notable cases where the toxic admixture of psychopathy, sexual violence, and digital writing have enabled acts of serial homicide in the vein of John Edward Robinson include at least six different murderers who inherited the moniker the Craigslist Killer, since defined as a psychopath who uses the popular online classified and personals ad service to locate and attract victims. The most notable case likely still remains that of German computer repairman Armin Meiwes, who, in 2001, located a consenting victim on the vore site known as the Cannibal Cafe, using the following straightforward want ad:

Seeking young, well-built men age 18-30 to slaughter.[27]

This unabashed call for volunteers was unexpectedly successful, and Meiwes did not even have to recruit from outside his native Germany. After providing the willing victim, a forty-three-year-old man named Bernd-Jurgen Brandes, with pain killers and peach schnapps, Meiwes made a video recording of the two men jointly consuming severed parts of Brandes's own body. Brandes was slightly older than the kind of man sought by Meiwes, but Brandes was himself aroused by this horrific cannibalistic act, which included having his own penis severed and flambéed, before he inevitably succumbed to the trauma and shock of his injuries. Meiwes then spent the next several months consuming the remainder of Brandes's body, which he kept in his freezer. Meiwes was identified and apprehended by authorities only once he returned to social media in an attempt to solicit other willing and eager victims. Eventually sentenced to just over eight years in prison for manslaughter, Meiwes later stated that, based on his experience, he believed there were at least eight hundred other homicidal cannibals who were operating undetected in Germany alone. But unlike Meiwes, who made no effort to conceal his true intentions, most cyberpsychos on social media operate and author content under various false pretexts and assumed online identities.[28]

One of the more unusual Internet want-ad homicides that intersects with coprographic writing, and can thus be recast as "hypertext coprographia," is the case of Mark Twitchell. It constitutes an example of how digital media can be a gateway to murder and a means of writing oneself into existence. In some ways, it is even more bizarre—and perhaps even more tragic—than the Brandes case, whose victim agreed to and volunteered for his own slaughter. In the Canadian city of Edmonton in 2008, an aspiring filmmaker and low-functioning psychopath named Mark Twitchell decided that he was going to provide a proof of concept for a screenplay he had authored and quite unoriginally titled *House of Cards*. Prepared to push the boundaries of both the law and cinematography—to force life to imitate art—the twenty-nine-year-old Twitchell used the screenplay along with a separate diary eerily reminiscent of Leonard Lake's transcripts of disturbed thoughts, titled *SK Confessionals* (the "SK" representing "serial killer"), to promulgate his scheme. But while Lake was inspired by and obsessed with the novel *The Collector*, Twitchell was inspired by the long-running Showtime network series *Dexter*, a controversial program about a serial killer who kills other serial killers. But it was less the thematic underpinnings of the series as much as its visual portrayals of surgically executed and gory murder and dismemberment that captivated Twitchell and which he sought to emulate.[29] Twitchell came to see himself as the eponymous and fictitious Dexter Morgan, casting himself as the "Killer" in his own screenplay that, as a transparent rip-off of *Dexter*, depicts a man who dupes his victim into attending an isolated location before murdering and dismembering him.

Consider the following amateurish and ungrammatical excerpt from the early pages of *House of Cards*, which was entered along with *SK Confessionals* as a key exhibit at Twitchell's murder trial in 2011:

INT. HOME OFFICE—NIGHT

Roger; a man in his early 40's surfs the web nervously. His hands shake in eager nervousness, he keeps peaking around the edge of the screen to keep an eye on the hallway. He can see the glow of the living room TV from down the hall and hear it's programming.

The website on his computer screen is an online matchmaking service for people who want to cheat on their spouses. He's checking his email when a message shows up from a very attractive woman. It reads: "Hey sexy, all set for tonight? See you soon, can't wait."

Roger quickly erases his browsing history and shut the computer down.[30]

In this passage, the reader is introduced to Roger, Twitchell's fictitious doomed victim in the screenplay. Like any roman à clef, the script is a thinly veiled façade for a true story, or, more accurately, one that Twitchell intended to make true. He would find someone to become "Roger" just as Twitchell would play the role of "Killer" in real life. After completing the screenplay, Twitchell went on to create a bogus profile on the Internet dating site PlentyOfFish, a free Canadian site that, as a forerunner to mobile applications like Tinder, was at the time largely populated by those with a penchant for infidelity, seeking casual sexual liaisons. Like the Hero murderer in *House of Cards*, Twitchell posed as a woman seeking a man and ultimately attracted the interest of at least two other users, both of whom he would lure to a rented garage under the pretense of a rendezvous. This is the same ruse Killer used to lure the hapless Roger in Twitchell's ridiculous screenplay. The first man to take Twitchell's online bait escaped with his life after he fought off Twitchell's attempts to subdue him when ambushed at the location. Out of embarrassment or for reasons we may never know, the man never reported the incident to police. His inaction left Twitchell free to lure a second victim, who would not be so lucky.

After the first victim escaped Twitchell's deathtrap and then chose to do nothing about it, a thirty-eight-year-old oil-pipeline technician named Johnny Altinger responded to the ad and went to the garage. Twitchell then ambushed and subdued Altinger before strapping him to a table. Twitchell then murdered, mutilated, and dismembered him, while filming the entire horrific event. This recording allowed the unhinged psychopath to visually document the fantasy that he had previously committed to writing:

KILLER: "Do you know what this is Roger? This is a work of art . . ."

The killer winds up and decapitates Roger in one smooth motion. The head slumps to the floor and as the neck spurts blood, the killer casually cleans the blade and puts it back into the scabbard, replacing it on the wall. He then picks up a power saw and goes to town on dismembering the body . . . packing the pieces into hefty bags and placing them in his trunk.[31]

In the end, Twitchell was as sloppy a murderer as he was a filmmaker and screenwriter. He was arrested and charged with murder and the earlier attempted murder in a matter of days. His first key mistake—sticking chapter-and-verse to the paltry seven-page script for *House of Cards*—was breaking into Altinger's apartment and, while posing as Altinger, sending a farewell e-mail to all of his victim's contacts, claiming to have found love with a woman he had met online, and with whom he was purportedly running away. But when friends and family immediately recognized the writing as fake (it was a departure from Altinger's usual style—a phenomenon in comparative and forensic linguistics known as markedness[32]), the e-mail immediately aroused suspicion. Once trace amounts of Altinger's blood were found on the keyboard of his computer, left there by Twitchell, a murder investigation was set into motion and eventually the police were led to Twitchell and his writings. This included his electronic file of *SK Confessionals*, which he had tried to delete but which was recovered by police computer analysts. It was perhaps the opening lines of that manifesto, even more than how *House of Cards* served as the blueprint for Altinger's murder, that confirmed to the police that they had the right suspect in custody:

> This story is based on true events. The names and events were altered slightly to protect the guilty. This is the story of my progression into becoming a serial killer.[33]

As both a diary and a cinematic companion—a kind of director's cut—to *House of Cards*, even Twitchell's private communications with himself are plagiarized rip-offs of existing media texts, including a parroting of the famed opening narration in the long-running NBC radio and television series *Dragnet*. However, when reading the screenplay, even without the diary as the decipherment key, no one would believe that Twitchell ever actually hoped to get the story produced, even as a short film. In reality, like the Zodiac's cryptograms and the Son of Sam's raving letters, we see in the Twitchell case rather strong anecdotal evidence for a narrative impulse closely tied to a compulsion to kill. For some murderers—serial, mass, or otherwise—writing is the rehearsal; for others, it is the end that justifies the means. For Twitchell it was both. It served a fantasy prop that allowed him to visualize his future crimes and develop an exemplar of himself—one part Hero, one part Professional—and at the same time to draw his victims out. The writing was both instrumental and expressive—part modus operandi and part paraphiliac signature.

By 2016, eight years after his brutal murder of Johnny Altinger, the lenient Canadian prison system allowed Twitchell to install an HD television in his prison cell so he could watch reruns of *Dexter* and reminisce about his crimes. In the same exact time frame, a chillingly similar scenario played out in South Carolina. On a ninety-five-acre farm in the town of Woodruff owned by forty-five-year old realtor, sex offender, and alleged mass murderer Todd Kohlhepp, authorities located a cache of dead bodies later identified as a string of young couples reported missing over the previous two years.[34] Following a tip that one couple had last been seen on Kohlhepp's rustic property, police eventually found a missing twenty-five-year-old woman chained up—but still alive—inside a metal storage container, where she had been held captive, raped, and tortured for months before being discovered. The bullet-riddled body of her boyfriend was located in a shallow grave nearby, as well as the bodies of another young couple that Kohlhepp apparently lured to his farm on an unknown date.

How and why Kohlhepp was not in prison in 2016 and able to commit these murders defies explanation. In 1987, at age fifteen while living in Arizona, he kidnapped another teenaged girl at gunpoint before tying her up and raping her at the house he shared with his father. After being arrested and serving fourteen years for the crime, he was paroled in 2001 and moved to South Carolina. Then, in 2003, following a minor customer-service dispute at a Superbikes Motorsport store in the town of Chesnee, South Carolina, Kohlhepp snuck into the business through the service bay and proceeded to shoot and kill all four employees on site, including the owner, the bookkeeper, and two mechanics. Kohlhepp somehow managed to avoid being a suspect in the mass murder, and the Superbikes massacre remained unsolved until he was arrested in November 2016 for the murders of the missing couples. He admitted to the 2003 mass murder and to other crimes that, at the time of this writing, remain under investigation. As not only a convicted rapist and registered sex offender but also a mass murderer *and* a serial killer displaying a wide range of motivations and methods, Kohlhepp is perhaps best classified as a multiple-event murderer and is a case study for evaluating the currently narrow definitions of mass and serial murder—since they fail to appropriately classify a murderer as dangerously versatile as Kohlhepp.

The confinement and murders of the couples on Kohlhepp's rural property recall with eerie similarity the modus operandi of Leonard Lake and Charles Ng, but with a digital twist in the vein of Mark Twitchell's online impersonation of his victim. Remarkably, Kohlhepp appears to have hijacked the social-media accounts of at least one of his male victims—thirty-two-year-old Charlie Carver—who was reported missing in August 2016 and later found dead on Kohlhepp's farm. After obtaining the password for Carver's Facebook account before killing him, Kohlhepp went on to assume the victim's identity online, making posts that appeared to have satisfied some paraphiliac and storytelling drive present in Kohlhepp. Like so many serial killers and mass murderers, the posts also amounted to allusions or parodies of existing works, in this case the iconic song "Hotel California" by The Eagles, originally released in 1976. On October 1, 2016, long after it was suspected that Carver had been shot to death and his girlfriend chained up as Kohlhepp's sex slave, the killer posted a transcription of the last verse of the song on Carver's Facebook account.

This entry—one part twisted joke, one part eulogy (or, more accurately, an elegy) for his victim, and one part communication to friends and family that he was still alive and well—is lifted verbatim from The Eagles song.[35] Like all acts of plagiarism by murderers who see themselves as poets, novelists, screenwriters, and songwriters, it is also uncredited. Stranger still, is what, in a new form of coprographia never before seen, which might be called "cybercoprographia," Kohl-hepp wrote on the website for online retail giant Amazon. It would seem that Kohlhepp bought many of the tools he needed to murder and bury his victims—as well as the implements necessary to confine and rape his female captives—from Amazon. But he didn't stop there. Following his crimes, Kohlhepp was compelled to write detailed customer reviews of the items that made cryptic reference to their use in his murders. Read some of these "reviews"[36]:

> A November 2015 review for a black folding knife: "its blacker than my soul and priced right."
> A September 2014 review for a black, infantry-style folding shovel: "keep in car for when you have to hide the bodies and you left the full size shovel at home…does not come with a midget, which would have been nice."
> A September 2014 review for a high-security padlock: "solid locks… have five on a shipping container…wont stop them…but sure will slow them down til they are too old to care." [Presumably a reference, based on the year, to one of Kohlhepp's earlier female victims, who was kept chained in the container and whose dead and decomposed body was later found on the property.]

The use of social media and dating apps—and now apparently online shopping reviews—allows psychopaths to entice victims, develop a fantasy persona, and chronicle their crimes by baking them into seemingly genuine but ominous posts that satisfy a need to prolong and relive their crimes through digital writing. Beyond serial killers, however, where the writing serves an obvious paraphiliac and fantasy-driven purpose, in some recent cases, social media have been leveraged to become an ideological platform for murderers not only before but also during and after their rampages. It has become a means of maximizing the spectacle they have devised in their minds. After the rise of public mass shootings in 2010, and the use of the Internet by psychopaths to plan and carry out their nefarious plans, it became obvious that the conventional methods of investigating the motives of killers needed to be expanded so as to include an understanding of how the killers expressed themselves in digital texts. In other words, the focus started to shift onto the narrative mechanisms within the dark psyche of the killers as both indicators and predicators of their motives and methods. Today, we are increasingly seeing the Internet serving as a narrative space that can be used to enter into the mind of the murderer as he plans, executes, and reflects on his actions.

GENERATION MEME

One of the more relevant cultural constructs of the digital age and its dependence on social media as a platform for disseminating murderous discourse has been the emergence of the so-called Internet meme, as discussed briefly earlier. *Meme* is Richard Dawkins's term for any cultural product or artifact (text, image, sound, idea, and so on) capable of being acquired and reproduced massively throughout the cultural sphere.[37] According to Dawkins, a meme, in evolutionary terms, is any unit of information that allows people to learn and share its content as it diffuses throughout that sphere. We depend on "memetic substance," the counterpart to genetic substance, to survive, thrive, and evolve socially and intellectually.

As scholars of semiotics—a branch of linguistics and anthropology that deals with the signs and hidden meanings of everyday life—and more specifically of *forensic* semiotics as the study of the symbols of crime and deviance, we see the term as really a substitute for "signs" that have migrated to cyberspace. While we dispute Dawkins's idea that memes are the media through which we encode and pass on information and knowledge—signs do that—we concede that in the world of the Internet Dawkins's term is a good one to indicate replicating or self-reproducing signs whose content is designed to be ephemeral and nonsignificant. It is for this reason that the term today applies almost exclusively to the Internet.

The Internet and its ability to intermix multiple media with cross-generational and socioeconomic boundaries has become the perfect environment where memes can emerge and travel, ranging from intentionally offensive memes to those cultivating nostalgia or disseminating propaganda. The study of memetics, as it is now called, has become a fertile area of scholarship and analysis by academics who specialize in communications and visual culture, since the "memescape" as some are calling it, has created news ways of sharing and processing information.[38] Whereas they once consisted of information that communicated practical and useful information to web users, many memes have devolved into essentially ephemeral and useless units of information that only small segments of society and specific subcultures are likely to understand. And, for the most part, these memes serve no functional purpose other than as novelties and diversions. These are "empty signifiers," as they have elsewhere been called.[39]

Fig. 4.4. An example of a mash-up meme where two images are combined with accompanying text to re-signify the original purpose of each. In this case, a well-known quote from the 2008 film *Taken* is juxtaposed against an image of the eponymous Waldo of the children's book series and media franchise fame, *Where's Waldo?* (known as *Where's Wally?* in the United Kingdom). *Taken* is a production of EuropaCorp. *Where's Wally?* by Martin Handford, was originally published in the United Kingdom by Walker Books, 1987.

Memes do have a social function, though, communicating coded messages that allow web denizens to self-identify as part of a virtual "in group" by virtue of their understanding of the memetic source of reference. In many cases, memes serve no other purpose than allowing those consuming them to identify with the in group, or what historian and acclaimed Cornell professor Benedict Anderson called the imagined community—that is, a hyperreal community that is constructed by loosely joined constituents.[40] The meme is more accurately, in semiotic terms, an index; it points to an imagined locus where people can interact in some way that they perceive as somehow meaningful. Anderson initially used the term to refer to nations, including those that, as recent crises in terrorism have reminded us, can exist in people's minds, having no recognized geographic locus or state status. Anderson recognized that the media could create imagined communities all their own, specifically through the use of images and a specific form of vernacular writing that stokes and foments ideological loyalties. The memescape is a metacommunity—one wholly imagined but with its own symbolism, discourse, rules of engagement, and rituals.

The memescape is also, perhaps not surprisingly, already having significant implications for the study of the relation between writing, technology, and murder. In the largely rural Wisconsin town of Waukesha in the spring of 2014, two twelve-year-old girls lured their friend into the woods to sacrifice her to the Internet meme known as Slender Man—the Internet's boogeyman who exists almost exclusively as a set of evolving memes and visual mash-ups, each more bizarre than the last. After composing a series of love letters to the ghoulish digital entity, without getting a response, the two grade-schoolers were so infatuated by the faceless online concoction that they believed they could summon him forth from cyberspace by murdering their classmate to win his affection. The intended victim managed to narrowly escape being the first human sacrifice to a memetic character.

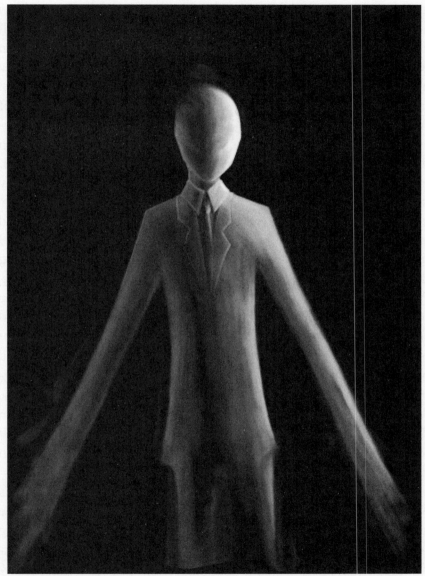

Fig. 4.5. One of countless online and typically anonymous renderings of the macabre Internet meme known only as Slender Man. In May 2014, two Wisconsin schoolgirls obsessed with the faceless ghoul tried to sacrifice their classmate and friend to him in the woods outside Milwaukee in order to conjure up a real-world version of the creature. Image from *Wikipedia* Creative Commons; user: LuxAmber. Licensed under CC BY-SA 4.0.

But while the attack on the Wisconsin girl was instigated by a meme and ended with the victim surviving, as we've seen, not all cases end so mercifully. Consider, by way of comparison, the more recent case of Dylann Roof, the man allegedly responsible for the massacre of nine parishioners at the Emanuel African Methodist Episcopal Church in Charleston, South Carolina. On the evening of June 17, 2015, Roof allegedly walked unannounced into a Bible-study session being held at the church, a predominantly black church that at the time also had a state senator serving as its senior pastor, and, after briefly sitting in on the session where he was welcomed by the group, opened fire with a handgun he had acquired using birthday-gift money from his family less than two months prior. His alleged attack left eight parishioners dead, as well as the pastor, who had hosted the study session. Roof was arrested the morning following the massacre, nearly 250 miles away while en route to Nashville. A sharp-eyed motorist had recognized him from surveillance video released to the media. The mass murder was immediately and rightfully flagged as a hate crime, thereby triggering the involvement of the FBI; however, little else was known about Roof's background or specific motivations. Aside from a pair of loitering and drug-possession run-ins with police, Roof had no notable criminal history. At twenty-two years old, Roof was essentially a drifter from a broken family, with no school or employment records. This made it difficult for the media and the police alike to dissect his background. Then the police discovered his website.

The site appeared to have been created—like Mark Twitchell's *SK Confessions* diary—as a means of mentally rehearsing the crime and foretelling his motives. Roof appeared, in effect, to be using writing to convince himself to commit the massacre. A chief distinction between Twitchell's memoirs (which were electronically composed but never published), Columbine shooter Eric Harris's website (which dated to the early Internet), and Roof's website is that the latter's manifesto was designed in a memescape environment. Allegedly created to maximize a perverted sense of spectacle,

Roof's online persona included a series of symbolic self-portraits used to advance a racist, hate-fueled worldview, intended clearly to leave a pictorial essay of his murders. Roof apparently admitted upon arrest that the massacre was at least six months in the planning,[41] implying that the site, registered under the domain lastrhodesian .com the previous February, was incidental to his plan to attack the church. It was a location, as he also later admitted, chosen because it was a known place of worship for blacks and a place of historical significance to the Charleston black community—even the whole of the American South. According to those who previously had some inkling that Roof was planning an attack of some kind, and who knew of his deep-seated racially motivated hate, it was logical for some (in retrospect) that the church would be a preferred location for Roof to target. This was especially the case once Roof realized that a previously contemplated attack site—the College of Charleston—was simply too hard a target to infiltrate.[42] Roof's reasons for selecting the college as the initial killing site—a large institution with a racially diverse student body—is bound to remain a mystery, especially given that his modus operandi was not generally in keeping with that used by prototypical school shooters.

At some point after Roof allegedly began turning his mind to committing murder in early 2015, he created his website "The Last Rhodesian," which, like Twitchell's private diary, was assigned a cryptic title. It was a title that, for those who understood the code, could serve as a key to deciphering his motives. Even if no other person clicked on the site, it would provide Roof with a platform for self-reflection. Yet, while the Twitchell case bears all the telltale signs of a malevolent psychopath (delusions of grandeur, unrealistic life goals, an inflated sense of self-worth, a complete lack of empathy for others, a willingness to put his own interests ahead of the lives of others, a penchant for risk taking and aggression, and so on), Roof's behaviors cannot be so easily classified under any psychopathic or schizoid rubric. He is an enigma save for one trait that he has in common with other mass murderers—hate.

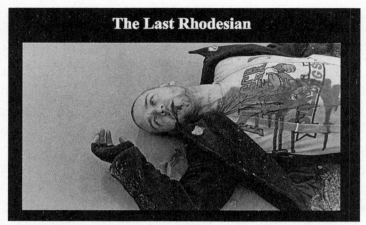

Fig. 4.6. The home page for Roof's website, "The Last Rhodesian" (which has since been taken down), where he employed the same pastiche and intermingling of coded text and images as a typical Internet meme.

Fig. 4.7. One of several images uploaded to the site by Dylann Roof that makes use of disparate props and symbols to communicate coded messages to his imagined community, once again replicating the architecture of the memescape.

Born and raised in the memescape, Roof would go on to create a website whose home page would reveal a twisted racist, paranoid set of beliefs forged in the memescape. His site, once launched live, consisted of a screenshot depicting a white male who can be described stereotypically as a skinhead or white supremacist, dead on the ground, covered in blood.[43] The image is overlaid on a black field with white font in much the same fashion as memes are visually constructed, according to a relatively standardized framing and font structure. Yet, the site is not purely about memetic spectacle, since it is accompanied by Roof's rambling manifesto, which itself is eerily reminiscent of Charles Manson's Helter Skelter prophecy; it is the literary prelude to what Roof hoped would be the incitation of a full-scale race war. Enraged about what he saw as slanted news reporting and political glad-handing surrounding the controversial 2012 shooting of black teenager Trayvon Martin in Florida, Roof went so far as to subtitle one section of his website, "An Explanation," where he discusses his anger about "black-on-white crime" and how the Martin shooting "awakened" him to the reality of the world. Indeed, while Roof is an avowed white supremacist and makes it clear in his writing that the alleged attack at the church targeted blacks and was hate-motivated, he does not limit his vitriol to African Americans. Other sections titled "Jews" and "Asians" make it clear that Roof's anger and resentment of other races knows no bounds. The origins of his hate-fueled beliefs remain for the most part unexplained; however, the handful of images that Roof uploaded to his site would seem to corroborate his written sentiments, acknowledging that he had researched the signs and symbols of hate that he needed.

In one image, Roof stops to pose for the camera while visiting a Confederate Army museum; in another, he is seen burning a miniature American flag. Both are apparently self-portraits taken by Roof using a timer. No one else was directly involved in the creation of these bizarre vignettes. In the most provocative and carefully staged image, Roof is seated in a lawn chair while holding a Confederate battle flag in one hand—a racist emblem—and a semiautomatic pistol in the other hand. It was, in fact, the same pistol Roof alleg-edly used later in the church massacre. All the while, he sits among potted plants, wearing aviator sunglasses. Some of these props, such as the Confederate flag, are clearly signifiers of widespread social ideologies rooted in Roof's Civil War–era nostalgia and closely held but cleverly concealed white–supremacist beliefs. In fact, it seems that Roof had at least one black friend prepared to vouch for him in the aftermath of the shooting, which suggests that his friend had no idea that Roof was a racist.[44] Other signs on the site, however, have a more theatrical than ideological function. If they do ultimately serve some larger purpose, they amount to a mash-up meme that only Roof himself understands—an imagined community for which he is the sole member. Had anyone bothered to visit the site and read its vitriolic content, his manifestos might have served as a revela-tory tableau of things to come—grounds to intervene and interdict Roof's intended massacre. But no one did.

The following excerpts are from Roof's nearly 2,500-word online manifesto.

> "I read the Wikipedia article and right away I was unable to understand what the big deal was. It was obvious that Zimmerman was in the right. But more importantly this prompted me to type in the words 'black on White crime' into Google, and I have never been the same since that day. The first website I came to was the Council of Conservative Citizens. There were pages upon pages of these brutal black on White murders. I was in disbelief. At this moment I realized that something was very wrong. How could the news be blowing up the Trayvon Martin case while hundreds of these black on White murders got ignored?"
>
> "I have no choice [. . .] I chose Charleston because it is [the] most historic city in my state, and at one time had the highest ratio of blacks to Whites in the country. We have no skinheads, no real KKK, no one doing anything but talking on the internet. Well someone has to have the bravery to take it to the real world, and I guess that has to be me."[45]

Roof clearly understood the distinction between the hyperreal Internet and the real world, otherwise he would not have taken the alleged action that he did, but the fact remains that it is in the hyperreal memescape that he first indulged his hate. This in turn fueled his hatred even more, inducing him to take action. It is relevant to note that Roof himself critiques those who deny a link between fantasy media such as video games, film, and Internet sites, and real actions. Cultivated and confessed online ahead of time through a toxic blend of racist ranting and white-supremacist propaganda combined with the coded images and text of Internet memetics, Roof's alleged hate-fueled and maniacal shooting spree at the church represents one of the more disturbing interplays between technology, expressive writing, and murder ever documented with respect to a mass murder in which the victims and the killer had no previous affiliation.

Beyond the dual nature of Roof's digital confessional, consider also the revelatory symbols and racist memes he used. These constitute coded messages that allude to a racially hateful view of American history. Here is a sampling of what we found.

White: Roof routinely differentiates between African Americans and whites by capitalizing the *W* in the word *White*, thereby making it a proper noun, whereas *black* is always spelled with a lowercase letter *b*. The distinction is subtle and went unnoticed by many; however, it is deliberate and provides an initial decoder key for the entries on the site.

Rhodesian: *Rhodesian* is also a proper noun and an implicit reference to the now-defunct nation of Rhodesia, a sub-Saharan African country that was itself an imagined community having no formal recognition as a nation-state other than by Apartheid-era South Africa, with whom it shared a border and diplomatic relations. Rhodesia (now modern-day Zimbabwe) effectively seceded from the British Empire in a bid to create its own short-lived white colony, enacting strict racial controls and segregation that mimicked the racist policies of its neighbor. Roof's proclamation of himself as the "last" Rhodesian is at once a parody of films like 1992's *The Last of the*

Mohicans and a renunciation of the ineffectual local Ku Klux Klan and skinhead communities. Roof considers himself the last denizen of the imagined community of Rhodesia. In an image posted to his Facebook account, Roof is also seen wearing a jacket emblazoned with the flags of both Rhodesia and Apartheid-era South Africa.

88: Beyond the use of specific grammatically based and lexically meaningful symbols, Roof also uses numerology. In one partic-ular photograph, he displays the number 88 written in sand at an unknown location. Like his other symbols, the number itself is innocuous to the untrained eye. However, in reality it is a cipher for "HH," as the letter *H* is the eighth letter in the alphabet and the two letters together are an abbreviation for *Heil Hitler*.

1488: As with 88, a second etching in the sand and captured on camera by Roof depicts the number 1488, which again has little signifi-cance to those who are unaware of its coded connotations. In this case, the origin of the symbol is highly convoluted, with 1488 often being alliterated as "Fourteen Words," a reference to the ideologies of infamous white-supremacist David Lane, founder of a paramilitary neo-Nazi group known as the Order, which was active in the United States in the early 1980s. The fourteen words in question were assembled by Lane as a mantra for the Order, with two separate versions, each fourteen words in length:

> "We must secure the existence of our people and a future for white children."

> "Because the beauty of the White Aryan woman must not perish from the earth."[46]

Actually, the 88 symbol has various other potential meanings, including a reference to the "88 Precepts," the title of a manifesto written by Lane and the basis for his self-styled religion of Wotanism, a modern-day Aryan cult. The title of Lane's manifesto, created while serving a prison sentence, is thought to stem from an eighty-eight-word excerpt from Hitler's infamous autobiography, *Mein Kampf* ("My Struggle"), which was written in two volumes between 1925 and 1926. Lane's preferred excerpt, appearing in chapter 8 of volume 1, runs exactly eighty-eight words in length:

What we must fight for is to safeguard the existence and reproduction of our race and our people, the sustenance of our children and the purity of our blood, the freedom and independence of the fatherland, so that our people may mature for the fulfillment of the mission allotted it by the creator of the universe. Every thought and every idea, every doctrine and all knowledge, must serve this purpose. And everything must be examined from this point of view and used or rejected according to its utility.[47]

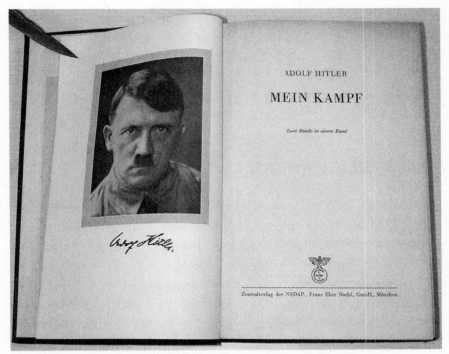

Fig. 4.8. The front matter of the original English translation of *Mein Kampf*, written by Adolf Hitler and edited by Nazi high commander Rudolf Hess, which served as hate-fueled inspiration for neo-Nazi militant David Lane's own essay, "88 Precepts," which, like *Mein Kampf*, was written in prison. Lane's writing subsequently inspired Dylann Roof's website.

By mishmashing racist ideology, visual spectacle, symbolism, numerology, and various hateful memes, Roof is likely to be the progenitor of a new breed of mass murderer. While his behavior in the weeks leading to the attack at the church falls generally in the realm of the behavior of other schizoid killers such as Elliot Rodger—self-imposed isolation, toiling away on a manifesto and its rationalization of the murders to come—Roof's engagement with hyperreality suggests the emergence of a frightening new trend. The enigmatic nature of his murders and the accompanying writings leads us to question how we can properly assess the writings of madmen posted to the Internet. Are they just spouting off for attention, like most people online, or does their writing constitute a preview of crimes to come—a harbinger of deadly acts and a window into their disordered minds? In a world pervaded by the theatrical and the hyperreal, it is becoming increasingly difficult to distinguish the truly dangerous killer in waiting from the legions of other cyberpsychos polluting the Internet. One thing is for certain—killers are writing now more than ever. The nature of the digital world has ensured it.

ANTI–SOCIAL MEDIA

Shortly after last call on June 16, 2016, a wife-battering, self-radicalized schizoid twenty-nine-year-old security guard named Omar Mateen walked into the Pulse nightclub—a popular LGBTQIA+ hangout in Orlando, Florida. After first exchanging fire with a police officer working an overtime security assignment outside the club, Mateen indiscriminately opened fire on the crowd inside with a semiautomatic rifle and pistol. Mateen would spend the next two hours making his way through the club, methodically and mercilessly executing everyone he could find. In an attack eerily reminiscent of the 1999 Columbine attack, but carried out as a solo venture, Mateen calmly, almost robotically, wandered through the club unmolested while police waited and marshaled outside. He ferreted out club-goers hiding in the bathroom and in other places, all the while laughing maniacally as he heartlessly moved from victim to victim. In the end, he killed forty-nine young men and women and injured fifty-three before police breached an exterior wall with a controlled-detonation device and killed Mateen in a volley of gunfire.

Like Roof, Mateen's massacre at the nightclub—the deadliest mass shooting in US history up to that time, and the deadliest attack targeted against the LGBTQIA+ community on record—represents a disturbing escalation in mass murder rationalized through the memescape. Mateen called 911 from his mobile phone during the attack to profess allegiance to the terror group Islamic State of Iraq and the Levant (ISIL), and he later told a police hostage negotiator that the attacks were in response to US bombings in Syria, a stronghold of ISIL occupation at the time. Indeed, while Mateen was born in America, he had already come under FBI scrutiny at least twice for harboring radical views and behaviors. These included cheering while watching the carnage of the 9/11 attacks in New York on school television.[48]

A typical malignant narcissist to the end, Mateen ensured, via the 911 operator and later a police negotiator, that the world was watching—that they knew why he was enacting his murderous scheme. He even called a local news station to alert them to his mass execution, and later he called his wife to ascertain if she had seen the story of him on television. Most incredibly, while walking through the club and murdering victims in cold blood, Mateen casually scrolled through the Facebook feed on his smartphone, checking to confirm that the rampage was eliciting attention from other users through posts and shares.[49] While ultimately ruled both an act of lone-wolf terrorism and a hate crime, the massacre at the Pulse nightclub in Orlando has a number of points in common with Roof's murder spree. Both were fueled by hatred. And both perpetrators employed the Internet to rationalize their actions and put themselves on public display.

Mateen was a half-witted loner who had shown evidence of schizoid thinking independent of his radical political leanings. He was a wife abuser and misogynist whose first spouse had filed for divorce just four months into their marriage. Mateen's behavior falls somewhere amidst emotional detachment, malignant narcissism, and the obsessive-schizoid thinking of the malignant narcissist. He also dabbled in the use of steroids and compulsively took selfies for upload to social media, though it is uncertain who exactly Mateen thought was his audience. The reality is that, like Roof's website and homemade memes, Mateen's social-media activity was ultimately about creating an online persona that he could later adopt in real life—a role he could convincingly take on after first rehearsing it online. In fact, whether Mateen was truly a supporter of ISIL and Roof truly a neo-Nazi and imagined Rhodesian are moot points. The bottom line is that the Internet has become the new environment for homicidal writing—Hypertext #Homicide, as we have called it here.

Fig. 4.9. A selfie taken by Mateen on an unknown date, vaguely reminiscent of the carefully rehearsed self-portrait captured by Seung-Hui Cho before the Virginia Tech shooting in 2007. This image was uploaded to Facebook a few weeks prior to the attack.

Mateen's ominous writings in the days before the shooting are also conceptually analogous to Roof's promise of "taking it to the real world" ahead of his attack at the church, and later posting about being in a "hurry" on the day of the attack. Like Roof, immediately prior to the rampage, Mateen's narrative impulse prompted him to take to Facebook and begin engineering the story in which he, in his twisted mind, was the Hero figure:

> In the next few days you will see attacks from the Islamic State in the usa.[50]

Like Roof's use of the term *White* with a capital *W* to denote supremacy, Mateen, capitalizes "Islamic State" while writing "usa" in lowercase letters to assign superiority and legitimacy to the former, and illegitimacy and inferiority to the latter—if only unconsciously. Also like Roof, it appears as though Mateen's strategy of crediting a specific terrorist or radical cause as inspiration for the attack only intensified or became fully formed as a narrative strategy after the attack was already past the planning stages and the murder weapons had been acquired. Yet, because social media are a lightning rod for the deranged and the disordered, it becomes difficult to assess the seriousness of such foreboding comments until it is, in many cases, too late.

Despite the number of innocuous profiles held by billions of social-media users, the reality is that the memescape can become a locus of gossip, ridicule, narcissism, exhibitionism, voyeurism, hypercompetiveness, and a number of other behaviors that straddle both antisocial and other psychopathological classifications discussed in this book. In many instances, it is therefore more accurate to call them "antisocial" rather than "social" media—antisocial behavior of course also being one of the cornerstones of psychopathy. These have become preferred platforms of murderers and other criminals to self-manage their public persona.[51] Some critics have already characterized social media as venues for the formation of "deviant cybercommunities,"[52] imagined communities of a toxic nature where abnormal and pathological individuals are not only tolerated but often celebrated because they have the virtual guts, so to speak, to take extraordinary risks—antihero bad boys for a brave new Orwellian counterworld. It should therefore come as little surprise that killers like Dorner, Roof, and Mateen mentally rehearse and transcribe their murders there. A world far beyond Orwell's worst nightmares.

Chapter 5

SO, WHY MURDER?

"Natural selection, as it has operated in human history, favors
not only the clever but the murderous."
—Barbara Ehrenreich, cited in Robert Andrews,
The Columbia Dictionary of Quotations
(New York: Columbia University Press, 1993), p. 294

"It didn't move him when he pulled her body out of the water or when he said that he'd put a shotgun to her head. It was as cold-blooded and premeditated as it could be. What pushed him to do it, none of us knew. Later on, when I put him in the squad car to take him to jail, I said, 'Mack, didn't you expect to get caught?' And he said, 'Not this quick.' He showed no emotion or regret or fear. It was like he was talking about shooting a dog."[1]

A 2007 true-crime book by Shelton L. Williams, *Washed in Blood*, can be read at one level as an account of a tragic murder but, at another more important level, as an essay on *why* people commit murder—often for no reason other than, to put it bluntly, killing someone. Williams, the first cousin of the victim described in this excerpt, recounts the story of seventeen-year-old would-be actress Elizabeth Jean Williams (Betty Williams), who was murdered in 1961 in Odessa, Texas, by Mack Herring, a former boyfriend and schoolmate, because, so he claimed, she had asked him to kill her. Also known as the "Kiss and Kill" murder, the case has since gone on to become both a poignant and troubling—yet lesser-known—cornerstone in the annals of American crime. The above statement is attributable to Odessa police detective Fred Johnson, who had brought Herring to the crime scene, and who had asked him to pull out Betty's cadaver from the pond where he had stashed it.

A Texas jury would later find Herring not guilty by reason of insanity. To this day, the case lingers in the collective memory of the people of Odessa, having become local legend—a local folk tale that includes purported sightings of Betty's ghost haunting her old high-school campus, Odessa High. Her parents had reported her missing after she had failed to show up for breakfast and then her scheduled morning classes. Betty had apparently slipped out of her bedroom the night before to meet up with a male paramour who, under interrogation, indicated that she left him soon after and was picked up by Herring, a popular football star at the school and her former boyfriend. Herring's statement to the police was an incredible one: he insisted that Betty had pleaded with him to murder her, claiming that she was allegedly in some suicidal state of mind. His story would become even more unbelievable when he claimed that, before being murdered, Betty asked for and gave him a good-bye kiss. Her parents and the police refused to believe Herring, and so did the jury. But in the end it bought the defense attorney's claim that Herring's crime was a result of insanity—that he was not criminally responsible for his actions. The outcome and the lurid details of the story ensured that the case would became an obsession not only in Texas but also across the whole of America and beyond—wherever word of the bizarre crime traveled. The case actually put murder itself in the spotlight. If Betty wanted to die, she would have done it privately, most people said, with some kind of discreet and comparatively nonviolent form of suicide. But imploring her ex-boyfriend to kill her—as he claimed—had implications that relate to virtually everything we have discussed in this book, the foremost of which being, why murder?

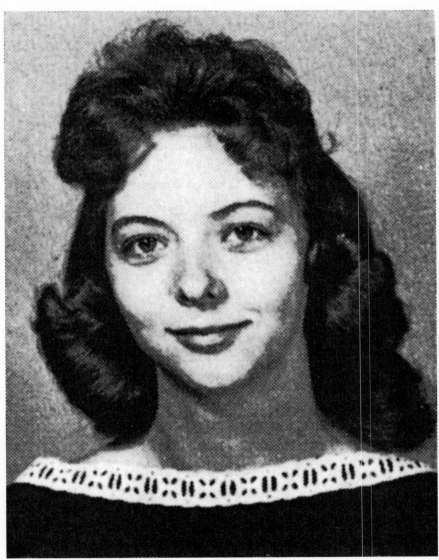

Fig. 5.1. Betty Williams's Odessa High School yearbook photo, 1960.

Whatever actually happened that night in Odessa, one thing is certain—Herring murdered his ex-girlfriend without any apparent qualm of conscience. No matter what Herring may have said or believed, the fact remains that murdering someone with no remorse, simply obeying a request to do so, jars us emotionally. The Kiss and Kill murder would in many ways foreshadow how both narrative construction and the physical act of writing, whether before the murder to facilitate it or after the murder to sensationally chronicle it—or both—would come of age in the digital era. The case in Odessa would prefigure murders like those of Armin Meiwes (chapter 4), who responded to an online classified to allow himself to be both murdered and cannibalized, as well as the even lesser-known case of Elaine O'Hara, murdered in Dublin, Ireland, in 2012. Depressed and despondent, the thirty-six-year-old O'Hara met successful architect and married father of three Graham Dwyer on the sexual fetish BDSM website Alt.com in 2011.[2] O'Hara first visited the site as part of a last-ditch effort to find companionship once the social stigma surrounding the BDSM subculture was mitigated through the obsession surrounding the Fifty Shades book series that same year. O'Hara and Dwyer soon moved off the site's conversation forum and began exchanging personal text messages. Among the quickly escalating texts sent by Dwyer to the victim, the following message from June 2011 was included:

I want to stick my knife in flesh while I am sexually aroused…I would like to stab a girl to death sometime.

Once Dwyer and the victim began engaging in consensual—though violent—sex acts in keeping with how they met, it was soon clear to Dwyer that O'Hara was, in fact, "that girl." Her depressed state of mind and the fact that she was intermittently suicidal—having committed herself to mental-health crisis facilities in the past—would, once Dwyer learned of this, make her the perfect victim. Her family, or so he thought, would in theory believe that, if she were to vanish, that she had finally taken her own life rather than simply talking about it. In reality, once he acted on his murderous plans, even the police believed the narrative he had reverse-engineered. Then they found the text messages, ones in which, in a relationship that recalled the modus operandi of the Internet's first serial killer, John Edward Robinson, Dwyer is known only as "Master." The police also found a short story written by Dwyer stored on his computer, a morbid piece of flash fiction—and like Mark Twitchell's screenplay, a script to the murder he was planning—titled *Killing Darci*. In the story, Dwyer, invoking a first-person narration, discusses stabbing and eviscerating a suicidal or terminally ill woman into "a ruined mess of guts" and then taking photographs of the body before dissolving it in lye.

As was later revealed, at roughly the same time in 2011 when Dwyer was authoring and editing this tale of murder, he was filming himself rehearsing the murder with other mistresses from the BDSM community. Initially, Dwyer would keep a knife in the room during sex acts, looking at the blade rather than his sex partner in order to become aroused. He later progressed to using a toy knife with a plastic spring-loaded blade to rehearse stabbing a woman during sexual intercourse. All of these acts, like most preparatory paraphilias—in this case a disorder known as picquerism (stabbing and puncturing as surrogate sex acts) as well as a specific fetish for knives—were progressing and escalating toward a more specific violent act—in this case, the murder of Elaine O'Hara as the true-to-life version of Dwyer's literary character "Darci." Eventually Dwyer was charged with O'Hara's murder and sentenced to life in prison—maintaining the entire time that, like Betty Williams, Elaine O'Hara wanted to be killed in this fashion. Dwyer's case remains a key case study. It is a foundational example of how violent fantasies, specific paraphilias, and writing and storytelling—including writing and storytelling *as* paraphilias—can all evolve in tandem and concomitantly escalate to real murders.

In 1961, at least in Odessa, Texas, such acts were considered "insane"; today, we have an improved understanding of how psychosexual disorders and specific paraphilias can exist in otherwise rational and seemingly normal individuals. In a secular and civilized society, we have made increasingly intricate attempts to explain murder psychologically, socially, legally, and even morally. Yet, still, we are left with questions we have perhaps tried to answer since the story of Cain and Abel: Is murder an inborn human trait, an act specific to the human condition? Is there a "murder instinct" within all of us? If writing, fantasizing, and murder are all acts unique to humans as a species, is there an evolutionary design or advantage to this triad? As we have asserted throughout this book, stories tell us more about murder than any scientific theory does—and stories might also help answer these same questions.

The analysis we have carried out of the writings and statements of murderers—some well-known, others lesser-known—suggests, in fact, that there is no one motive for murder. Perhaps this is why we feel impelled to write tales about it, so as to come to grips with it. We have seen that murder has many contextual triggers—a bid for revenge, an inner urging provoked by wrath, jealousy, outright hatred (of someone or of some group), and so on. Of course, these are especially powerful triggers in those who have a schizoid or psychopathic personality; however, in the end we are *all* capable of murder. Many of the murders that have become part of civilization's history are explained, in fact, as being motivated by some inner emotional response—something innate, something that is, like the act of writing, in our hardwiring as humans.

Across the ages, we as a species have relished in tales of murder, perhaps because these stories represent—as the Aarne-Thompson index suggests—attempts to explain such a horrific thing in a creative, imaginative way. We are all attracted powerfully to murder mysteries, whether these mysteries are packaged as literature, films, television series, oral gossip, or board games. There is an old journalistic saying that encapsulates this penchant: "There's nothing like a good murder case to sell newspapers." Historian Bill James sees this fascination as a consequence of living in a "popular crime culture."[3] He maintains that showcasing how crimes have been committed, investigated, and prosecuted in media and pop culture generally has profoundly influenced our understanding of what murder is; it has also provided a stage for serial killers and mass murderers on which to play out their twisted fantasies in the public limelight. But we beg to differ—somewhat. While it is true that the media create a frenzy of emotions surrounding the act of murder, the inherent attraction to these stories is not an invention of pop or Internet culture; they have simply tapped into it. Murder tales are part of a universally understandable über-narrative that goes back to our origins as humans—to our biology.

Through their own statements and writings, we have seen how murderers do not, by and large, see their actions as anything other than necessary, or certainly advantageous. Even Carl Jung, who developed the archetype theory on which a portion of our own analyses of murder have been based, suspected that the archetypes that surface in behaviors, symbols, texts, and rituals may be embedded in the human DNA. If so, they are embedded forms of the human imagination's quest to understand its own impulses. Writing is one of the ways we use to understand ourselves. The words of none other than the infamous philanderer the Marquis de Sade—from whom the term "sadism" as both a practice and a documented attack paraphilia is derived—encapsulate the essence of this dilemma eloquently:

> Murder is a horror, but an often necessary horror, never criminal, which it is essential to tolerate in a republican state. Is it or is it not a crime? If it is not, why make laws for its punishment? And if it is, by what barbarous logic do you, to punish it, duplicate it by another crime?[4]

A MURDER INSTINCT?

Animals kill for survival. There is no intentionality in their killing; that is, they do not *murder*, in the service of self-interestedness. They are programmed by biology to *kill* in order to survive and to protect their territories. Evolution has equipped each species on this planet with innate killing mechanisms, from poisonous venom to antlers, to deadly, razor-sharp teeth. In our evolutionary history, humans have also killed for survival and for territory. But what truly distinguishes humans from other animals is the fact that we have developed the ability to make our own killing truly versatile and incredibly effective, inventing all kinds of weapons to carry out this act. In sum, there is a "killing instinct" that is imprinted in all animals, human and nonhuman alike, through biology. It is there for reasons of survival—not only to survive in a given environment but also to thrive and to dominate it. It is likely rooted in the limbic system, or mammalian brain, the group of interconnected cerebral structures that are common to all mammals. The same system is involved in emotion, motivation, behavior, and various autonomic functions. In other words, the killing instinct serves as a survival instinct.

Evolution has provided the human brain with another system—the neocortex—with which we have developed the unique capacity for language, conscious thought, and other rational faculties—including imagination and writing. This brain structure is distinctive. Now, since murder and the neocortex are specific to the human species, the question becomes, Has the neocortex allowed us to transform the killing instinct into a conscious act of killing that we have come to call *murder*? To put it hypothetically in neurological terms, is killing limbic and murder neocortical? Murder involves thinking about death, not just reacting to some threat or responding to some survival urge. The act of murder is, arguably, an exaptation, or a trait that acquires functions for which it was not originally adapted or selected.

In some people, the murder instinct or impulse is, of course, more easily activated than in others. We call them murderers. Researchers at the Karolinska Institute in Sweden have confirmed a previously outstanding claim by neuroscientists, published in *Molecular Psychiatry* in 2014, that two genes may be associated with violent behavior—*MAOA* and *CDH13*.[5] These are present in the genomes of up to 10 percent of all violent offenders. The rest of us, apparently, do not have a higher-than-normal prevalence of these genes. Nevertheless, they are there, perhaps to be activated by the right triggers.[6] Of course, there are many factors that may lead to murder, as we have discussed throughout this book. But it is legitimate to ask whether or not these are essentially sparks, not causes. Having said this, we are well aware that we cannot reduce humans to their genetics; humans are much more complex than that. But when all the layers of complexity are removed, those two damn genes are there (pardon our plain English)! A murder-instinct hypothesis would also allow us to entertain various other hypotheses that we have explored indirectly in this book. For example: Is the male genome particularly predisposed toward activation of the murder instinct? This hypothetical question is not meant, in any way, to diminish the atrocities committed by women. But the statistics tell a rather suggestive story on this count, as we have seen. This would, after all, be consistent with the traditional evolutionary narrative that males have, by and large, been the hunters and thus the killers. A perusal of the FBI's homicide data, based on their Uniform Crime Reporting (UCR) Program, lends some credence to this tentative supposition.[7]

Of the nearly thirteen thousand murder victims in a given year, most (on average almost 80 percent) are male. Of the offenders for whom gender is known, over 90 percent are also males. Single-victim and single-offender cases account for roughly half of all murders. Although mass murders are apparently on the rise, the single killer–single victim scenario is still the most prevalent one. This suggests that murder and male genetics may be linkable in some way. A perusal of other databases, such as the Murder Accountability Project, corroborates the same pattern of homicides by gender, on an annual basis. The manifestos we have examined in this book were also drafted primarily—if not almost exclusively—by male murderers. We looked for as many female manifestos as possible, but we came up somewhat short, with exceptions of course also discussed in this book. Let us make no mistake about it—women are also murderers. But men are more so. And this could have an evolutionary origin.

A relevant footnote to the FBI statistics is that in those cases of murder for which the relationships of victims and offenders are known, roughly half of all victims are killed by someone they knew (acquaintance, neighbor, friend, boyfriend, etc.), while a little over one quarter (about 27 percent on average over the last decade) of victims are slain by family members.

These figures cast an ominous pall over gender relations—namely, the possibility that, all other socio-cultural factors aside, males may feel impelled to control women sexually and through violence. The loss of this control through social factors, with women becoming increasingly independent over the last three generations, may be behind the spousal and partner slayings that have caught the media's attention recently. Femicide, defined as the murder of women specifically because they are women, remains a global problem, one generally perpetrated by intimate partners or family members. Even in the face of gender-equality movements in the world, or perhaps because of them, the femicide rates are still unbearably high, as reported by the United Nation's Entity for Gender Equality and the Empowerment of Women on its website.[8] Femicide happens everywhere, no matter what kind of society and political system in which women live.

One murders a spouse or romantic partner not out of love but out of fear of losing her. It is not a romantic impulse that spurs men to kill their partners but a lack of one.[9] The number of studies on the phenomenon of femicide is extensive. There is one study in particular that is pertinent to the present discussion; that is the book *When Men Murder Women*, by Rebecca and Russell Dobash. The book is based on interviews, over a ten-year period, of men serving life sentences in British prisons for killing women.[10] The researchers found that those who killed their partners did so mainly from sexual jealousy or for some other emotionally controlling impulse. The interviewees seemed to believe that they literally had an intrinsic right to possess their sexual partners, and it was the fear of losing them that spurred them on to murder. Upbringing, incidentally, did not surface as a factor in provoking the murders. However, upbringing cannot be eliminated from any theory of murder, as will be discussed later. Rather, as the researchers suggest, the men believed that they had a proprietary right toward their partners. It was the loss of their property that induced them to destroy it completely. Some even killed the children involved in the relationship, new boyfriends, or others connected with the females. The underlying subtext in the murders was, If I can't have her, nobody else can.

Now, if our hypothesis is a viable one, a fundamental question arises: What about women who kill? Over the decades, a number of authors and filmmakers, most recently and famously novelist Gillian Flynn, have attempted to depict female murderers and their motives, with varying degrees of plausibility. In reality, the percentage of women murderers when compared to male murderers is miniscule, falling at the lower ends of any murder curve. And even women who kill multiple victims typically tend not to do so for the psychopathic and narcissistic reasons that drive men to commit murder. The motives tend to be (though not always) instrumental (such as financial gain) rather than expressive (fantasy fulfillment or ego-driven) in nature. Sometimes, women will simply join the men in the act of murder, either out of some misplaced loyalty or to indulge the rare and obscure paraphilia known as hybristophilia, discussed at length earlier in this book. As we have seen, there are many women who are attracted to the proverbial bad-boy serial killer; and there have been many "Bonnie and Clyde" pairs going out to kill for the thrill of it, from Ian Brady and Myra Hindley (the Murders on the Moor) to Paul Bernardo and Karla Homolka (the Schoolgirl Murders), along with a notable list of other disordered losers who somehow manage to find each other. Obviously, as these remarkable male-female team-killer scenarios suggest, emancipation from our mammalian killer-instinct past is very hard to achieve, for both men and women alike. Perhaps women may have acquired some of the same genetic material as males over time, but less so. We leave this line of reasoning because it is, after all, still a matter of guesswork.

A particularly notable case in this regard is that of Charlene Gallego, who joined her husband, Gerald, on a killing spree of ten victims, mostly teenagers, in Sacramento between 1978 and 1980.[11] The Gallegos kept teenage girls as sex slaves before murdering them, a modus operandi common to many male-dominated male-female team killers, with husband/wife teams being the most common relationship between team killers, and female strangers being the most common victims.[12] In many of these cases, the women later claim that they were forced to participate, that they were not willing participants and were essentially carrying out orders rather than being twisted and pathetic hybristophiliacs who enjoyed it. In 1980, authorities similarly questioned whether Charlene Gallego was forced to commit the ten murders of innocent strangers in order to cater to her husband's urges, or whether she was a complicit partner. Her chilling words are revelatory:

> We had this sexual fantasy see, so we just carried it out. I mean, like it was easy and fun and we really enjoyed it, so why shouldn't we do it?[13]

Kinky, cruel, and generally heinous sexual acts drawn out of disordered fantasy worlds are the driving force behind these kinds of murders—team murders for which over one quarter of those committed since 1850, like the heinous crimes of the Gallegos, have occurred in California alone.[14] These are acts that are also more common, sadly, than one might think. The Gallego murders certainly raise the ominous possibility that despite cultural restraints, some deranged individuals, male and female, need some engagement in "partnered murder."

Another (lesser-known) murderous sex couple is David John Birnie and Catherine Margaret Birnie, a malicious, sadistic duo from Perth, Australia, who murdered four women in their home in the 1980s; their crimes are today referred to as the "Moorhouse murders." When police asked Catherine why she didn't show any mercy towards a victim around whose neck she had tightened a cord slowly (as her husband stood beside the bed, watching), Catherine made the following statement:

> I wanted to see how strong I was within my inner self. I didn't feel a thing. It was like I expected. I was prepared to follow him to the end of the earth and do anything to see that his desires were satisfied. She was a female. Females hurt and destroy males.[15]

Fig. 5.2. Catherine Margaret Birnie.

But Catherine did have a qualm of conscience in the end, as her resigned words also show:

I think I must have come to a decision that sooner or later there had to be an end to the rampage. I had reached the stage when I didn't know what to do. I suppose I came to a decision that I was prepared to give her [Referring to one of the couple's victims] a chance. I knew that it was a foregone conclusion that David would kill her, and probably do it that night. I was just fed up with the killings. I thought if something did not happen soon it would simply go on and on and never end. Deep and dark in the back of my mind was yet another fear. I had great fear that I would have to look at another killing like that of Denise Brown, the girl he murdered with the axe. I wanted to avoid that at all costs. In the back of my mind I had come to the position where I really did not care if the girl escaped or not. When I found out that the girl had escaped, I felt a twinge of terror run down my spine. I thought to myself: David will be furious. What shall I tell him?[16]

Clearly, of the two, Catherine was the one who had at least some sense of moral conscience. Maybe the limbic sexual pull between such partners is so strong that women concede to it, despite the internal moral turmoil within them. Whatever the case, there is much more to murder than we will ever really know. Just as Catherine's statements demonstrate, we all are both fascinated and repelled by murder. This is a clear symptom of the psychic tug of moral war that is going on in all of our minds.

It is said that murder is irrational; and yet, it is also thought to be "normal" to the murderer, as the analysis of the writings of various murderers has revealed. In fact, murder can always be rationalized and even normalized. Some cultures endorse it to avenge family dishonors, especially by or against women, as discussed earlier. Rationality, it might be argued, is a construct; it varies according to place and time and is historically relative. Sacrificing humans was once thought by some societies to be a rational act—the clerics of antiquity even thought it to be morally and spiritually righteous. This would hardly be the case today—or so we hope. The truth is that when we strip away culturally arbitrary notions of normality and irrationality, we are left with a true paradox: once killing for survival is transformed into murder for some "reason," anyone is capable of murder—depending on the circumstances.

The film *Se7en*, first mentioned at the outset of this book, certainly understood this psychic (and moral) conflict within us. In the film's story, retiring Los Angeles detective William Somerset decides to tackle a final case with the help of newly transferred detective David Mills. They soon discover a number of grisly murders and realize that they are dealing with a remarkable breed of serial killer, the generically named John Doe (the Everyman of medieval theater), who is targeting people he thinks are committing one or more of the seven deadly sins. The film concludes in horrific fashion when Mills finds that the last murder victim, after the killer is captured, is his wife, who was pregnant at the time of her murder. The anguish on Mills's face is excruciating. John Doe claims to represent the deadly sin of envy, saying that he was envious of Mills's normal life and especially of his wife; thus, he decapitated her. Detective Mills learns of his wife's murder when a box containing his dead wife's head is delivered to him. John Doe taunts Mills, imploring him to kill him in revenge and thus commit the sin of wrath—in essence an early and bizarrely convoluted version of suicide by cop. Mills, in a frenzied state of rage, acquiesces and shoots the killer repeatedly in the head. In so doing, he actually allows the antagonist of the story to complete his mission—to show that we are all capable of murder. In truth, anyone in Mills's situation would likely have resorted to shooting John Doe. We call it revenge, but it is still murder.

What is particularly ominous about the final scene of the film is that it suggests that the only appropriate form of justice in this case is visceral and unavoidable, recalling the ancient murders encoded in myths and legends. The scene leaves us in a veritable state of moral angst. There seems to be no other way for Mills to come to grips with his tragedy but to enact murderous revenge. An eye for an eye is the biblical way of rationalizing murder; there seems to be no way around this dilemma. Murder is as part of life as is living—an existential oxymoron if there ever was one.

Of course, as we have seen throughout this book, revenge is not the only trigger for murder. In fact, there may be no trigger at all, as the Mack Herring case (the Kiss and Kill murder) implies. A recent confession by a heinous Australian serial killer also falls in the same category of truly "senseless" murder. His name is Mark "Chopper" Read. A few weeks before dying of cancer, Read confessed to four murders in a qualm of conscience. He had become internationally famous—or infamous—following the release of the 2000 film *Chopper*, which depicted with varying accuracy his violent life. Read was also known as a writer, after his autobiographical 1993 book, *How to Shoot Friends and Influence People*, became widely read.

After recounting his murders—three shootings and the hanging of a child killer in his jail cell—Read said that he felt "nothing at all" during the killings. It is perhaps too easy to assign his murderous activities to some form of insanity. But his book made a compelling counterargument to the insanity explanation: he killed just for the sake of killing, as if impelled to do so unexplainably. When asked why he killed, he answered rather glibly:

> "Can't really tell you why, I haven't the faintest idea and . . . I couldn't care less."
> "When I killed Sammy the Turk that wasn't self defence, that was outright fucking murder."[17]

Fig. 5.3. Mark Read.

Of course, one can interpret these as the statements of a psychopath or a schizoid, but there was no clinical evidence to suggest that he was either of these. His murders can be designated only as senseless. Perhaps it can be said that in someone like Read the balance that most of us maintain between limbic and neocortical states of mind breaks down under certain conditions (including through aberrant upbringing). The words of vampire serial murderer and so-called Chessboard Killer Andrei Chikatilo, discussed previously, are in keeping with this hypothesis:

> My inconsistent behaviour should not be misconstrued as an attempt to avoid responsibility for any acts I have committed. One could argue that even after my arrest, I was not fully aware of their dangerous and serious nature. My case is peculiar to me alone. It is not fear of responsibility that makes me act this way, but my inner psychic and nervous tension. I am prepared to give testimony about the crimes, but please do not torment me with their details, for my psyche would not be able to bear it. It never entered my mind to conceal anything from the investigation. Everything which I have done makes me shudder. I only feel gratitude to the investigating bodies for having captured me.[18]

Fig. 5.4. Andrei Chikatilo, better known as the "Rostov Ripper," as depicted in an undated Soviet-Era police mug shot.

Obviously, the moral impulses within Chikatilo were at odds with his urges. His claim that these murders were unconscious—"I was not fully aware of their dangerous and serious nature"—is a rather concrete articulation of what we are talking about here. This inner angst we feel with regard to murder is arguably why we are so fascinated by tales of murder. They mirror the sense of tragedy and mystery that murder elicits. Such tales are truly treatises on one of the greatest dilemmas of human existence—Why murder? As French writer Colette has so aptly put it:

> A bestial and violent man will go so far as to kill because he is under the influence of drink, exasperated, or driven by rage and alcohol. He is paltry. He does not know the pleasure of killing, the charity of bestowing death like a caress, of linking it with the play of the noble wild beasts: every cat, every tiger, embraces its prey and licks it even while it destroys it.[19]

CULTURE, EVOLUTION, AND MURDER

We are not so naïve as to believe that a murder-instinct hypothesis will suffice to explain the phenomenon of murder. As we have seen throughout this book, there is more to murder than anyone can ever satisfactorily explain. The appearance of murder in the human chronicle may even explain the origin of culture and even religion as systems for controlling and hopefully eliminating murder as something unique to us as a species.

Indeed, as various scripts and holy texts have asserted, the antidote to killing is altruism—grace and piety. Religions, philosophical systems, art, and all the other culture-based human activities are directly or indirectly founded on this very principle—even when, or perhaps especially when, these activities revolve around the phenomenon of murder, such as the many stories of murder throughout history. There may well be, in a phrase, a "kindness instinct" that evolution has provided as an antidote to the murder instinct. Culture puts murder on a leash via laws, ritualistic constrictions, moral codes, and the like. But that leash has not been very successful in eliminating the limbic triggers for murder—anger, betrayal, dishonor, control, hatred, and so on. As the acerbic English philosopher Thomas Hobbes once put it, "The condition of man is a condition of war of everyone against everyone."[20] Or as the poet Samuel Taylor Coleridge put it, in his marvelous poem "Kubla Khan," there are within us, "Ancestral voices prophesying war!"[21] The sociobiologist E. O. Wilson, on the other hand, has claimed that cultures are nothing more than part of our genetic heritage. As he puts it, "genes hold culture on a leash."[22] We would make the reverse claim—namely that cultures hold genes on a leash. Without culture, we may indeed end up killing one another for any kind of perceived reason on a routine daily basis. The "purge" (of movie fame) may give way to the "urge" (for murder).

Although ascertaining *why* culture came about in the first place remains difficult, determining *when* it appeared in human life poses much less of a conundrum. The most likely estimate is that the first true human cultures came into existence around one hundred thousand years ago—a period from which the plaster casts of skulls reveal that both Neanderthal and Cro-Magnon hominids had brains of similar size to ours. The physical characteristics that distinguished the Cro-Magnons from the Neanderthals were a high forehead and a well-defined chin. Artifacts attributed to the earliest period of Cro-Magnon culture demonstrate clearly that they had mastered the art of fashioning many useful instruments from stone, bone, and ivory—including weapons. They made fitted clothes and decorated their bodies with ornaments of shell and bone. A number of colored paintings left on the walls of caves near their habitats provide clear evidence that their form of social life was indeed one based on culture. About ten thousand years ago, they started to domesticate plants and animals, initiating an agricultural revolution that set the stage for the events in human history that eventually led to the founding of the first civilizations. It is not clear if they used their weapons for murder; at this point in prehistory, they most likely used them for hunting. But the killing-effectiveness with which they were made certainly suggests that murder was around the corner, if it had not already arrived.

Human culture today is descended from this same culture and is a product of neocortical planning. Murder emerged, arguably, in this context, like a fire that could not be extinguished, only controlled. As the ancient tales and accounts that form the Aarne-Thompson index tell us, from the outset murder has been as much a part of human civilized life as anything else. Now, a caveat about portrayals of this very kind is in order at this point. Ours is, like all other theories, a specific view derived from our *interpretation* of the relevant facts. It is one explanatory tale among many other possible ones. We are also aware that our account of the evolutionary antecedents to murder is by far an incomplete one because it does not encompass the question of why, at a certain point in our evolution, we decided to fashion culture to control our killer instinct. Nevertheless, any coherent discussion of murder cannot ignore the biology-culture dynamic that marks human existence, even though it must be taken with the proverbial grain of salt.

Some scholars, such as Richard Dawkins (mentioned in the previous chapter), have been very clever in arguing the case that genes have culture on a leash—in juxtaposition to our reverse hypothesis. Although their arguments might appear to an outsider to be merely a matter of academic or philosophical quibbling, the differences between evolutionists like Dawkins and other kinds of theorists actually reflect a profound chasm in worldview that exists in the modern world. With advances in genetics and artificial forms of intelligence, we are already changing our ethical and moral systems significantly, including our view of murder. So it is hardly a moot academic disputation.

Let's briefly encapsulate here the relevant facts, for the sake of argument. Evolution starts with the origin of life, defined in terms of a tiny simple organism with the capacity to reproduce itself.

Next comes a more complex cell—the basis of all higher life-forms, including human body tissues. The next step leads to larger multicellular organisms (flatworms, crustaceans, etc.) with the capacity to develop more complex organs like eyes and brains. The last, giant step is the emergence of the human mind. Sociobiologists maintain that the change from largely instinctive behavior to reflective thought occurred via a gene-culture *coevolution* process. This was set in motion in *Homo habilis*, the species of hominids that had learned how to use their hands to make tools around 1.5 and 2.0 million years ago. *Homo habilis* hominids lived in groups as hunter-gatherers on the savanna plains of Africa. Threatened by larger mammals, but desperately needing to catch game in order to survive, they had to learn how to act cooperatively, to think logically, and to communicate among themselves in some fashion. So they developed communal rules for hunting, food sharing, the division of labor, mating, and so on. Theirs was likely the earliest human culture. Evidently, killing was an intrinsic part of cultural ritual and symbolism, as archeology has revealed.[23]

Now the sociobiological argument is that as cultures became more complex, so did the human mind. Humans were forced to make choices that conferred upon them greater survival and reproductive abilities. Gene evolution gradually gave way to cultural evolution. The body's survival mechanisms were eventually replaced by the survival formats provided by culture.[24] The functions of genes were replaced by memes (see chapter 3). The memetic code was thus responsible for cultural progress, advancement, and betterment, having become the primary agent in the human species's evolutionary thrust forward. This clever proposal is, however, just that. There is no evidence that this substitution paradigm ever occurred. To sociobiologists, memes have evolved simply to help human beings cope with their particular form of consciousness, thus enhancing their collective survivability as a species—no more, no less. Therefore, one can legitimately ask, Is murder a meme? If it is, then what coping mechanism does it reflect? If not, why do we kill intentionally? We cannot imagine any plausible, and meaningful, sociobiological answers to these questions.

In the end, meme theory is no more than that—a theory of human nature. So is ours, as we readily admit. To paraphrase the French philosopher and semiotician Michel Foucault, human beings have, since their origins, sought to understand and define themselves.[25] They have done so by resorting to Nature or God. As others have done in the past, the sociobiologists have simply placed most of their bets on Nature.

So where does this leave our own hypothesis that a murder instinct has developed over time in the human species as a derivative of the mammalian killer instinct and that culture may be an antidote to this instinct? It leaves it as a working hypothesis. Murder is a reflective form of killing, seemingly guided by inner impulses and urges. Culture is the leash for controlling these impulses and urges. Those who have been highly adept at the control levers have become cultural leaders in various ways, including artists, musicians, scientists, philosophers, and the like. They are the real survivors of Nature's experiment, and the murderers are those who have failed it. To quote British author H. G. Wells, "Biologically the species is the accumulation of the experiments of all its successful individuals since the beginning."[26]

Within this hypothetical paradigm, one can claim that human habits are formed so that we can perhaps tame the tug of psychic war within us, relieving us from its angst. Reactions to these very habits as "mind-numbing" have been the causes behind various Nietzschean murders. Even deranged Minnesota serial killer and serial arsonist Carl Panzram (discussed previously) was aware that murder presented a moral and logical paradox—a deranged way of "doing good," as his words, uttered from prison, reveal:

> "I would have gone into the murder business on a wholesale scale instead of being a piker and only killing 21 human beings. My intentions were good because I am the man that goes around the world doing people good."[27]

"I am sorry for only two things. These two things are: I am sorry that I
have mistreated some few animals in my life time and I am sorry
that I am unable to murder the whole damed [*sic*] human race."[28]

Panzram's statements are both rational and irrational at once,
highlighting the conflicted culturally guided sense of murder. There
may be no other way to explain murder other than in such terms.
What is true, though, is that murder has communal consequences.
We all have a stake in any murder that is committed, because we
are all emotional participants in it by proxy. As British writer W.
H. Auden so eloquently pointed out, "Murder is unique in that it
abolishes the party it injures, so that society has to take the place of
the victim and on his behalf demand atonement or grant forgiveness;
it is the one crime in which society has a direct interest."[29]

BACK TO FREUD

The ideas of Sigmund Freud have always been controversial and dis-
carded by some, perhaps many, as products of his own fanciful imagination. Freud was a teller of psychic über-tales, which were derived
from his deep understanding of myths as central to human identity
and character. Famed science-fiction author Michael Crichton encap-
sulated Freud's understanding of the link between story, sexuality,
morality, and identity by extolling him as "undoubtedly the greatest
novelist of the 20th century."[30] Freud's ideas remain so incisive and
believable today because, arguably, they represent timeless mythic
narratives recycled in clinical terms. One of these is highly relevant
to the discussion at hand, namely the Eros versus Thanatos mythic
dichotomy that Freud saw as operative in the human unconscious
as a conflictual one—paralleling our own hypothesis about murder.

In Greek mythology, Eros was the god of love (the counterpart
of the Roman god Cupid). He was represented as the son of Chaos
and the embodiment of harmony and creative power. In Greek art,
he was depicted as a winged youth, often with eyes covered to sym-

bolize the blindness of love. He is a metaphor of our sexual desires and thus of a life force within us. In the Eros legend, sex is more than sex; it is a creative impulse that is the source of new life, of art, and of reflection, and, as such, it unites all of us on a common creative-civilized ground. Here's how Freud put it:

> Civilization is a process in the service of Eros, whose purpose is to combine single human individuals, and after that families, then races, peoples and nations, into one great unity, the unity of mankind. Why this has to happen, we do not know; the work of Eros is precisely this.[31]

One way to explain sexually based murders is to say that the Eros impulse is out of balance. It morphs into a destructive rather than a constructive force. The statements of several sexual serial killers discussed previously can easily be seen to support this possibility. Of course, not all murders have a sexual motive, as we have also seen. Murders are deranged creative acts, unless they are reactive and spontaneous responses to a threat or to the enactment of some revenge.

Many of the other murder writings that we have examined here show a fascination with death, and even an experimentation with it. This is traceable to a death instinct that Freud called Thanatos, the Greek god standing for a primitive desire for destruction, decay, and death, manifested by a turning away from pleasure. Freud claimed that the death instinct coexisted with the life instinct. Eros impels us to create; Thanatos, to engage in acts of self-destruction. We have seen many instances of the Eros versus Thanatos tension in the statements of the murderers in previous chapters.

Like our own hypothesis, there is very little empirical evidence to support the validity of the Freudian model. Psychoanalysis, like literary criticism, stands on its own as an interpretation of the facts. It can be counterargued, but it cannot be refuted offhand simply because it cannot be empirically tested or validated. Not everything in human life can be subjected to the normal curve, at least in our opinion. There have been many clever ways around Freud's ideas in the works of contemporary psychologists who have, in our view, simply renamed them, claiming that this eliminates them from clinical practices *ipso facto*. Psychologists now prefer to see the Freudian impulses as part of regular processes, called "salience biases," whereby someone would be drawn to crime because of the promise of immediate pleasure, and "risk calculations," where someone would do something reckless because of the potential for increase in social status.[32] There is no need to comment on these lexical reworkings of Freud—they are simply that. The fact remains that we all intuitively understand the Eros versus Thanatos conflict within us, as did the ancient myths and murder stories.

Life impulses and concomitant death impulses seem to consti-tute a paradoxical partnership in our brains. We ritualize both, and when death is brought about intentionally through murder, then we lament it and write about it as bearing great consequences, because it throws this partnership out of balance. Of course, all this is plausible if we admit to a level of mind that is below the conscious one—an unconscious level. Some say that this is Freud's greatest discovery; others say that it is instead a clever renaming of memory (individual and cultural). So, let's briefly revisit this concept in the light of the murder hypothesis we are elaborating here.

Let's start with Freud's description of the unconscious:

It was a triumph for the interpretative art of psychoanalysis when it succeeded in demonstrating that certain mental acts of normal people, for which no one had hitherto attempted to put forward a psychological explanation, were to be regarded in the same light as the symptoms of neurotics: that is to say that had a meaning, which was unknown to the subject but which could easily be dis-covered by analytic means. . . . A class of material was brought to light which is calculated better than any other to stimulate a belief in the existence of unconscious mental acts even in people to whom the hypothesis of something at once mental and uncon-scious seems strange and even absurd.[33]

It may well be that those "unconscious mental acts," which we do not comprehend, are the very ones that might lead a Bundy or a Rader to do what they did. Maybe the unconscious is where the limbic versus neocortical tug plays out, shaping our conscious behaviors, which are vulnerable to various emotional and irrational impulses within us that Freud categorized under the notion of the id, as we have already discussed:

> We can come nearer to the Id with images, and call it chaos, a cauldron of seething excitement. We suppose that is somewhere in direct contact with somatic processes, and takes over from them instinctual needs and gives them mental expression. These instincts fill it with energy but it has no organization and no unified will, only an impulsion to obtain satisfaction for the instinctual needs, in accordance with the pleasure-principle.[34]

If this "cauldron of seething excitement" overwhelms us, it is because we are constrained by social rules and cultural constraints—these are the forces that shape the role of the superego. One might therefore explain many murders, and especially serial murders, in these terms; namely, these crimes are the aberrant product of a repressed id. It's a concept that, while perhaps not using this precise terminology, has allowed crime fiction to evolve tremendously as a genre over the last thirty years. As those novelists who depict the criminal mind with particular clinical and procedural credibility have shown, including James Ellroy and Michael Connelly—and more so the Scandinavian crime writers constituting the "Nordic noir" tradition such as Jo Nesbø and the late Stieg Larsson—murder as an act and an idea is rooted in repressed or otherwise disordered impulses inevitably linked to the id, the superego, and the libido (sex drive). As the eminent psychiatrist Charles Brenner once explained, the superego manifests itself in human behavior and actions as follows:

1. the approval or disapproval of actions and wishes on the grounds of rectitude;

2. critical self-observation;
3. self-punishment;
4. the demand for reparation or repentance of wrong-doing; and
5. self-praise or self-love as a reward for virtuous or desirable thoughts and actions.[35]

Looking back on the writings and statements discussed in this book, we can see the presence of these elements in various murderer manifestos. We saw, for example, how mass murderers viewed their actions as self-righteous (1), perceiving them in terms of a Hero mythology. As for (2), critical self-observation, we have seen time and again murderers like Chikatilo, who are critically aware of the consequences of their actions. Their statements bear this out rather explicitly. Many engage in self-punishment (3) or a need to enact repentance (4). But the most common manifestation of a warped id-superego dynamic is in (5), culminating in the pursuit of self-interestedness. Some of the more relevant defense mechanisms as documented in the murderers reveal, in fact, classic psychoanalytic symptoms, such as an obsessive fixation with, or attachment to, something or someone, a rationalization offering excuses, and a distortion of basic Eros impulses, which lead to murderous behavior.

These mechanisms are of great interest to literary criminology because they produce typical symbolic and ritualistic behaviors, as we saw with many serial killers. In psychoanalytic theory, symbolism stems from the unconscious. Freud put it as follows:

> Symbolism is not peculiar to dreams, but is characteristic of unconscious ideation, in particular, among people, and is to be found in folklore, and in popular myths, legends, linguistic idioms, proverbial wisdom and current jokes, to a more complete extent than in dreams.[36]

One Freudian idea that we have already explored and that can be recalled here is the Oedipus complex. To reiterate, he thought that in all children there is hostility toward the parent of the same sex and an attraction to the parent of the opposite sex; this attraction eventually manifests itself in some neurotic behavior. He wrote about his notion in a letter to a friend:

> Being entirely honest with oneself if a good exercise. Only one idea of general value has occurred to me. I have found love of the mother and jealousy of the father in my own case too, and now believe it to be a general phenomenon of early childhood. If that is the case, the gripping power of Oedipus Rex, in spite of all the rational objections to the inexorable fate that the story presupposes, becomes intelligible. Our feelings rise against any arbitrary individual fate but the Greek myth seizes on a compulsion which everyone recognizes because he has felt traces of it in himself. Every member of the audience was once a budding Oedipus in fantasy, and this dream-fulfillment played out in reality causes everyone to recoil in horror, with the full measure of repression which separates his infantile from his present state.[37]

As we have seen, some serial murderers may be reliving their Oedipal sexual fantasies in a warped and perverted way. What is interesting to emphasize here is that, whether right or wrong, concepts such as the Oedipus complex are born through the study of literature, which Freud himself saw as a source of recording unconscious desires and processes. Our literary criminological approach has many parallels with this approach, since it posits that the tales of murder, both real and fictional, are keys to understanding "the emotional, unconscious or only partly comprehended bases of our behavior," as Simon Lesser puts it.[38] In a way, Dostoyevsky's *Crime and Punishment* or Poe's tales of murder and terror are really fictional versions of Freudian theory. They offer deep insights into the irrational forces that shape murderous behavior.

LITERARY CRIMINOLOGY

Our inroad into the meaning of murder has been through the template of writing—both literary and nonliterary (actual statements of murderers). Many theories in traditional criminology favor social conditions as the causes for murder. But, as we have seen, people do not murder only because their upbringing conditioned them to do so; they murder for a host of aberrant emotional reasons. As briefly mentioned, medieval society had a very straightforward theory of murder that did not distinguish among different motives. It saw murder as a sin, a transgression of the moral order. Within the last century, we have recast murder into a different domain—that of psychology and criminology—so that it can be interpreted in secular, scientific terms. Predictably, this has led to all kinds of theoretical paradigms to explain it. In the process, though, we have lost the unity of thought that envisions murder as emanating from a singular source. By using literary criminology, our intent has been to sift out of the writings of murderers and fictional murder stories alike some common denominator. The one that stands out is the presence of a narrative mechanism that translates motives into stories that attempt, either directly or indirectly, to come to grips with the reality of murder as part of our evolutionary heritage.

Even terrorists—perhaps above anyone else—display a compulsion to use this mechanism as they weave their tales of justification not only to explain their otherwise senseless killings of human beings but also to fuel them. The narrative mechanism goes both ways—it both rationalizes and instigates murder. Narrative has always been an effective yardstick for exploring the human condition. As the Argentine writer Jorge Luis Borges suggested in his *Ficciones* (1944), the human mind is inherently predisposed to understand life as a narrative. Literary criminology presents us with a model of how the motives for murder are rationalized through expressive writing and at how the ensuing stories become a source for future murders, as we are seeing on a daily basis in terrorist-based murders.

We hardly realize the presence of unconscious forces at work within us, which manifest themselves in the words and phrases that we use as we speak and write. Words and texts are clues to the murderer's inner world. As we have suggested throughout this book, the literary approach may even be a way to solve or prevent murders. There are, actually, a number of existing literary-based investigative methods that have been used by law enforcement. A common one is handwriting analysis, with its focus on identifying details of a person's handwriting in order to construct a handwriting-based profile of a murderer. It comes as no surprise to a literary criminologist to discover that the method was first conceived in a fictional context, namely in Dickens's *Bleak House* (which we have already discussed). The plot revolves around a contested handwritten will litigated before the courts in England. While at the time handwriting analysis was still a junk pseudoscience known as graphology, which was concerned foremost with using handwriting as a means for analyzing behavioral traits, Dickens suggested that it might also be used for criminological purposes—to identify a genuine text versus a forged facsimile.[39] In the subsequent century, the FBI's Questioned Document Unit similarly began relying on the use of an exemplar (an existing sample with a confirmed author) in order to compare it to suspected fakes. It is the same method that helped rule out a number of the copycat Zodiac letters as being genuine.

The detailed analysis of a murderer's writing offers a general rubric under which murder, narrative, style, and other cultural forms can be seen to interact.

SCAN OF MURDER

Beyond the theoretical application of psychoanalysis and forensic semiotics to the writings of killers, it is obvious to us that language can help penetrate the darkened recesses of the criminal mind. A technique of particular relevance to literary criminology is known as Scientific Content Analysis (SCAN). It is a technique that helps investigators decode the writer's thoughts through the language used.[40] SCAN helps hypothetically illuminate the underlying rationale for murder in terms of the latent narrative archetypes found in the murderer's discourse, including how he puts ideas—and fantasies or other imaginary scenarios—into writing based on education and background. The method can also reveal whether the writer is being truthful or deceptive in retelling his version of events or in making assertions, which, parenthetically, is applicable not only to murders but also to any criminal investigation. And, perhaps most important, in the case of murder inquiries, it might actually reveal why a killer does what he or she does. When killers feel compelled to commit their crimes to writing and discuss them in their own words, we have before us a true source of insight into the meaning of murder.

SCAN examines linguistic patterns, revealing telltale signs of deception or of motivation through the structure and contents of the writing itself. By going over the statements line by line, theme by theme, it is possible to tease out relevant and often subtle aspects of a murderer's intentions and state of mind. We have attempted to do this throughout this book. As we have seen, elements such as pronoun use reveal the subject's relation to the crime; a shift in pronoun use also indicates a shift in the murderer's perspective. Even writing with capitals versus lowercase letters, as we have seen, tells us an awful lot about the murderer's perspectives and autobiographical narrative—what archetypal character he sees himself as assuming. The basic idea of the SCAN technique is similarly to get at the underlying meaning of a text through its form and the various hidden meanings in it. Let's look at a few final cases to show how SCAN can constitute an effective investigative tool.

Consider the infamous case of disgraced NFL star, small-time actor, and corporate shill, O. J. Simpson. As the 2016 ESPN sport-crime documentary *OJ: Made in America* details, the acquittal of Simpson by a rogue Los Angeles jury for the brutal 1994 murder of his ex-wife Nicole Brown and her friend Ron Goldman—crimes now almost universally recognized as having been committed by Simpson, as corroborated by a subsequent civil-court ruling—underscored inherent defects in the American jury system. In this case, the jury simply chose to overlook the physical evidence and Simpson's obvious motive, namely his proprietary obsession over Nicole (a common motive, as we have seen previously). And while Simpson's interminable 1995 murder prosecution was referred to as the "trial of the century" by the media of the day and raised the bar in terms of permissible courtroom theatrics, little attention was paid to one of the earliest pieces of evidence to emerge in the original investigation pointing to Simpson's culpability. It is an exhibit that has also curiously seen little discussion or analysis in the countless books and media productions that have emerged in the years since the case became a public sensation. We are referring here to Simpson's "suicide" letter. Using the SCAN technique, the letter turns out to be as much a confession to murder as it is a final good-bye—perhaps more so.

To Whom It May Concern:

First, everyone understand. I have nothing to do with Nicole's murder. I loved her; always have and always will. If we had a problem, it's because I loved her so much.

Recently, we came to the understanding that for now we were not right for each other, at least for now. Despite our love, we were different and that's why we mutually agreed to go our separate ways.

It was tough splitting for a second time, but we both knew it was for the best. Inside, I had no doubt that in the future we would be close friends or more. Unlike what has been written in the press, Nicole and I had a great relationship for most of our lives together. Like all long-term relationships, we had a few downs and ups.

I took the heat New Year's 1989 because that's what I was supposed to do. I did not plead no contest for any other reason but to protect our privacy and was advised it would end the press hype.

I don't want to belabor knocking the press, but I can't believe what is being said. Most of it is totally made up. I know you have a job to do, but as a last wish, please, please, please, leave my children in peace. Their lives will be tough enough.

I want to send my love and thanks to all my friends. I'm sorry I can't name every one of you, especially A.C. Man, thanks for being in my life. The support and friendship I received from so many: Wayne Hughes, Lewis Marks, Frank Olson, Mark Packer, Bender, Bobby Kardashian. I wish we had spent more time together in recent years. My golfing buddies: Hoss, Alan Austin, Mike, Craig, Bender, Wyler, Sandy, Jay, Donnie, thanks for the fun.

All my teammates over the years: Reggie, you were the soul of my pro career. Ahmad, I never stopped being proud of you. Marcus, you've got a great lady in Catherine, don't mess it up. Bobby Chandler, thanks for always being there. Skip and Kathy, I love you guys. Without you, I never would have made it through this far.

Marguerite, thanks for the early years. We had some fun. Paula, what can I say? You are special. I'm sorry I'm not going to have, we're not going to have, our chance. God brought you to me, I now see. As I leave, you'll be in my thoughts.

I think of my life and feel I've done most of the right things. So why do I end up like this? I can't go on. No matter what the outcome, people will look and point. I can't take that. I can't subject my children to that. This way, they can move on and go on with their lives.

Please, if I've done anything worthwhile in my life, let my kids live in peace from you, the press.

I've had a good life. I'm proud of how I lived. My mama taught me to do unto others. I treated people the way I wanted to be treated. I've always tried to be up and helpful. So why is this happening?

I'm sorry for the Goldman family. I know how much it hurts.

Nicole and I had a good life together. All this press talk about a rocky relationship was no more than what every long-term relationship experiences. All her friends will confirm that I have been totally loving and understanding of what she's been going through.

At times, I have felt like a battered husband or boyfriend, but I loved her; make that clear to everyone. And I would take whatever it took to make it work.

Don't feel sorry for me. I've had a great life, great friends. Please think of the real O.J. and not this lost person.

Thanks for making my life special. I hope I helped yours.

Peace and love, O.J.[41]

Fig. 5.5. Mug shot of O. J. Simpson.

The letter was read on national television by Simpson's friend and lawyer Robert Kardashian, prefacing a bizarre, televised chase through Los Angeles in which Simpson's servile friend Allen Cowlings—in perhaps the greatest folie à deux ever captured live on television—drove Simpson's infamous white Ford Bronco in circuitous fashion along freeways and suburban roads, with LAPD prowl cars following cautiously behind. All the while, Simpson cowered in the back with a gun to his head, vowing suicide, having absconded from an appointment to turn himself in to police and instead leaving behind the letter before fleeing.

Simpson was a documented wife batterer with explosive rage issues comingled. At the same time, he had a certain glib charm that led to a cult of personality—one that attracted hordes of fans both before and even after the accusations of murder. Simpson is, by definition, both a malignant narcissist and a tyrannical psychopath, one who harbored a toxic sense of ownership over his ex-wife. Simpson claimed in his letter that he was innocent of all allegations, and that he loved Nicole, who also bore him two children during their mercurial marriage. Simpson's written words, however, gave him away—they revealed what his convincing affectations and façade of innocence concealed:

> "First, everyone understand. I have nothing to do with Nicole's murder."
> "I'm sorry for the Goldman family."
> "Unlike what has been written in the press, Nicole and I had a great relationship."
> "I want to send my love and thanks to all my friends."
> "Let my kids live in peace."[42]

A quick SCAN of the words reveals Simpson's unconscious thoughts: The first statement indicates what is known as a weak denial or an avoidance strategy; at no point does Simpson assert that he did not kill Nicole. Opting for the present tense of "have" (versus "had") is also suggestive of deception or perhaps of his mental inability, at this point, to distinguish between past and current events under stress. In the second statement, Simpson offers an apology and does not deny killing Ron. Note that the victim is not mentioned by name, a recurring feature seen in similar documents, and an omission that might suggest that Ron was simply collateral damage or else that he was the lover of Simpson's possession—Nicole. So, Ron must be effaced—he is the indirect object in a grammatical construction where Nicole is the subject. In the third statement, Simpson uses the past tense, suggesting that he is aware of his actions and that he committed them because of Nicole's betrayal. By using the personal pronoun ("I") as part of the phrase "Nicole and I," he clearly identifies himself as a victim along with Nicole. It also suggests that he never actually intended to take his own life. In the fourth statement, Simpson's narcissism crystallizes conspicuously, using first-person pronoun forms to put himself at the center of the narrative. In the fifth statement, Simpson does not name his children, using instead the possessive pronoun "my," which suggests that he sees them as his property as well.

Simpson's letter says as much about his motivation for murdering Nicole Brown and Ron Goldman as any confession would. Its omissions and discourse strategies of avoidance linguistically flesh out Simpson's own pathological egocentricity and sense of entitlement, providing us with an unobstructed view into a killer's mind. When comparing Simpson's letter to the thousands of other written denials and bona fide suicide letters, it becomes evident that it was simply the next act in an elaborate piece of theater that Simpson was directing. His true passion was, after all, not so much professional football as being a Hollywood actor. After being acquitted by the jury in his criminal trial, Simpson was later found to be responsible in a wrongful-death civil trial filed by Ron Goldman's family. Simpson was ordered to pay $33 million in damages. Undeterred by the ruling, and in keeping with his compulsion to write about his crime in an exculpatory manner—as well as a convenient backdrop to boast about himself—in 2007 Simpson had a book ghost-written about the murder, tauntingly titled *If I Did It*. He was later arrested on felony kidnapping and armed robbery charges for his shakedown of a Las Vegas sports-memorabilia dealer, and he was sentenced to serve thirty-three years in a Nevada prison in 2008.

Between Simpson's acquittal on murder charges in 1995 and his subsequent felony charges, the SCAN technique would find increased use as an effective mechanism for entering the minds of killers. In fact, the year after Simpson's acquittal in Los Angeles, the technique would come of age and reveal itself as very helpful in a different and truly enigmatic murder case. It was a case that constituted one of the most puzzling unsolved child murders in recent memory—the slaying of six-year-old JonBenét Ramsey.

Fig. 5.6. The gravesite of JonBenét Ramsey, murdered in her home on Christmas night, 1996. Image from *Wikipedia* Creative Commons; author: Taurusrus. Licensed under CC BY-SA 3.0.

The day after Christmas in 1996, socialite and former beauty queen Patsy Ramsey discovered what appeared to be a ransom note left on the stairs of the family's upscale home in Boulder, Colorado. The note claimed that Patsy's daughter and child beauty contestant, JonBenét, had been kidnapped by a "foreign faction" and that she would be executed if exactly $118,000 was not paid in specific denominations and the instructions not followed with precision. While the absurdity of the letter suggested a hoax, sure enough, Patsy proceeded to her daughter's room to find it empty. A frenzied panic soon surged throughout the family. Police, family members, and neighbors soon descended on the house, without any control over the primary crime scene, and the body of a murdered JonBenét was found in the basement roughly eight hours after the discovery of the note. An autopsy confirmed that she had been beaten and strangled with ligature fastened with an intricate knot, and that she had been tenuously fondled in a sexual manner, but there had otherwise been no verifiable sexual assault.

Erring on the side of statistics showing that children are frequently murdered by family members, the police immediately zeroed in on the parents; their suspicion was buoyed by the fact that there was no sign of forced entry, and that after being snatched from her room by her killer, JonBenét was fed a bowl of pineapple—the remnants of which were found in the kitchen and in JonBenét's stomach at autopsy. The police immediately assumed that the note was a diversionary tactic. It was written with a nondominant hand, indicating that the author was likely looking to outwit handwriting-analysis experts. The parents were eventually cleared by DNA analysis, however, questions—largely with respect to the girl's circumspect older brother—linger on to this day. The parents had always insisted that JonBenét's brother, Burke—who was nine years old at the time and whose fingerprints were found on the half-eaten bowl of pineapple—was asleep the entire time. The case remains unsolved; however, as revealed in a penetrating documentary produced by the CBS network to coincide with the twentieth anniversary of the murder, a modern-day reanalysis suggests that the family was directly involved in the girl's death and subsequent staging of the scene. It also implicates the police and district attorney's office in a cover-up, the motive for which is unclear. But the documentary is based on speculation, and in our view, really does not solve the case. In fact, other documentaries through the years have reached different conclusions. Perhaps the most enduring clue, however, is the writing of the killer, a text that can be put to analysis via SCAN.

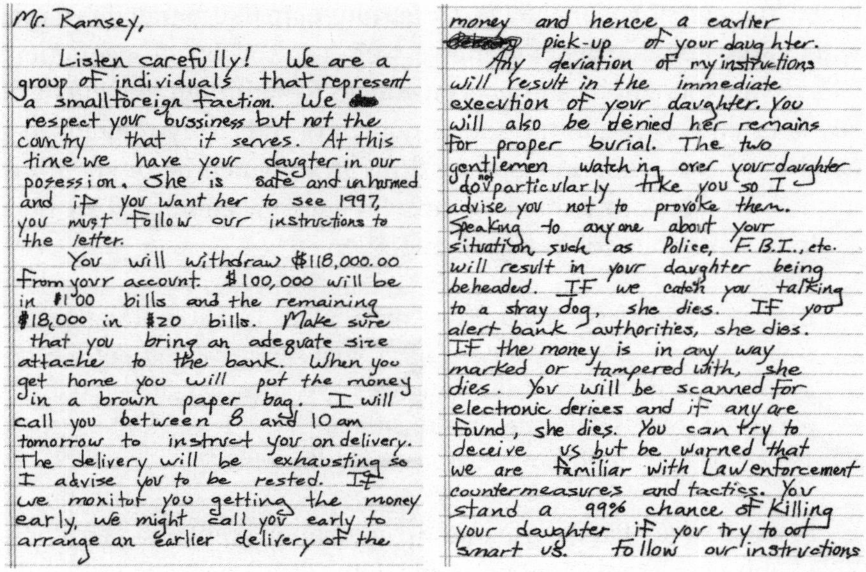

Mr. Ramsey,

Listen carefully! We are a group of individuals that represent a small foreign faction. We ~~do~~ respect your bussiness but not the country that it serves. At this time we have your daughter in our posession. She is safe and unharmed and if you want her to see 1997 you must follow our instructions to the letter.

You will withdraw $118,000.00 from your account. $100,000 will be in $100 bills and the remaining $18,000 in $20 bills. Make sure that you bring an adequate size attache to the bank. When you get home you will put the money in a brown paper bag. I will call you between 8 and 10 am tomorrow to instruct you on delivery. The delivery will be exhausting so I advise you to be rested. If we monitor you getting the money early, we might call you early to arrange an earlier delivery of the

money and hence a earlier ~~delivery~~ pick-up of your daughter. Any deviation of my instructions will result in the immediate execution of your daughter. You will also be denied her remains for proper burial. The two gentlemen watching over your daughter do particularly like you so I advise you not to provoke them. Speaking to anyone about your situation such as Police, F.B.I., etc. will result in your daughter being beheaded. IF we catch you talking to a stray dog, she dies. IF you alert bank authorities, she dies. IF the money is in any way marked or tampered with, she dies. You will be scanned for electronic devices and if any are found, she dies. You can try to deceive us but be warned that we are familiar with Law enforcement countermeasures and tactics. You stand a 99% chance of killing your daughter if you try to out smart us. Follow our instructions

Fig. 5.7. The first two pages of the handwritten ransom note left by the intruder at the Ramsey home overnight on December 25–26, 1996, as it appeared once located by Patsy Ramsey the next morning. While the note was left after Jon-Benét had already been sexually molested and strangled to death, its length and implausible cloak-and-dagger detail—far longer and more elaborate than any known ransom letter—suggested to police that it was either authored before-hand and brought to the scene, or was otherwise prepared via the luxury of time after the girl was dead.

When this note is compared with other ransom notes bearing threats or instructions, there is little doubt that this one is likely to be a fake or a narrative construction of sorts. It also reveals elaborate and ideological motives other than ransom—essentially distractors and pure subterfuge—for the death of young JonBenét. But perhaps its defining feature is its allusions to other key texts, a phenomenon known as *intertextuality* in literary theory. Intertexuality is a feature of many criminal texts. Recall here the Zodiac's murderous plagiarizing of existing works ranging from Edgar Allan Poe to Richard Connell in his letters and cryptograms, the serial-killer manifestos that inspired several killers to reenact the circumstances in John Fowles's novel *The Collector*, and the way Mark Twitchell based his screenplay on the *Dexter* narrative. In like-minded fashion, whoever killed JonBenét Ramsey was inspired by crime fiction. Clearly inexperienced and unaccustomed to writing a document of any substantive length, the author quoted or indirectly referenced a number of crime and kidnapping films from which he or she drew inspiration. These intertextual sources shaped the content of the note itself. Consider the following segment.

> Listen carefully! We are a group of individuals that represent a small foreign faction. We do respect your bussiness but not the country that it serves. At this time we have your daughter in our posession. She is safe and unharmed and if you want her to see 1997, you must follow our instructions to the letter.[43]

First, we note that the use of the exclamation point is superfluous. This habit will likely show up in the author's other writings, should they ever become available. At the same time, the imperative "listen carefully" is lifted from films where a phone call is placed in a kidnapping scheme and where "listen" as a verbal order would be more appropriate than in a written note. This is the first of several direct or indirect references to crime-film clichés. Also, foreign factions do not describe themselves as "foreign," a detail that adds nothing to the note; it is put there for obfuscation—claiming that the kidnapping is part of an international plot. Counterintuitively, this makes the admission that the plot is "small" stand out as disingenuous. Thus, the supposed geopolitical or terrorist agenda to the kidnapping is nothing more than a ruse, it's hiding some other motive.

> You will withdraw $118,000.00 from your account. $100,000 will be in $100 bills and the remaining $18,000 in $20 bills. Make sure that you bring an adequate size attaché to the bank. When you get home you will put the money in a brown paper bag. I will call you between 8 and 10 am tomorrow to instruct you on delivery. The delivery will be exhausting so I advise you to be rested. If we monitor you getting the money early, we might call you early

to arrange an earlier delivery of the money and hence a earlier delivery pick-up of your daughter.[44]

The weirdly specific amount requested is perhaps the most revelatory element of the instructions in the letter. First, this is a low sum for any kidnapper to demand, particularly from a notably wealthy family. Second, it is an awkward amount to compile. Most important, this is precisely the amount that John Ramsey received as a work bonus earlier in 1996. The killer must have been aware of that bonus. Further, the use of "adequate" to describe the attaché case, much like how "hence" is used as a conjunctive adverb elsewhere in the letter, reinforces that author is well-educated and a native speaker of English—no true kidnapper would have used such expressions based on a review of catalogued ransom notes. In fact, the letter, upon our analysis, was found to yield a score on the Flesch-Kincaid scale—a standardized formula for calculating readability—of roughly 40/100. With lower scores being indicative of greater reading difficulty, the note falls somewhere between *Time* magazine (50/100) and a peer-reviewed academic or scientific journal (30/100) in terms of its grammatical and lexical complexity. Given that the author is clearly college-educated or at the very least well-read, the misspellings are therefore intentional and deceptive, used as clear identity-obfuscation techniques. The sentence "The delivery will be exhausting so I advise you to be rested," is an obvious intertextual allusion to the 1971 film *Dirty Harry* (discussed previously), in which the psychopathic killer, Scorpio (a reference to the Zodiac Killer), asks the protagonist if he has had a "good rest" before requiring him to run between pay phones around San Francisco. As specified in the letter:

Any deviation of my instructions will result in the immediate execution of your daughter. You will also be denied her remains for proper burial. The two gentlemen watching over your daughter do not particularly like you so I advise you not to provoke them. Speaking to anyone about your situation, such as Police, F.B.I., etc., will result in your daughter being beheaded. If we catch you talking to a stray dog, she dies. If you alert bank authorities, she dies. If the money is in any way marked or tampered with, she dies. You will be scanned for electronic devices and if any are found, she dies. You can try to deceive us but be warned that we are familiar with law enforcement countermeasures and tactics. You stand a 99% chance of killing your daughter if you try to out smart us. Follow our instructions and you stand a 100% chance of getting her back.[45]

The reference to denial of proper burial is clear evidence that the killer knew the Ramseys were devout Episcopalians. The reference to "two gentlemen" might suggest that the killer—or at least the author—was female, a possibility reinforced by the phrase "watching over," which denotes a sense of caring for and protecting—in contrast to "watching," which would denote guarding or holding. Prior to the more-terrorist practice of beheading captives that has become synonymous with ISIL, the use of the word "beheaded" as a means of execution had, as far as we know, never been used in other kidnapping notes. Its significance in the letter is still not entirely understood. It might simply be a way of reinforcing the deception that it was a "foreign faction" that was responsible for the kidnapping. The repeated "she dies" rejoinders to hypothetical scenarios is, however, once again a verbatim rehashing of the film *Dirty Harry*, this time referencing the conversations between Scorpio and Dirty Harry in which "the girl dies" is used by the killer to punctuate his sentences. Significantly, the same phrase ("she dies") also appears in the kidnapping film *Ransom*, which was released just months before JonBenét's murder in 1996.

You and your family are under constant scrutiny as well as the authorities. Don't try to grow a brain John. You are not the only fat cat around so don't think that killing will be difficult. Don't underestimate us John. Use that good southern common sense of yours. It is up to you now John! Victory! S.B.T.C.[46]

"Don't try to grow a brain John" is lifted directly from the 1994 hostage film *Speed*, and it marks a significant deviation from the "Mr. Ramsey" salutation at the start of the letter. This is fairly strong evidence that the killer-kidnapper not only knew the Ramseys but likely hated the father for some reason—or was otherwise pretending to. The coaxing to use "good southern common sense" is a bizarre statement. John Ramsey was born in Nebraska, attended college in Michigan, and lived in a number of places in his life—including in Georgia for a few years, where he met Patsy, a native Georgian and southerner. It may be that much of the information on the family came through Patsy, and that the author made the assumption that John was a southerner himself. This would support the theory that the killer is someone who ingratiated himself or herself with the family through beauty pageants attended by Patsy and JonBenét—or even that he or she was a member of the family. It is unclear what the "S.B.T.C." signature reveals. Some have believed that it stands for "Saved by the Cross," yet another religious reference. However, it may harbor something more cryptic. One possibility is: "Stupid bitch, take care."

Patsy Ramsey died of ovarian cancer in 2006 with many still believing, rightly or wrongly, that she was the author of the ransom note. Some, including a Boulder grand jury, have speculated that the evidence overwhelmingly pointed to JonBenét having been killed by someone in the house, versus an intruder, and that the note was created after the fact as a scripted kidnapping plot to hide what really happened so as to divert authorities. If true, this would mean that Patsy—who was never properly eliminated as the author of the letter, following an expert analysis of her handwriting samples, known as exemplars—discovered the murder and then instinctively created the document to stage the scene. It is, however, an excessively long note, especially if authored under duress. There are also simply too many loopholes in the critical first few hours of the investigation—crime-scene contamination, police tunnel vision, witnesses not being isolated—to draw an informed conclusion on what happened over the course of that day, December 26, 1996. And while there are indeed some indicators of a linguistic female voice in the document, it strikes us as having been written *before* rather than during or after the murder. The author was clearly a crime-film aficionado, and whether by DNA or through the use of this letter—or both—the reality is that this case remains very solvable today.

The final case we wish to discuss here regarding the viability of the SCAN technique as an investigative tool in unsolved murders is the even more horrifying case of April Tinsley, an eight-year-old girl who was murdered in Fort Wayne, Indiana, on Good Friday in 1988. It's a Midwestern cold case that few people have heard of—yet it prevails as among the most disturbing. Tinsley was last seen walking home from a visit to a friend's house just two blocks away; witnesses claimed that they saw April being dragged into a blue pickup truck soon after. The young girl's body was found three days later, over twenty miles away in Amish farm country, where she had been thrown into a ditch. April had been sexually assaulted and then strangled. The offender's DNA was recovered at the scene. Even though she lived in a small community, and the murder of a child typically galvanizes police and citizens to close their ranks, the case soon went cold and the killer remained at large. Then, in 1990, the killer returned. He left his calling card on a barn door, in wax crayon, not far from where he had disposed of April's body just two years earlier.

Fig. 5.8. Eight-year-old April Tinsley as she appeared at the time of her abduction and murder in the spring of 1988.

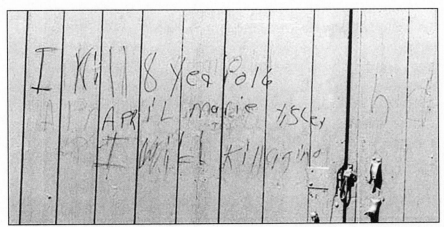

Fig. 5.9. An ominous scrawl left by April's killer on a barn door in rural DeKalb County, Indiana, in 1990, in which the killer vows to murder again.

In 1990, standardized DNA testing in criminal cases was still a few years away. In the meantime, investigators had an alternative clue: an anonymous confession left by the killer, who was seemingly compelled to return to the scene and relive the crime—as child killer Albert Fish once did—through the use of taunting coprographic writings similar to those we have discussed previously. Barely legible and written in crayon, the scrawl on a barn board read as follows:

I kill 8 year old April Marie Tisley. I will kill again. ha ha[47]

The killer cites the victim's full name, including her middle name, as it would have been reported in the media and death notices in 1988, as well as on her tombstone; however, the surname is misspelled, and there is a notable grammatical error, with "kill" being used as a present-tense form. Investigators at the time were unsure if the errors in the letter were intentional, so as to obfuscate identity, or if they simply suggested limited literacy. The case stayed cold, this time for another fourteen years. Then, yet again, the killer resurfaced to publish more of his thoughts—a lot more.

Over the period of several days in 2004, fourteen years after having left his last piece of writing on the barn, April's killer returned to the city of Fort Wayne, where he had kidnapped her in 1988. He then composed four new letters on yellow, lined paper and left them at various locations throughout the city, including in the mailboxes of homes with small children and even in the basket of a young girl's bicycle, where it sat in front of her house. To make it clear that the notes weren't hoaxes written by a copycat, and that he was in fact April's killer, the author went so far as to seal two of the notes in plastic baggies along with a used condom in one of the bags. The DNA on the condom was later found to match the DNA left at the original murder scene, which had been entered into the DNA database by police. The cowardly pedophile was not only sadistically aroused by the terror and panic he was sowing but also obsessed with prolonging media coverage of his crimes. Like the Zodiac before him, the letters became an end in themselves.

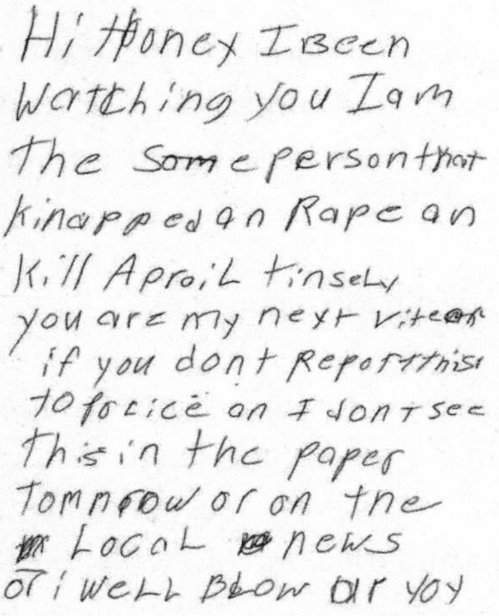

Fig. 5.10. A partial copy of one of four hand-written notes delivered, along with a used condom in one case to various Fort Wayne addresses in 2004. All of the notes consisted of generally the same content and keywords, including recurring and apparently deliberate misspellings, like in the 1990 barn-door scrawl.

The notes consisted of the same general overtures and threats made against unnamed children as the intended recipients of the writings. Read the full pathetic and twisted plea for attention and predatory taunting, as laid out in the longest of the letters recovered in 2004:

> Hi honey I been watching you I am the same person that kidnapped an rape an kill Aproil Tinsely you are my next victim if you don't report this to police an I don't see this in the paper tommrow or on the local news or I well blow up [your] house killing everyone but you you will be mine. I am the same person are knapped an rape an murder Aprol Tinsley you our next. Ha Ha.[48]

What the maniacal author never realized was that his linguistic errors were so egregious and exaggerated that they painted for police a very specific picture of the type of psychopath he was. So intense was his penchant for theatrics—the paraphiliac need to cause fear and command protracted public attention—that the killer was prepared to take extraordinary risks at revealing himself in order to further his quest for sadistic gratification. The intentionally introduced spelling and grammatical irregularities coupled with the DNA sample constituted a rather precise profile of his identity. One note was also accompanied by a photograph of a tattered bedspread that likely had souvenir value, and it was probably connected to April's murder in 1988. Of all the killers whose writings have been analyzed in this book, this one stands out as the most malignant of narcissists and psychopaths, which exemplifies the twisted Hero archetype perhaps more than any of the other sexual murderers-as-writers we've discussed here.

Just as significant to the offender profile was the number of locations where the killer elected to leave these writings. Unbeknownst to him, these locations, coupled with the 1990 scrawl and the 1988 crime scene, allowed for the application of geographic profiling to complement the use of SCAN analysis.

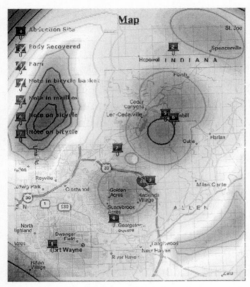

Fig. 5.11. A graphic rendering of the Fort Wayne area after inputting all of the known crime-scene locations attended by the offender between 1988 and 2004. The geo-profiling program, known as RIGEL, overwhelmingly points to the northwest suburb of, ironically, Huntertown, Indiana, as being the home base for April Tinsley's murderer. This includes the likely place of residence of the killer at the time the notes were distributed in 2004. Graphic treatment of RIGEL profile courtesy of Michael Arntfield's Cold Case Society, with special thanks to Peter Leimbigler of the University of Toronto.

Developed by police officer turned criminologist Kim Rossmo, the geo-profiling program, known as RIGEL, has been used to identify the home base of serial killers and serial rapists—the greater the number of data points, the more accurate the estimated residence of an offender.[49] Rooted in geometry and the understanding that all people, including murderers—and especially murderers with access to a vehicle, as in April Tinsley's case—navigate space in only a handful of ways, and the greater the number of times they repeat those steps, the greater the chance that the paths they take—either habitually and instinctively or deliberately to avoid authorities—can be used to extrapolate the location of their home residence. It is interesting that, analogous to literary criminology, Rossmo has developed a comprehensive taxonomy of four offender types who navigate their action spaces and acquire targets in relation to their home bases. These can be summarized as follows.

> *The Hunter*: an offender who targets a specific victim or type of victim in the immediate area of his home base, staying within the action space where he knows the terrain.

The Poacher: a killer on the road, that is, an offender with a great degree of mobility who targets victims—usually of a specific type—while away from his home base, to guarantee his anonymity.

The Troller: an opportunistic and impulsive offender—often disorganized—who will attack whenever and wherever opportunity strikes while he is going about his daily business or when he is marauding around in search of such an opportunity.

The Trapper: often associated with older and more organized offenders, this criminal is synonymous with a deathtrap, or worm-on-a-hook scenario, in which the victim is lured to a specific location and into a premeditated locale for murder.

Today, police have a DNA profile of April's killer that has allowed them to estimate with some degree of accuracy (using an innovative system known as *phenotyping*) what the killer looked like in 1988 and what he looks like today. It's a type of reverse-engineered genetic composite that has also confirmed that the killer's ethnic background is in France. On top of this, they know that he drove a blue pickup truck in 1988; that he likely lived in or passed through Huntertown with regularity en route to the scenes where the writings were left; and that they are dealing with a psychopath, as well as a Hero and Hunter offender type. The killer is highly organized and motivated, and he had likely seen April before that Good Friday when he snatched her. Moreover, there is no question that he killed again in the intervening years. His intermittent absences from the Fort Wayne area likely reflect his being incarcerated for other crimes that have not yet been linked. It is somewhat puzzling why a DNA match has not yet been made, though there are a few scientific and administrative reasons why that might be the case. Either way, he remains out there. The police, presumably, are still working this investigation as hard as they can. The fact that they have, finally, enlisted the assistance of the FBI all but confirms that it remains a priority. However, the geo-profile was sent to them by us, but we have never received an acknowledgement. They are no doubt too busy still following up other leads—now over thirty years after the fact. At least we hope this to be the case. However, sadly, the city's homicide-clearances rate, as filed with the US Justice Department—a baseline performance indicator of how effectively a police department investigates murder cases— suggests otherwise. Never mind the fact that Fort Wayne's murders more than doubled in the five years after the Tinsley murder, the city's clearance rate since 1988 confirms the Fort Wayne police manage to solve only a little more than *half* of its murders, on average.

The murders discussed previously all underscore how powerful an investigative tool SCAN can be in the detection and solution of crimes. In keeping with the theme of this final chapter, it also leads us to believe that murder does not occur solely in the individual mind; it is connected to history, culture, and possibly evolutionary genetics. The murderers all seem to react instinctually to either their impulses or their motivations, be they revenge, lust or envy, or some other emotional source. Murder has a long history behind it, and it continues to play a much-too-dominant role in human life.

THOU SHALT NOT KILL

Many homicide detectives summarize the reasons for murder in three words: sex, money, revenge. All three have a forbidden command-ment or deadly sin associated with them. At the dawn of civilization, we combined these into a master commandment: Thou shalt not kill. It is an interdiction that comes from deep inside us. Murderers like Herring or Read clearly ignored this primary commandment, inner voice, or whatever else we might want to call it. Why they did so defies any explanation, including our own as offered in this chapter. Murder is a mystery and will likely remain so. It is relevant to note that the Bible allows for some killings, such as the one we discussed at the beginning of this book, by the heroine Judith. This too is a mystery—we must both kill and not kill. We will never be able to resolve why this is so. We will continue to write about it, though, as if impelled to do so in order to understand it in our own peculiar way.

Our trek through the various tales of murder, as we have called them, led us to realize that whatever lies within us, it provokes murder—the opposite of life and the thirst for life—as a remedy to any host of conditions. The literary approach to murder is akin to that of literary critics who analyze texts of poetry, prose, or drama. It is as revelatory as any forensic or criminological technique. As writer Samuel Butler appropriately put it, "It is our less conscious thoughts and our less conscious actions which mainly mould our lives and the lives of those who spring from us."[51]

Maybe the whole purpose of civilized life is to overcome the instincts, at least the destructive ones. As Albert Einstein put it, "If men as individuals surrender to the call of their elementary instincts, avoiding pain and seeking satisfaction only for their own selves, the result for them all taken together must be a state of insecurity, of fear, and of promiscuous misery."[52] Surely, the commandment "Thou shalt not kill" is a profound warning; if we do kill, in a world where the purge gives way to the urge, we will lose civilization and all the benefits that it has bestowed on us. Maybe and hopefully the dilemma of murder will resolve itself through further evolution. As British writer and travel raconteur W. Winwood Reade so perceptively remarked:

> We live between two worlds; we soar in the atmosphere; we creep upon the soil; we have the aspirations of creators and the propensities of quadrupeds. There can be but one explanation of this fact. We are passing from the animal into a higher form, and the drama of this planet is in its second act.[53]

Let's hope that we are beginning the second act, where murder no longer exists.

NOTES

PROLOGUE: PEN NAMES AND CRIMINAL MINDS

1. Setepenra," *Los Angeles Times*, July 18, 2016, http://www.latimes.com/books/la-et-jc-cosmo-setepenra-books-20160718-snap-story.html (accessed July 25, 2016).

2. Liam Casey, "Nurse Accused of Killing Seniors Posted Dark Poem Written From Perspective of Serial Killer," *National Post*, October 25, 2016, http://news.nationalpost.com/news/canada/nurse-accused-of-killing-seniors-posted-dark-poem-written-from-perspective-of-serial-killer (accessed October 29, 2016)

3. *The Wire*, directed by David Simon, *The Wire: Season 5* (HBO Original Programming, 2008), disc for episodes 3–8.

4. Gareth Norris, "The Evolution of Criminal Profiling: From Whitechapel to Quantico & Beyond," in *Profiling & Serial Crime: Theoretical & Practical Issues*, 3rd ed., edited by Wayne Petherick (Waltham, MA: Academic, 2014), pp. 3–16.

5. Michael Arntfield, "Necrophilia in Literature, Poetry & Narrative Prose," in *Understanding Necrophilia: A Global Multidisciplinary Approach* (San Diego: Cognella Academic Publishing, 2016), pp. 109–20.

6. Jean Rostand, *Pensées d'un Biologiste* (1939), reprinted in *The Substance of Man* (London: Greenwood, 1962), p. 68.

7. Michael Arntfield, *Gothic Forensics: Criminal Investigative Procedure in Victorian Horror & Mystery* (New York: Palgrave-Macmillan, 2016), p. 4.

8. Rita Charon, *Narrative Medicine: Honoring the Stories of Illness* (New York: Oxford University Press, 2008).

CHAPTER 1: THE TALE OF MURDER

1. Richard Slotkin, *Gunfighter Nation: The Myth of the Frontier in Twentieth-Century America* (New York: Macmillan, 1998), p. 655.

2. William Blackstone, *Commentaries on the Laws of England* (London: Clarke and Sons, 1628), p. 47.

3. Eric W. Hickey, *Serial Murderers and Their Victims*, 7th ed. (Boston: Cengage, 2015), pp. 4–5.

4. John E. Douglas, Anne W. Burgess, Allen G. Burgess, and Robert K. Ressler, *Crime Classification Manual: A Standard System for Investigating and Classifying Violent Crime* (New York: Lexington Books, 1992), pp. 12ff.

5. For which, see, Antonio Nicaso and Marcel Danesi, *Made Men: Mafia Culture and the Power of Symbols, Rituals, and Myth* (Lanham: Rowman & Littlefield, 2013).

6. Paul Lunde, *Organized Crime: An Inside Guide to the World's Most Successful Industry* (London: Dorling Kindersley, 2004), p. 57.

7. René Girard, *Violence and the Sacred* (Baltimore: Hopkins Press, 1979).

8. *Wikipedia*, s.v. "Richard Kuklinski," https://en.wikipedia.org/wiki/Richard_Kuklinski (accessed November 2, 2016).

9. Sara Jean Green, "Gunman Sentenced to 29 Years for Killing Wine Steward in August 2012," *Seattle Times*, http://blogs.seattletimes.com/today/2015/01/gunman-sentenced-to-29-years-for-killing-wine-steward-in-aug-2012/ (accessed November 2, 2016).

10. *Wikipedia*, s.v. "Megan's Law," https://en.wikipedia.org/wiki/Megan%27s_Law (accessed November 2, 2016).

11. Adam Gabbatt, "French Woman Admits Killing Six Newborn Babies," *Guardian,* March 15, 2010, https://www.theguardian.com/world/2010/mar/15/french-woman-admits-killing-babies (accessed November 2, 2016).

12. Radhika Sanghani, "My Aunt Died Because Doctors Assumed Domestic Violence Is Normal for Asian Women," *Telegraph*, February 12, 2015, http://www.telegraph.co.uk/women/womens-life/11408535/Asian-women-doctors-assume-domestic-violence-is-normal-for-them.html (accessed November 2, 2016).

13. Michael Arntfield, *Gothic Forensics: Criminal Investigative Procedure in Victorian Horror and Mystery* (New York: Palgrave-Macmillan, 2016).

14. Christine A. Jackson, *The Tell-Tale Art: Poe in Modern Popular Culture* (Jefferson, NC: McFarland, 2012).

15. Elizabeth Merrill, "The Woman Forever Tied to Steve McNair," *ESPN* July 4, 2010 http://www.espn.com/blog/afcsouth/post/_/id/12757/the-woman-forever-tied-to-steve-mcnair (accessed November 1, 2016)

16. *Wikipedia*, s.v. "Beltway Sniper Attacks," https://en.wikipedia.org/wiki/Beltway_sniper_attacks (accessed November 2, 2016).

17. Gideon Long, "Daniel Zamudio: The Homophobic Murder That Changed Chile," *BBC News*, October 29, 2013, http://www.bbc.com/news/world-middle-east-24722180 (accessed November 2, 2016).

18. Fyodor Dostoyevsky, *Notes from the Underground* (New York: Vintage Classics, 1994), p. 1.

19. *Wikipedia*, s.v. "Mont Vernon Murder," https://en.wikipedia.org/wiki/ Mont_Vernon_Murder (accessed November 2, 2016).

20. *Wikipedia*, s.v. "List of Alleged *Natural Born Killers* Copycat Crimes," https://en.wikipedia.org/wiki/List_of_alleged_Natural_Born_Killers_copycat _crimes (accessed November 2, 2016).

21. Cited in Jeff Guinn and Douglas Perry, *The Sixteenth Minute: Life In the Aftermath of Fame* (New York: Jeremy F. Tarcher / Penguin, 2005), p. 4.

22. "Bernhard Goetz," *Alchetron*, last modified August 31, 2016, http:// alchetron.com/Bernhard-Goetz-572264-W (accessed September 15, 2016).

23. Marcel Mauss, "Les techniques du corp," *Journal de Psychologie* 32 (1934): 3–4.

24. Karl Marx, *Economic & Philosophic Manuscripts of 1844* (1844; repr., Moscow: Progress Publishers, 1944).

25. Emile Durkheim, *The Elementary Forms of Religious Life* (New York: Collier, 1912).

26. Phil Chalmers, *Inside the Mind of a Teen Killer* (New York: Nelson, 2010).

27. Steve Clemons, "'We Were Bored . . So We Decided to Kill Somebody," *Atlantic*, August 20, 2013, http://www.theatlantic.com/national/archive/2013/08/we -were-bored-so-we-decided-to-kill-somebody/278858/ (accessed November 2, 2016).

28. Cesare Lombroso, *L'uomo delinquente* (Milano: Hoepli, 1876).

29. Genesis 4:3–7.

30. Genesis 4:2–16.

31. Genesis 4:9.

32. *Wikipedia*, s.v. "Inanna," https://en.wikipedia.org/wiki/Inanna (accessed November 2, 2016).

33. Sigmund Freud, "Instincts and Their Vicissitudes," in *The Standard Edition of the Complete Psychological Works of Sigmund Freud*, vol. 14, *1914– 1916: On the History of the Psycho-Analytic Movement, Papers on Metapsychology and Other Works* (London: Hogarth, 1957), pp. 109–40.

34. 1 John 3:15.

35. Aristotle, *Poetics* (written 335 BCE), in *The Works of Aristotle*, vol. 11, edited by W. D. Ross (Oxford: Clarendon, 1952).

36. Euripides, *Medea*, trans. E. P. Coleridge, http://classics.mit.edu/Euripides/ medea.html (accessed November 2, 2016).

37. John Gottman and Nan Silver, *What Makes Love Last?* (New York: Simon and Schuster, 2013), p. 14.

38. Sophocles, *Oedipus the King*, trans. F. Storr, http://classics.mit.edu/ Sophocles/oedipus.html (accessed November 2, 2016).

39. Ralph Waldo Emerson, *The Annotated Emerson* (1844; repr., Cambridge: Harvard University Press, 2012), p. 243.

40. Euripides, *Medea*.

41. St. Augustine discusses the notion of free will extensively in his *De Libero Arbitrio*, trans. Dom Mark Pontifex (Westminster: Newman, 1955).

42. The tale comes from the work of Sir Thomas Malory, *The Winchester Malory: A Facsimile* (London: Early English Text Society, 1976).

43. Dante, *The Divine Comedy, Inferno* (New York: Vintage Classics, 2013), circle 2, canto 4.

44. William Shakespeare, *Romeo and Juliet*, I.5, http://shakespeare.mit.edu/romeo_juliet/full.html (accessed November 2, 2016).

45. William Shakespeare, *The Tragedy of Hamlet, Prince of Denmark*, 1.5.31–37, http://shakespeare.mit.edu/hamlet/full.html (accessed November 2, 2016).

46. Arntfield, *Gothic Forensics*.

47. Ronald R. Thomas, *Detective Fiction and the Rise of Forensic Science* (Cambridge: Cambridge University Press, 1999).

48. Oscar Wilde, *Intentions* (London: Methuen, 1891), p. 94.

49. Philip Simpson, *Psycho Paths: Tracking the Serial Killer through Contemporary American Film and Fiction* (Chicago: Southern Illinois University Press, 2000), p. 31.

50. Michael Arntfield, *Gothic Forensics: Criminal Investigative Procedure in Victorian Horror & Mystery* (New York: Palgrave-Macmillan, 2016)

51. Richard von Krafft-Ebing, *Psychopathia Sexualis* (Stuttgart: Ferdinand Enke, 1886).

52. David Canter and Donna Youngs, *Investigative Psychology: Offender Profiling and the Analysis of Criminal Action* (Hoboken, NJ: Wiley, 2009).

53. William Shakespeare, *As You Like It*, II.7.1, http://shakespeare.mit.edu/asyoulikeit/full.html (accessed November 2, 2016).

54. Associated Press, "US Serial Killer Richard Ramirez Dies in Hospital," *Guardian*, June 7, 2013, https://www.theguardian.com/world/2013/jun/07/richard-ramirez-night-stalker-dies (accessed June 4, 2016).

55. "Charles Manson—Love of Bees—5-9-2013," YouTube video, 5:25, posted by "ATWARwithlies" on May 11, 2013, http://www.youtube.com/watch?v=puWmSC-RmRg (accessed November 14, 2016).

56. Vincent Bugliosi, *Helter Skelter: The True Story of the Manson Murders* (New York: W. W. Norton, 2001).

57. *Murderpedia*, s.v. "Pedro Alonzo López," http://murderpedia.org/male.L/l/lopez-pedro.htm (accessed November 14, 2016). Laytner's interviews

were published in the *Chicago Tribune* on Sunday, July 13, 1980, and in the *Toronto Sun* and the *Sacramento Bee* on July 21, 1980.

58. Ibid.

59. Ibid.

60. David A. Lieb, "Mo. Teen Gets Life, with Possible Parole, for Killing 9-Year-Old Girl," Associated Press, February 8, 2012, http://bangordailynews .com/2012/02/08/news/nation/mo-teen-gets-life-with-possible-parole-for-killing -9-year-old-girl/ (accessed October 27, 2016).

61. Daily Mail Reporter, "'I Just F***ing Killed Someone and It was Ahmazing': The Sick Diary Entries of Teen Who Strangled and Stabbed Neighbor, 9," *Daily Mail*, February 7, 2012, http://www.dailymail.co.uk/news/ article-2097307/Alyssa-Bustamante-sentence-Missouri-teens-diary-says-killing -Elizabeth-Olten-felt-ahmazing.html (accessed November 2, 2016).

62. Friedrich Nietzsche, *Beyond Good and Evil* (New York: Dover Publications, 1997), chap. 9.

63. Rachel Eddie, "'We Were All Drunk and She'd F***ing Seen All of Us . . . So I Cut Her': Listen to Anita Cobby's Killer John Travers Confess to Raping and Murdering Her in Never Before Heard Tape," *Daily Mail* (Australia), February 8, 2016, http://www.dailymail.co.uk/news/article-3437303/Listen-Anita-Cobby-s -killer-John-Travers-confess-gang-rape-murder-tape.html (accessed November 2, 2016).

64. Keegan Kyle and Tony Saavedra, "Grand Jury Transcripts: Prosecutors Say Gruesome Text Messages Reveal Suspects' Plan to Kill Prostitute," *Orange County Register*, November 24, 2014, http://www.ocregister.com/articles/gordon -643341-cano-jackson.html (accessed November 1, 2016).

65. Raymond Chandler, "The Simple Act of Murder," *Atlantic Monthly*, December 1944.

66. John Dickie, *Cosa Nostra: A History of the Sicilian Mafia* (London: Hodder and Stoughton, 2004), p. 11.

67. George F. Will, *Statecraft as Soulcraft: What Government Does* (New York: Touchstone, 1984), p. 30.

68. Robert Grimminck, "10 Chilling Social Media Confessions to Murder," *Listverse*, August 26, 2016, http://listverse.com/2015/08/26/10-chilling-social -media-confessions-to-murder/ (accessed November 14, 2016).

69. Jacob Rogers, Facebook post [personal page], ca. 2015, at http://www .facebook.com/jacobrogers453 (accessed August 31, 2016; site discontinued).

70. Kashawn Hines, Facebook post [personal page], ca. 2012, at http://www .facebook.com/hines754453 (accessed August 31, 2016; site discontinued).

71. Rosemarie Farid, Facebook video, June 30, 2014, https://www.facebook

.com/rosemarie.farid, cited in "Alleged Murderer Uses Social Media to Brag about Beating Man," *CBS Miami*, July 7, 2014, http://miami.cbslocal.com/2014/07/07/alleged-murderer-uses-social-media-to-brag-about-beating-man/ (accessed November 2, 2016).

72. Dee Gyp Blancharde, Facebook post [personal page], June 14, 2015, https://www.facebook.com/deegyp.blancharde/posts/10206865671021262?pnref=story (accessed November 2, 2016)

73. For example, Marshall McLuhan, *Understanding Media: The Extensions of Man* (Cambridge: MIT Press, 1964).

74. "Murder-Suicide Facebook Post: Nancy Lopez Calls Fort Wayne, Ind., Police after Seeing Bart Heller's Status," *Huffington Post*, December 12, 2012, http://www.huffingtonpost.com/2011/12/12/murder-suicide-facebook-p_n_1143358.html (accessed November 2, 2016).

75. Girard, *Violence and the Sacred*, p. 23.

76. *The Perfect Husband: The Laci Peterson Story*, TV movie directed by Roger Young (October 26, 2004); Catherine Crier, *A Deadly Game: The Untold Story of the Scott Peterson Investigation* (New York: William Morrow, 2006).

77. Barbara A. Oakley, *Evil Genes* (New York: Prometheus Books, 2008).

78. Quoted in Leland E. Hinsie and Robert Jean Campbell, *Psychiatric Dictionary* (New York: Oxford University Press, 1970), p. 372.

79. Bill James, *Popular Crime: Reflections on the Celebration of Violence* (New York: Scribner, 2011).

80. Joseph de Maistre, *The Works of Joseph de Maistre*, edited by Jack Lively (1821; repr., New York: Macmillan, 1965).

CHAPTER 2: THIS IS THE ZODIAC SPEAKING

1. Adam Karlin, "11 Creepy Serial Killer Quotes," Lineup, 2016, http://www.the-line-up.com/serial-killer-quotes/ (accessed October 27, 2016).

2. There are, of course, various theories. See, for example, Gary Stewart's book, *The Most Dangerous Animal of All* (New York: Harper, 2015), in which he argues that it was Earl Van Best Jr., his biological father, who died in 1984.

3. All typos and grammatical errors in this letter (and others in this book) are not corrected, since these are also part of the style or narrative of the writer, or else reveal something about his or her background.

4. David Schmid, *Natural Born Celebrities: Serial Killers in American Culture* (Chicago: University of Chicago Press, 2005).

5. Carl Jung, *The Portable Jung* (Harmondsworth: Penguin, 1971), p. 12.

6. Michael Arntfield, *Murder City: The Untold Story of Canada's Serial Killer Capital* (Victoria: Friesen Press, 2015).

7. From Mike G. Aamodt, "Serial Killer Statistics," Radford University/FGCU Serial Killer Database, November 23, 2015, http://maamodt.asp.radford.edu/serial killer information center/project description.htm (accessed April 19, 2016).

8. Murder Accountability Project, "Clearance Rates," murderdata.org (accessed November 3, 2016).

9. Allan Branson "African American Serial Killers: Overrepresented but Underacknowledged," *Howard Journal of Crime and Justice* 52, no. 1 (2013): 1–18.

10. Murder Accountability Project, "Charts & Maps," murderdata.org (accessed November 3, 2016).

11. Eric Hickey, *Serial Murderers and Their Victims*, 7th ed. (Boston: Cengage Learning, 2016), p.273.

12. Michael Arntfield, *Mad City: The True Story of the Campus Murders That America Forgot* (New York: Little A Books, 2016).

13. Erik Larson, *The Devil in the White City: Murder, Magic and Madness at the Fair That Changed America* (New York: Crown, 2002).

14. Michael Arntfield, *Practical Criminology* (Toronto: Nelson, 2017).

15. Kieran Crowley, *Sleep My Little Dead: The True Story of the Zodiac Killer* (New York: St. Martin's, 1997).

16. Cited in *CrimeZZZnet*, s.v. "Seda, Heriberto," http://www.crimezzz.net/serialkillers/S/SEDA_heriberto.htm (accessed November 4, 2016).

17. Gary Ridgway, confession text, November 2003, reported by the Associated Press; transcript can be found at "Green River Killer Confession: Text," BBC News, November 5, 2003, http://news.bbc.co.uk/2/hi/americas/3245301.stm (accessed August 1, 2016).

18. Gary Ridgway, as reported in "Green River Killer Confesses: 'I Killed So Many Women I Have a Hard Time Keeping Them Straight," *Seattle Post-Intelligencer*, November 4, 2003, http://www.seattlepi.com/local/article/Green-River-Killer-confesses-1128925.php (accessed November 15, 2016).

19. Statements made in Leavensworth Federal Penitentiary in 1930, as found in many sources, including *Murderpedia*, s.v. "Carl Panzram," http://murderpedia.org/male.P/p/panzram-carl.htm (most quotes are no longer available, as they have been taken down).

20. Schmid, *Natural Born Celebrities*.

21. Cited in "The BTK Strangler Serial Killer Poems by Dennis Rader," http://www.freewebs.com/thebtksite/raderletters.htm (accessed November 4, 2016).

22. Ibid.

23. Alfred Loeb, as quoted in the Clarence Darrow Digital Collection, University of Minnesota Law Library, "Friedrich Wilhelm Nietzsche (1844–1900)," http://darrow.law.umn.edu/photo.php?pid=862 (accessed October 27, 2016).

24. Words spoken by Angel Maturino Reséndiz, after a Houston judge ruled that Reséndiz was mentally competent to be executed, on June 21, 2006 (cited in *The Evil Within: A Top Murder Squad Detective Reveals The Chilling True Stories of the World's Most Notorious Killers*, by Trevor Marriott [London: John Blake, Amazon Digital Services, 2013]).

25. Cited in Hadness Fontenot, *Killer Quotes: Quotes from Serial Killers* (Munich: BookRix, GMBH, 2015).

26. Ibid.

27. Albert Fish, "Albert Fish Quotes," *AZQuotes*, http://www.azquotes.com/author/40485-Albert_Fish (accessed November 4, 2016).

28. Hickey *Serial Murderers and Their Victims*, p. 203.

29. H. H. Holmes, cited in Harold Schechter, *Depraved* (New York: Pocket Star, 1994).

30. Tom Philbin, *I, Monster: Serial Killers in Their Own Chilling Words* (New York: Prometheus Books, 2011).

31. Robert Bartholomew, "The Great Clown Scare of 2016," *Psychology Today*, October 7, 2016, https://www.psychologytoday.com/blog/its-catching/201610/the-great-clown-scare-2016 (accessed November 5, 2016).

32. Cited in *Wikiquote* (unsourced), "Talk: John Wayne Gacy," last modified February 28, 2016, https://en.wikiquote.org/wiki/Talk:John_Wayne_Gacy (accessed November 15, 2016).

33. Cited in "I Knew I Was Sick or Evil," *Chicago Tribune*, February 18, 1992, http://articles.chicagotribune.com/1992-02-18/news/9201150876_1_jeffrey-dahmer-dahmer-case-insanity-defenses (accessed November 15, 2016).

34. From "Jeffrey Dahmer Quotes," http://www.azquotes.com/author/37830-Jeffrey_Dahmer (accessed November 4, 2016); and "Serial Killer Quotes," SerialKillerCalendar.com, http://www.serialkillercalendar.com/Serial-Kilelr-quotes.html (accessed November 15, 2016).

35. Cited in Carlton Smith, *The BTK Murders: Inside the "Bind Torture Kill" Case That Terrified America's Heartland* (New York: St. Martin's, 2006), p. 78.

36. Michael Arntfield, *Gothic Forensics: Criminal Investigative Procedure in Victorian Horror & Mystery* (New York: Palgrave Macmillan, 2016), pp. 26–27.

37. Cited in Dirk Cameron Gibson, *Clues from Killers' Serial Murder and Crime Scene Messages* (Westport: Praeger, 2004), p. 28.

38. Michael Newton, *Hunting Humans: An Encyclopedia of Modern Serial Killers* (New York: Breakout Productions, 1990), p. 312.

39. Cited in Gibson, *Clues from Killers' Serial Murder and Crime Scene Messages*, pp. 13–14.

40. Chris McNab, *Serial Killer Timelines* (Berkeley: Ulysses, 2010), p. 117.

41. Cited in "Murderous Love: Why Are So Many Women Aroused by Serial Killers?" *Telegraph*, February 27, 2014, http://www.telegraph.co.uk/women/womens-life/10665003/Murderous-love-Why-are-so-many-women-aroused-by-serial-killers.html (accessed November 4, 2016).

42. Barry Bearak, "Bundy Is Executed as Crowd of 500 Cheers," *Los Angeles Times*, January 25, 1989, http://articles.latimes.com/1989-01-25/news/mn-992_1_ted-bundy (accessed November 6, 2016)

43. Ibid., p. 41.

44. Hervey Cleckley, *The Mask of Sanity: An Attempt to Clarify Some Issues about the So-Called Psychopathic Personality* (Maryland Heights: Mosby, 1941). Fifth edition facsimile reprinted in 1988 by Emily Cleckley.

45. Cited in "Theodore Robert Bundy #106: Clark County Prosecuting Attorney," Clark Prosecutor, http://www.clarkprosecutor.org/html/death/US/bundy106.htm (accessed November 15, 2016).

46. Ted Bundy, interviewed by James Dobson for the Meese Commission, Florida State Prison, "Ted Bundy's Final Interview," January 23, 1989. A transcript of the interview can be found at "A Transcript of Ted Bundy's Final Interview," uploaded by Tiffany Princep, Academia, http://www.academia.edu/4921305/A_Transcript_of_Ted_Bundys_Final_Interview (accessed October 27, 2016).

47. Gary Lachman, *Turn Off Your Mind: The Mystic Sixties and the Dark Side of the Age of Aquarius* (New York: Disinformation Books, 2001), p. 396.

48. Ibid., p. 397.

49. Andrei Chikatilo, statement in court made before Judge Leonid Akubzhanov, cited in Moira Martingale *Cannibal Killers: The History of Impossible Murderers* (1993; repr., New York: St. Martin's, 1995), p. 175. First published in London by Robert Hale Limited.

50. A good account of vampire killers is the one by Sondra London, *True Vampires: Blood-Sucking Killers Past and Present* (Los Angeles: Feral House, 2013).

51. Newton, *Hunting Humans*.

52. For a summary of the relevant research, see Marcel Danesi, *Signs of Crime: Introducing Forensic Semiotics* (Berlin: Mouton de Gruyter, 2013), pp. 93–97.

53. Richard Ramirez, bragging to others in jail, cited in "Richard Ramirez Quotes," *Quote Authors*, http://www.quoteauthors.com/richard-ramirez-quotes/ (accessed November 4, 2106).

54. Richard Ramirez, statement to Deputy Sheriff Jim Ellis, cited in ibid.

55. Hickey *Serial Murderers and Their Victims*, pp. 313–18.

56. Peter Vronsky, *Female Serial Killers: How and Why Women Become Monsters* (New York: Berkley, 2007).

57. Tony Thorne, *Countess Dracula: The Life and Times of the Blood Countess, Elisabeth Báthory* (London: Bloomsbury, 1998), p. 3.

58. Cited in the film *Aileen: Life and Death of a Serial Killer*, directed by Nick Broomfield and Joan Churchill (Lafayette Films, 2003). For more information, see "Aileen: Life and Death of a Serial Killer," IMDb, http://www.imdb.com/title/tt0364930/?ref_=ttqt_qt_tt (accessed October 27, 2016).

59. Cited in "Arthur Shawcross Quotes," *AZ Quotes*, http://www.azquotes.com/quote/904900 (accessed November 4, 2016).

60. Cited in Mikhail Krivich and Ol'gert Ol'gin *Comrade Chikatilo: Russia's Most Notorious Serial Killer* (Los Angeles: Graymalkin Media, 1992).

61. McNab, *Serial Killer Timelines*, p. 16.

62. Ibid.

63. Cited in Krivich and Ol'gin, *Comrade Chikatilo*.

64. Hickey *Serial Murderers and Their Victims*, p. 172.

65. Cited in *Wikipedia*, s.v. "Ed Gein," last updated October 9, 2015, https://simple.wikipedia.org/wiki/Ed_Gein (accessed November 15, 2016).

66. Cited in Colin Wilson and Donald Seaman, *The Serial Killers: A Study in the Psychology of Violence* (New York: Virgin, 2007), p. 72.

67. "Edmund Kemper: The Co-Ed Killer," Crime & Investigation Network, http://www.crimeandinvestigation.co.uk/crime-files/edmund-kemper (accessed October 27, 2016).

68. Edmund Kemper, statement in court, cited in "Edmund Kemper Quotes," *AZ Quotes*, http://www.azquotes.com/author/42856-Edmund_Kemper (accessed November 15, 2016).

69. Cited in Lawrie Reznek, *Evil or Ill? Justifying the Insanity Defence* (London: Routledge, 1997), p. 213.

70. David Canter, *Criminal Shadows: Inside the Mind of the Serial Killer* (New York: HarperCollins, 1994).

71. Peter Vronksy, *Serial Killers: The Method and Madness of Monsters* (New York: Berkley, 2004), p. 31.

72. Mark Seltzer, *True Crime: Observations on Modernity* (New York: Routledge, 2007), p. 9.

73. *Se7en*, directed by David Fincher (New Line Cinema in the United States, 1995).

CHAPTER 3: DARK ODYSSEYS

1. Elliot Rodger, "My Twisted World: The Story of Elliot Rodger," May 2014, available at http://abclocal.go.com/three/kabc/kabc/My-Twisted-World.pdf (accessed May 20, 2016).

2. Ibid.

3. James A. Fox and Jack Levin, *Extreme Killing: Understanding Serial and Mass Murder* 3rd ed. (Los Angeles: Sage, 2015), p. xii.

4. Susan Scutti, "Why Millennials Are Having Less Sex than Generation Xers," *CNN*, August 16, 2016, http://www.cnn.com/2016/08/02/health/millennials-less-sex-than-gen-x/ (accessed November 9, 2016).

5. Ronald M. Holmes and Stephen T. Holmes, *Profiling Violent Crimes: An Investigative Tool*, 4th ed. (Thousand Oaks, CA: Sage, 2009); Ronald M. Holmes and Stephen T. Holmes, "Understanding Mass Murder: A Starting Point," *Federal Probation* 56 (1992): 53–61.

6. John Olsson, *Word Crime: Solving Crime through Forensic Linguistics* (London: Continuum, 2009), p. 55.

7. Ibid.

8. Cited in the *Texas Monthly* 14, no. 8 (August 1986): 169.

9. George Hennard, in a letter written to Jill Fritz and Jana Jemigan, as cited in Paula Chin, "A Texas Massacre: George Hennard's Mounting Fury—and the Lives of 23 Victims—Ends in a Rampage That Became a Texas Massacre," *People* 36, no. 17 (November 4, 1991), http://www.people.com/people/archive/article/0,,20111193,00.html (accessed October 26, 2016).

10. Theodore Millon, *Disorders of Personality*, 3rd ed. (Hoboken, NJ: Wiley, 2011).

11. Rodger, "My Twisted World."

12. "James Holmes Files," Tumblr blog, 2013, http://james-holmes-files.tumblr.com/post/55563049910/james-holmes-online-dating-profiles-adult (accessed May 29, 2016).

13. Michael Arntfield and Joan Swart, "The X-Factor: Corporate & Occupational Psychopathy in Law Enforcement Management & the Operational Impact on Cold Case Homicides," *Journal of Cold Case Review* 1 (2015): 50–68.

14. Cited in Christopher Dorner, "Christopher Dorner's Manifesto (Disturbing Content and Language)," posted by Kennedy Ryan, *KTLA 5 News*, February 13, 2013, http://ktla.com/2013/02/12/read-christopher-dorners-so-called-manifesto/ (accessed November 15, 2016).

15. James A. Fox and Jack Levin, *Extreme Killing: Understanding Serial and Mass Murder*, 3rd ed. (Thousand Oaks, CA: Sage, 2015).

16. Michael W. Chapman, "Sandy Hook Killer Had 'Movie Depicting Man/ Boy Relationship' on His PC," *CSN News*, January 30, 2014, http://www.cnsnews .com/news/article/michael-w-chapman/sandy-hook-killer-had-movie-depicting -manboy-relationship-his-pc (accessed August 1, 2016).

17. Pamela Engel, "Adam Lanza Had Files about Pedophilia and Other Disturbing Content on His Computer," *Business Insider*, January 2, 2014, http:// www.businessinsider.com/adam-lanza-had-files-about-pedophilia-2014-1   (accessed August 2, 2016).

18. Fox and Levin, *Extreme Killing*.

19. Yair Neuman, Dan Assaf, Yochai Cohen, and James L. Knoll, "Profiling School Shooters: Automatic Text-Based Analysis," *Frontiers in Psychiatry* 6, no. 86 (June 3, 2015), http://www.ncbi.nlm.nih.gov/pmc/articles/PMC4453266/ (accessed September 9, 2016).

20. James P. McGee and Caren R. DeBernardo, "The Classroom Avenger: A Behavioral Profile of School-Based Shootings," *Forensic Examiner* 8 (1999):16–18.

21. Mary E. O'Toole, *The School Shooter: A Threat Assessment Perspective* (Quantico, VA: Critical Incident Response Group, National Center for the Analysis of Violent Crime, FBI Academy, 2000).

22. Neuman et al., "Profiling School Shooters."

23. Cited in M. Alex Johnson, "Gunman Sent Package to NBC News," *MSNBC*, April 19, 2007, http://www.nbcnews.com/id/18195423#.V9UrcUsxH8s (accessed September 11, 2016).

24. See William van Ornum, "The Secret Service on Preventing School Violence," *National Review*, December 2012, http://www.nationalreview.com/ corner/335825/secret-service-preventing-school-violence-william-van-ornum (accessed October 3, 2016).

25. Eric W. Hickey, *Serial Murderers and Their Victims*, 7th ed. (Boston: Cengage, 2015).

26. Dave Cullen, *Columbine* (New York: Hachette Book Group, 2009).

27. Ibid.

28. Fox and Levin, *Extreme Killing*.

29. Donna Youngs, David Canter, and Nikki Carthy, "The Offender's Narrative: Unresolved Dissonance in Life as a Film (LAAF) Responses," *Legal and Criminological Psychology* 21 (2016): 251–65.

30. Cullen, *Columbine*.

31. Hickey, *Serial Murderers*, p. 287.

32. Hickey, *Serial Murderers*.

33. Jack Anderson, "Broken Cookies Vex Death Row Serial Killer," *Warsaw*

Times-Union, February 19, 1997, https://news.google.com/newspapers?id=J6U _AAAAIBAJ&sjid=WFYMAAAAIBAJ&dq=&pg=3520%2C4031941 (accessed November 10, 2016).

34. Hickey, *Serial Murderers*, pp. 302–303.

35. Don Lasseter, *Die for Me: The Terrifying True Story of the Charles Ng and Leonard Lake Torture Murders* (New York: Pinnacle Books, 2000).

36. Hickey, *Serial Murderers*.

37. Ibid.

38. Citations from various sources, including, YouTube, https://www .youtube.com/watch?v=DzSJQ2-hI0A (this video is "private" and is not available for public viewing; Patrick Bellamy, "Charles Ng: Cheating Death," in crimelibrary, February 9, 2015, http://web.archive.org/web/20150209235111/ http://www.crimelibrary.com/serial_killers/predators/ng/call_1.html (accessed September 11, 2016); and *Murderpedia*, s.v. "Leonard Lake," http://murderpedia .org/male.L/l/lake-leonard.htm (accessed November 15, 2016).

39. Grover Maurice Godwin, *Hunting Serial Predators*, 2nd ed. (Boston: Jones and Bartlett Publishers, 2008), p. 210.

40. Edwin H. Sutherland and David R. Cressey, *Principles of Criminology*, 10th ed. (Philadelphia: Lippincott, 1978).

CHAPTER 4: HYPERTEXT #HOMICIDE

1. Cited in Basil Kates, "FBI Arrests New York Cop for Plan to Cook, Eat Women," *Reuters*, October 25, 2012, http://news.nationalpost.com/news/ fbi-charges-new-york-cop-for-plan-to-cook-eat-women (accessed November 2, 2016).

2. Michael Arntfield, "New Media and Necrophilia," in *Understanding Necrophilia: A Global Multidisciplinary Approach* (San Diego: Academic Publishing, 2016).

3. Michael Arntfield, "Cybercrime & Cyberdeviance," in *Criminology: A Canadian Perspective*, 8th ed. (Toronto: Nelson Education, 2017), pp. 500–17.

4. Jean Baudrillard, *Simulations* (New York: Semiotext(e), 1983).

5. Dareh Gregorian, Robert Gearty, Joanna Molloy, and Frank Miller, "Cannibal Cop Gilberto Valle Faces Life in Prison after Jury Finds Him Guilty of Conspiracy to Kidnap and Illegal Use of Federal Databases," *New York Daily News*, March 12, 2013, http://www.nydailynews.com/new-york/cannibal-faces -life-guilty-conspiracy-kidnap-illegal-databases-article-1.1286075 (accessed November 2, 2016).

6. "NY Policeman Gilberto Valle Acquitted in Cannibal Plot," BBC News, July 1, 2014, http://www.bbc.com/news/world-us-canada-28113850 (accessed November 2, 2016).

7. Cited in "Accused NYPD 'Cannibal Cop' Gilberto Valle: Facebook Postings, Instant Messages Paint Picture of Twisted Mind," *New York Daily News*, October 24, 2012, http://www.nydailynews.com/new-york/mind-accused -cannibal-article-1.1192701 (accessed November 2, 2016).

8. William Gibson, *Neuromancer* (London: Grafton, 1984), p. 67.

9. Michael Benedikt, *Cyberspace: First Steps* (Cambridge: MIT Press, 1991), p. 1.

10. Richard Dawkins, *The Selfish Gene* (Oxford: Oxford University Press, 1976).

11. See *R. v. Sharpe* (2001) 1 S.C.R. 45, 2001 SCC 2.

12. *Thought Crimes: The Case of the Cannibal Cop*, directed by Erin Lee Carr (New York, NY: HBO, 2015).

13. Eric Kraepelin, *Psychiatrie: Ein Lehrbuch für Studierende und Ärzte*, 7th ed., vol. 2, *Klinische Psychiatrie* (Leipzig: Verlag Barth, 1904).

14. Hervey Cleckley, *The Mask of Sanity: An Attempt to Clarify Some Issues about the So-Called Psychopathic Personality* (Maryland Heights: Mosby, 1941). Fifth edition facsimile reprinted in 1988 by Emily Cleckley.

15. Robert Hare, *Psychopathy: Theory & Research* (New York: Wiley, 1970).

16. Robert Hare, *The Hare Psychopathy Checklist: Revised* (Toronto: Multi-Health Systems, 1970); and Robert Hare, *Without Conscience: The Disturbing World of Psychopaths among Us* (New York: Guilford, 1998).

17. Canadian Broadcasting Corporation, "The Psychopath Next Door," *Doc Zone* (original air date: November 27, 2014).

18. Theodore Millon and Roger Davis, *Disorders of Personality: DSM IV and Beyond* (Hoboken, NJ: Wiley, 1996).

19. Ibid.

20. Michael Arntfield and Joan Swart, "The X-Factor: Corporate and Occupational Psychopathy in Law Enforcement Management and Its Operational Impact on Cold Case Homicides," *Journal of Cold Case Review* 1 (2015): 50–68.

21. James Ellroy, *My Dark Places* (New York: Vintage, 1997).

22. Michael Arntfield, *Murder City: The Untold Story of Canada's Serial Killer Capital, 1959–1984* (Victoria: Friesen Press, 2015).

23. See Michael Arntfield, "Cybercoprographia: Where Cyberbullying Meets Deviant Fantasy," Michael Arntfield, June 11, 2015, http://michaelarntfield.com/ cybercoprographia-where-cyberbullying-meets-deviant-fantasy/ (accessed June 20, 2016).

24. Arntfield *Murder City*, p. 32.

25. Michael Largo, *Final Exits: The Illustrated Encyclopedia of How We Die* (New York: HarperCollins, 2006).

26. Eric W. Hickey, *Serial Murderers and Their Victims*, 7th ed. (Boston: Cengage, 2015).

27. Ibid., p. 168.

28. "German 'Cannibal' Tells of Regret: A German Accused of Killing and Eating a Man He Met on a Website for Cannibals Has Expressed Regret for His Actions," BBC News, November 23, 2003, http://news.bbc.co.uk/2/hi/europe/3230774.stm (accessed November 1, 2016).

29. Alexandra Zabjek, "Friends Worried about Murder Victim's Date, Twitchell Trial Hears," *Edmonton Journal*, March 20, 2011, http://www.edmontonjournal.com/life/friends+worried+about+murder+victim+date+twitchell+trial+hears/4484524/story.html (accessed June 30, 2016).

30. Cited in Associated Press, "HL: Movie Script Crown Says Alleged Killer Used as a Road Map for Murder," Yahoo News, March 22, 2011, https://www.yahoo.com/news/hl-movie-script-crown-says-alleged-killer-used-20110322-150835-334.html (accessed July 13, 2016).

31. Ibid.

32. John Olsson, *Forensic Linguistics: An Introduction to Language, Crime and the Law*, 2nd ed. (London: Continuum, 2008).

33. Cited in Rob Kovitz, *According to Plan* (Winnipeg: Treyf Books, 2014), p. 587.

34. Credit for the term "multiple-event killer" goes to Professor Michael Aamodt at Radford University and Enzo Yaksic of the Murder Accountability Project, both of whom are also members of the Northeastern University Atypical Homicide Research Group along with author Arntfield.

35. Sarah Dean, "Serial Killer Posed as One of His Victims with Eerie Hotel California Facebook Post," *Daily Mail*, November 8, 2016, http://www.dailymail.co.uk/news/article-3917344/Did-South-Carolina-serial-killer-post-woman-s-dead-boyfriend-Facebook-Kidnapper-shared-Hotel-California-lyrics-online-referencing-song-creepy-Amazon-reviews.html (accessed November 11, 2016).

36. Tim Stelloh, "Blacker Than My Soul: Alarming Amazon Reviews Linked to Alleged S.C. Serial Killer Todd Kohlhepp," *NBC News*, November 7, 2016, http://www.nbcnews.com/news/us-news/blacker-my-soul-alarming-amazon-reviews-linked-alleged-sc-killer-n679231 (accessed November 11, 2016).

37. Dawkins, *Selfish Gene*.

38. Bradley E. Wiggins and G. Bret Bowers, "Memes as Genre: A Structurational Analysis of the Memescape," *New Media & Society* 17 (2015): 1886–1906.

39. For an overview of forensic semiotic theory, see Marcel Danesi, *Signs of Crime: Introducing Forensic Semiotics* (Berlin: Mouton de Gruyter, 2013).

40. Benedict Anderson, *Imagined Communities: Reflections on the Origin and Spread of Nationalism* (London: Verso, 1983).

41. Associated Press, "Dylann Storm Roof, Alleged Charleston Gunman, Had Confederate Flag, but Friends Didn't Think He Was Racist," *National Post*, June 18, 2015, http://news.nationalpost.com/news/world/dylann-storm-roof-alleged -charleston-gunman-had-confederate-flag-but-friends-didnt-think-he-was-racist (accessed November 21, 2016).

42. Ibid.

43. The webpage has since been taken down, but the image Roof used (illegally) appears to be a still from a 1992 film titled *Romper Stomper*, produced by Film Victoria.

44. Ibid.

45. Cited in Brendan O'Connor, "Here Is What Appears to Be Dylann Roof's Racist Manifesto," *Gawker*, June 20, 2015, http://gawker.com/here-is-what-appears -to-be-dylann-roofs-racist-manifest-1712767241 (accessed July 19, 2016).

46. Cited in *Wikipedia*, s.v. "Fourteen Words," last modified on September 6, 2016, https://en.wikipedia.org/wiki/Fourteen_Words (accessed July 19, 2016).

47. Ibid.

48. Laura Collman, "Orlando Gunman 'Cheered the Terrorists on 9/11 and Made Plane Noises to Taunt Others on the School Bus,' Former Classmates Claim," *Daily Mail*, June 14, 2016, http://www.dailymail.co.uk/news/article -3639632/Orlando-gunman-cheered-terrorists-9-11-plane-noises-taunt-school -bus-former-classmates-claim.html (accessed September 15, 2016).

49. Harriet Alexander, "Omar Mateen Searched for Facebook Posts about Orlando Shooting while He Was Carrying It Out," *Telegraph*, June 16, 2016, http:// www.telegraph.co.uk/news/2016/06/16/omar-mateen-searched-for-facebook -posts-about-orlando-shooting-w/ (accessed September 15, 2016).

50. Cited by Holly Yan, Pamela Brown, and Evan Perez, "Orlando Shooter Texted Wife during Attack, Source Says," CNN, updated June 17, 2016, http:// www.cnn.com/2016/06/16/us/orlando-shooter-omar-mateen/ (accessed September 21, 2016).

51. Michael Arntfield, "Towards a Cybervictimology: Digital Predation, Routine Activity Theory & the Anti-Sociality of Social Media," *Canadian Journal of Communication* 40 (2015): 371–88.

52. Sun S. Lim, Shobha Vadrevu, Yoke Chan, and Iccha Basnyat, "Facework on Facebook: The Online Publicness of Delinquents and Youths-at-Risk," *Journal of Broadcasting & Electronic Media* 56 (2012): 346–61.

CHAPTER 5: SO, WHY MURDER?

1. Cited in Pamela Coloff, "A Kiss before Dying," *Texas Monthly*, February 2006, http://www.texasmonthly.com/articles/a-kiss-before-dying/ (accessed October 12, 2016).

2. Paul Williams, *Almost the Perfect Murder* (London: Penguin Random House UK, 2015).

3. Bill James, *Popular Crime: Reflections on the Celebration of Violence* (New York: Scribner, 2011).

4. Marquis de Sade, *Philosophy in the Bedroom* (1795; repr., New York: Grove, 1994), p. 23.

5. J. Tiihonen et al., "Genetic Background of Extreme Violent Behavior," *Molecular Psychiatry* 20 (June 2015): 786–92, doi:10.1038/mp.2014.130.

6. An excellent program on the neuroscience of murder is the BBC one, which is shown on various other public broadcasting channels, *Are Murderers Born or Made?* (BBC, "Are Murderers Born or Made?" March 9, 2015, http://www.bbc.com/news/magazine-31714853 [accessed November 15, 2016]). One of the conclusions is that the amygdala of the brain, which controls emotions, is involved in the act. The program indicated that the trigger for the emotional centers to go amok is upbringing, concluding that "murderers are both born and made."

7. For expanded data on homicide rates in 2010, see US Department of Justice, Federal Bureau of Investigation, "Crime in the United States," https://ucr.fbi.gov/crime-in-the-u.s/2010/crime-in-the-u.s.-2010/offenses-known-to-law-enforcement/expanded/expandhomicidemain/ (accessed October 2, 2016).

8. See "Fast Facts: Statistics on Violence against Women and Girls," UN Women, http://www.endvawnow.org/en/articles/299-fast-facts-statistics-on-violence-against-women-and-girls-.html (accessed November 12, 2016).

9. Interesting accounts of the reasons for femicide are those by Zygmunt Bauman, *Liquid Love: On the Frailty of Human Bonds* (Cambridge: Polity, 2003); David Adams, *Why Do They Kill? Men Who Murder Their Intimate Partners* (Nashville: Vanderbilt University Press, 2007); and Aaron Ben-Ze'ev and Ruhama Goussinsky, *In the Name of Love: Romantic Ideology and Its Victims* (Oxford: Oxford University Press, 2008).

10. Rebecca Dobash and Russell Dobash, *When Men Murder Women (Interpersonal Violence)* (Oxford: Oxford University Press, 2015).

11. See Harold Schechter, *The Serial Killer Files: The Who, What, Where, How, and Why of the World's Most Terrifying Murders* (New York: Random House, 2003), pp. 70ff.

12. Eric Hickey, *Serial Killers and Their Victims*, 7th ed. (Boston: Cengage Learning, 2016), pp. 283 and 299.

13. Charlene Gallego, as quoted in Schechter, *Serial Killer Files*, p. 70.

14. Hickey, *Serial Killers and Their Victims*, p. 296.

15. 5. Cited in Kristen Laurence, *The Murder Stories*, GooglePlay ed. (Lulu, 2014), p. 89.

16. Ibid.

17. Cited in "Chopper Confesses: 'I Murdered Four People': A Notorious Australian Criminal Who Was Never Convicted of Murder Confesses to Four Killings in His Last TV Interview," *Sky News*, October 21, 2013, http://news .sky.com/story/chopper-confesses-i-murdered-four-people-10430853 (accessed September 19, 2006).

18. Cited in Mikhail Krivich and Ol'gert Ol'gin, *Comrade Chikatilo: Russia's Most Notorious Serial Killer* (Los Angeles: Graymalkin Media, 1992).

19. Colette, "Assassins," in *Quatre Saisons* (Paris: Ferenczi, 1928), p. 123.

20. Thomas Hobbes, *Leviathan* (London: Andrew Crooke, 1651), p. 34.

21. Samuel Taylor Coleridge, "Kubla Khan" (text available at Poetry Foundation, https://www.poetryfoundation.org/poems-and-poets/poems/detail/ 43991 [accessed November 15, 2016]).

22. E. O. Wilson, *On Human Nature* (New York: Bantam, 1978), p. 167.

23. An overview with relevant bibliographical relevance of *Homo habilis* can be found on the Smithsonian National Museum of Natural History, "*Homo habilis*," What Does It Mean to Be Human? last updated February 9, 2016, http:// humanorigins.si.edu/evidence/human-fossils/species/homo-habilis (accessed November 15, 2016).

24. Richard Dawkins, *The Selfish Gene* (Oxford: Oxford University Press, 1976); *The Blind Watchmaker* (Harlow: Longmans, 1987); and *River out of Eden: A Darwinian View of Life* (New York: Basic, 1995).

25. Michel Foucault, *The Archeology of Knowledge*, translated by A. M. Sheridan Smith (New York: Pantheon, 1972).

26. H. G. Wells, *A Modern Utopia* (London: Penguin, 1905), p. 56.

27. Carl Panzram, *Killer, A Journal of Murder*, ed. Thomas E. Gaddis and James O. Long (New York: Macmillan, 1970), p. 23.

28. Cited in Brian King, ed., *Lustmord: The Writings and Artifacts of Murderers* (Burbank, CA: Bloat Books, 1997), p. 192.

29. W. H. Auden, "The Guilty Vicarage," *Harper's*, May 1948.

30. Michael Crichton, interview with *Book Reporter* (November 2002), interview posted on Readers Read, http://www.writerswrite.com/books/interview -with-michael-crichton-110120023 (accessed November 15, 2016).

31. Sigmund Freud, *Civilization and Its Discontents* (1931; repr., London: Hogarth, 1963), p. 48.

32. The reworkings of Freud have been oriented toward the neuroscience field. A recent good overview of the concept of salience is by Lucina Q. Uddin, *Salience Network of the Human Brain* (New York: Academic, 2016).

33. Ibid., pp. 235–36.

34. Quoted in Leland E. Hinsie and Robert Jean Campbell, *Psychiatric Dictionary* (New York: Oxford University Press, 1970), p. 372.

35. Charles Brenner, *An Elementary Textbook of Psychoanalysis* (Garden City: Doubleday, 1974), pp. 111–12.

36. Sigmund Freud, *The Interpretation of Dreams* (New York: Avon 1901), p. 286.

37. Cited in Martin Grotjahn, *Beyond Laughter: Humor and the Subconscious* (New York: McGraw-Hill, 1966), p. 84.

38. Simon Lesser, *Fiction and the Unconscious* (Boston: Beacon, 1957), p. 15.

39. Michael Arntfield, *Gothic Forensics: Criminal Investigative Procedure in Victorian Horror & Mystery* (New York: Palgrave-Macmillan, 2016), p. 45.

40. The two definitive textbooks on this topic remain John Olsson, *Forensic Linguistics: An Introduction to Language, Crime and the Law*, 2nd ed. (London: Continuum, 2008); and John Olsson, *Wordcrime: Solving Crime through Forensic Linguistics* (London: Bloomsbury, 2012).

41. From CNN, "The OJ Pages: O.J.'s Suicide Note," www.cnn.com/US/OJ/suspect/note/ (accessed November 15, 2016); Copyright © 1995 Cable News Network, Inc. This transcript has been edited to account for minor typos and strike-through annotations, given the extended length of the document and because they have been deemed immaterial to the excerpts being analyzed here.

42. The LSI Laboratory for Scientific Interrogation has both analyzed and published Simpson's letter on its website at "Analysis of the O.J. Simpson Suicide Letter," http://www.lsiscan.com/o_j__simpson_suicide_letter_.htm (accessed October 28, 2016).

43. Cited in John Olsson, *Forensic Linguistics: An Introduction to Language, Crime, and the Law* (London: Continuum, 2004), p. 82.

44. Ibid.

45. Ibid.

46. Ibid.

47. Cited in "Remember Me," True Crime Diary, May 16, 2012, http://www.truecrimediary.com/index.cfm?page=cases&id=178 (accessed August 12, 2016).

48. Cited in Chris Hanson, "New Forensic DNA Analysis Produces

Image of Cold-Case Killer at Large," *Crime Watch Daily*, May 2, 2016, http://crimewatchdaily.com/2016/05/02/young-girl-murdered-police-receive-series-of-disturbing-taunts/ (accessed August 13, 2016).

49. See: D. Kim Rossmo, *Geographic Profiling* (Boca Raton, FL: CRC, 2000).

50. Murder Accountability Project, "Clearance Rates: Uniform Crime Report for Homicides: 1965–2014," www.murderdata.org/p/blog-page.html (accessed November 16, 2016).

51. Samuel Butler, *The Way of All Flesh* (1903; repr., London: Courier, 2004), p. 57.

52. Albert Einstein, *Out of My Later Years* (New York: Citadel, 1956), p. 34.

53. W. Winwood Reade, *The Martyrdom of Man* (1872; repr., Honolulu: University Press of the Pacific, 2004), p. 94.

SELECT BIBLIOGRAPHY

Aamodt, Mike G. "Serial Killer Statistics." Radford University/FGCU Serial Killer Database (last modified November 23, 2015), http://maamodt.asp.radford.edu/serial killer information center/project description.htm (accessed April 19, 2015).

Adams, David. *Why Do They Kill? Men Who Murder Their Intimate Partners*. Nashville, TN: Vanderbilt University Press, 2007.

Alexander, Harriet. "Omar Mateen Searched for Facebook Posts about Orlando Shooting while He Was Carrying It Out," *Telegraph*, June 16, 2016, http://www.telegraph.co.uk/news/2016/06/16/omar-mateen-searched-for-facebook-posts-about-orlando-shooting-w/ (accessed October 28, 2016).

Anderson, Benedict. *Imagined Communities: Reflections on the Origin and Spread of Nationalism*. London: Verso, 1983.

Aristotle. *Poetics* (written 335 BCE). In *The Works of Aristotle*. Vol. 11. Edited by W. D. Ross. Oxford: Clarendon, 1952.

Arntfield, Michael. "Cybercoprographia: Where Cyberbullying Meets Deviant Fantasy." Michael Arntfield, June 11, 2015), http://michaelarntfield.com/cybercoprographia-where-cyberbullying-meets-deviant-fantasy/ (accessed August 25, 2016).

———. "Cybercrime & Cyberdeviance." In *Criminology: A Canadian Perspective*. 8th ed. Toronto: Nelson Education, 2017.

———. *Gothic Forensics: Criminal Investigative Procedure in Victorian Horror and Mystery*. New York: Palgrave-Macmillan, 2016.

———. *Mad City: The True Story of the Campus Murders That America Forgot*. New York: Little A Books, 2016.

———. *Murder City: The Untold Story of Canada's Serial Killer Capital*. Victoria: Friesen Press, 2015.

———. "Necrophilia in Literature, Poetry & Narrative Prose." *Understanding Necrophilia: A Global Multidisciplinary Approach*. San Diego: Cognella Academic Publishing, 2016. 109–20.

———. "New Media and Necrophilia." *Understanding Necrophilia: A Global Multidisciplinary Approach*. San Diego: Cognella Academic Publishing, 2016. 161–72.

———. *Practical Criminology*. Toronto: Nelson (Forthcoming 2018).

———. "Towards a Cybervictimology: Digital Predation, Routine Activity Theory & the Anti-Sociality of Social Media." *Canadian Journal of Communication* 40 (2015): 371–88.

Arntfield, Michael, and Joan Swart. "The X-Factor: Corporate & Occupational Psychopathy in Law Enforcement Management & the Operational Impact on Cold Case Homicides." *Journal of Cold Case Review* 1 (2015): 50–68.

Auden, W. H. "The Guilty Vicarage," *Harper's*, May 1948.

Baudrillard, Jean. *Simulations*. New York: Semiotext(e), 1983.

Bauman, Zygmunt. *Liquid Love: On the Frailty of Human Bonds*. Cambridge: Polity, 2003.

BBC News. "German 'Cannibal' Tells of Regret: A German Accused of Killing and Eating a Man He Met on a Website for Cannibals Has Expressed Regret for His Actions,"

BBC News, November 23, 2003, http://news.bbc.co.uk/2/hi/europe/3230774.stm (accessed September 1, 2016).

———. "NY Policeman Gilberto Valle Acquitted in Cannibal Plot," BBC News, July 1, 2014, http://www.bbc.com/news/world-us-canada-28113850 (accessed September 1, 2016).

Benedikt, Michael. *Cyberspace: First Steps*. Cambridge: MIT Press, 1991.

Ben-Ze'ev, Aaron, and Ruhama Goussinsky. *In the Name of Love: Romantic Ideology and Its Victims*. Oxford: Oxford University Press, 2008.

Blackstone, William. *Commentaries on the Laws of England*. London: Clarke and Sons, 1628.

Book Reporter, "An Interview with Michael Crichton," *Book Reporter* (November 2002). Interview posted on Readers Read, http://www.writerswrite.com/books/interview -with-michael-crichton-110120023 (accessed November 15, 2016).

Brenner, Charles. *An Elementary Textbook of Psychoanalysis*. Garden City: Doubleday, 1974.

Bugliosi, Vincent. *Helter Skelter: The True Story of the Manson Murders*. New York: W. W. Norton, 2001.

Butler, Samuel. *The Way of All Flesh*. Reprint, North Chelmsford, MA: Courier, 2004. First published in 1903.

Canter, David. *Criminal Shadows: Inside the Mind of the Serial Killer*. New York: HarperCollins, 1994.

Canter, David, and Donna Youngs. *Investigative Psychology: Offender Profiling and the Analysis of Criminal Action*. Hoboken, NJ: Wiley, 2009.

Carr, Erin Lee, director. *Thought Crimes: The Case of the Cannibal Cop*. HBO, 2015.

Casey, Liam. "Nurse Accused of Killing Seniors Posted Dark Poem Written from Perspective of Serial Killer," *National Post*, October 25, 2016. http://news.nationalpost.com/ news/canada/nurse-accused-of-killing-seniors-posted-dark-poem-written-from -perspective-of-serial-killer (accessed October 29, 2016).

Chalmers, Phil. *Inside the Mind of a Teen Killer*. New York: Nelson, 2010.

Chandler, Raymond. "The Simple Act of Murder," *Atlantic Monthly*, December, 1944.

Cleckley, Hervey. *The Mask of Sanity: An Attempt to Clarify Some Issues about the So-Called Psychopathic Personality*. Maryland Heights: Mosby, 1941. Fifth edition facsimile reprinted in 1988 by Emily Cleckley.

Colette. "Assassins." In *Quatre Saisons*. Paris: Ferenczi, 1928.

Collman, Laura. "Orlando Gunman Cheered the Terrorists on 9/11 and Made Plane Noises to Taunt Others on the School Bus, Former Classmates Claim," *Daily Mail*, June 14, 2016, http://www.dailymail.co.uk/news/article-3639632/Orlando-gunman -cheered-terrorists-9-11-plane-noises-taunt-school-bus-former-classmates-claim.html (accessed June 29, 2016).

Crowley, Kieran. *Sleep My Little Dead: The True Story of the Zodiac Killer*. New York: St. Martin's, 1997.

Cullen, Dave. *Columbine*. New York: Hachette Book Group, 2009.

Danesi, Marcel. *The "Dexter Syndrome": The Role of the Serial Killer in Popular Culture*. New York: Peter Lang, 2016.

———. *Signs of Crime: Introducing Forensic Semiotics*. Berlin: Mouton de Gruyter, 2013.

Dawkins, Richard. *The Blind Watchmaker*. Harlow: Longmans, 1987.

————. *River out of Eden: A Darwinian View of Life*. New York: Basic, 1995.

————. *The Selfish Gene*. Oxford: Oxford University Press, 1976.

de Maistre, Joseph. *The Works of Joseph de Maistre*. Edited by Jack Lively. Reprint, New York: Macmillan, 1965. First published in 1821.

de Sade, Marquis. *Philosophy in the Bedroom*. Reprint, New York: Grove, 1994. First published in 1795.

Dickie, John. *Cosa Nostra: A History of the Sicilian Mafia*. London: Hodder and Stoughton, 2004.

Dobash, Rebecca, and Russell Dobash. *When Men Murder Women (Interpersonal Violence)*. Oxford: Oxford University Press, 2015.

Douglas, John E., Anne W. Burgess, Allen G. Burgess, and Robert K. Ressler. *Crime Classification Manual: A Standard System for Investigating and Classifying Violent Crime*. New York: Lexington Books, 1992.

Durkheim, Emile. *The Elementary Forms of Religious Life*. New York: Collier, 1912.

Edmonton Journal. "Agreed Statement of Facts in the Twitchell Case," *Edmonton Journal*, April 5, 2011, http://www.edmontonjournal.com/news/twitchell-case/Read+Agreed +statements+facts+Twitchell+case/4563142/story.html (accessed October 28, 2016).

Einstein, Albert. *Out of My Later Years*. New York: Citadel, 1956.

Ellroy, James. *My Dark Places*. New York: Vintage, 1997.

Emerson, Ralph Waldo. *The Annotated Emerson*. Reprint, Cambridge: Harvard University Press, 2012. First published in 1844.

Engel, Pamela. "Adam Lanza Had Files about Pedophilia and Other Disturbing Content on His Computer," *Business Insider*, January 2, 2014, http://www.businessinsider.com/ adam-lanza-had-files-about-pedophilia-2014-1 (accessed August 16, 2016).

Foucault, Michel. *The Archeology of Knowledge*. Translated by A. M. Sheridan Smith. New York: Pantheon, 1972.

Fox, James A., and Jack Levin. *Extreme Killing: Understanding Serial and Mass Murder*. 3rd ed. Thousand Oaks, CA: Sage, 2015.

Freud, Sigmund. *Civilization and Its Discontents*. Reprint, London: Hogarth, 1963. First published in 1931.

————. "Instincts and Their Vicissitudes." In *The Standard Edition of the Complete Psychological Works of Sigmund Freud*. Vol. 14 *1914–1916: On the History of the Psycho-Analytic Movement, Papers on Metapsychology and Other Works*. London: Hogarth, 1957.

————. *The Interpretation of Dreams*. New York: Avon 1901.

Gibson, William. *Neuromancer*. London: Grafton, 1984.

Gill, Ann. *Rhetoric and Human Understanding*. Prospect Heights, IL: Waveland, 1994.

Girard, René. *Violence and the Sacred*. Baltimore: Hopkins, 1979.

Gottman, John, and Nan Silver. *What Makes Love Last?* New York: Simon and Schuster, 2013.

Gregorian, Dareh, Robert Gearty, Joanna Molloy, and Frank Miller. "Cannibal Cop Gilberto Valle Faces Life in Prison after Jury Finds Him Guilty of Conspiracy to Kidnap and Illegal Use of Federal Databases," *New York Daily News*, March 12, 2013, http:// www.nydailynews.com/new-york/cannibal-faces-life-guilty-conspiracy-kidnap -illegal-databases-article-1.1286075 (accessed July 7, 2016).

Grotjahn, Martin. *Beyond Laughter: Humor and the Subconscious*. New York: McGraw-Hill, 1966.

Hare, Robert. *The Hare Psychopathy Checklist—Revised.* Toronto: Multi-Health Systems, 1970.

———. *Psychopathy: Theory & Research.* New York: Wiley, 1970.

———. *Without Conscience: The Disturbing World of Psychopaths among Us.* New York: Guilford, 1998.

Hickey, Eric W. *Serial Murderers and Their Victims.* 7th ed. Boston: Cengage, 2015.

Hinsie, Leland E., and Robert Jean Campbell. *Psychiatric Dictionary.* New York: Oxford University Press, 1970.

Hobbes, Thomas. *Leviathan.* London: Andrew Crooke, 1651.

Holmes, Ronald M., and Steven T. Holmes. *Profiling Violent Crimes: An Investigative Tool.* 4th ed. Thousand Oaks, CA: Sage, 2009.

———. "Understanding Mass Murder: A Starting Point." In *Federal Probation* 56 (1992): 53–61.

Jackson, Christine A. *The Tell-Tale Art: Poe in Modern Popular Culture.* Jefferson, NC: McFarland, 2012.

James, Bill. *Popular Crime: Reflections on the Celebration of Violence.* New York: Scribner, 2011.

Jung, Carl. *The Portable Jung.* Harmondsworth: Penguin, 1971.

Kraepelin, Eric. *Psychiatrie: Ein Lehrbuch für Studierende und Ärzte.* 7th ed. Vol. 2. *Klinische Psychiatrie.* Leipzig: Verlag Barth, 1904.

Lachman, Gary. *Turn Off Your Mind: The Mystic Sixties and the Dark Side of the Age of Aquarius.* New York: Disinformation Books, 2001.

Largo, Michael. *Final Exits: The Illustrated Encyclopedia of How We Die.* New York: HarperCollins, 2006.

Larson, Erik. *The Devil in the White City: Murder, Magic and Madness at the Fair That Changed America.* New York: Crown, 2002.

Lasseter, Don. *Die for Me: The Terrifying True Story of the Charles Ng and Leonard Lake Torture Murders.* New York: Pinnacle Books, 2000.

Lesser, Simon. *Fiction and the Unconscious.* Boston: Beacon, 1957.

Lim, Sun. S., Shobha Vadrevu, Yoke Chan, and Iccha Basnyat. "Facework on Facebook: The Online Publicness of Delinquents and Youths-at-Risk," *Journal of Broadcasting & Electronic Media* 56 (2012).

Lombroso, Cesare. *L'uomo delinquente.* Milano: Hoepli, 1876.

Lunde, Paul. *Organized Crime: An Inside Guide to the World's Most Successful Industry.* London: Dorling Kindersley, 2004.

Marx, Karl. *Economic & Philosophic Manuscripts of 1844.* Reprint, Moscow: Progress Publishers, 1944. First published in 1844.

Mauss, Marcel. "Les techniques du corp," *Journal de Psychologie* 32 (1934).

McGee, James P., and Caren R. DeBernardo. "The Classroom Avenger: A Behavioral Profile of School Based Shootings," *Forensic Examiner* 8 (1999): 16–18.

McLuhan, Marshall. *Understanding Media: The Extensions of Man.* Cambridge: MIT Press, 1964.

McNab, Chris. *Serial Killer Timelines.* Berkeley: Ulysses, 2010.

Millon, Theodore. *Disorders of Personality: DSM IV and Beyond.* 3rd ed. Hoboken, NJ: Wiley, 2011.

Millon, Theodore, and Roger Davis. *Disorders of Personality: DSM IV and Beyond*. 1st ed. Hoboken, NJ: Wiley, 1996.

Neuman, Yair, Dan Assaf, Yochai Cohen, and James Knoll. "Profiling School Shooters: Automatic Text-Based Analysis," *Frontiers in Psychiatry* 6, no. 86 (2015), http://www.ncbi.nlm.nih.gov/pmc/articles/PMC4453266/ (accessed September 10, 2016).

Newton, Michael. *Hunting Humans: An Encyclopedia of Modern Serial Killers*. New York: Breakout Productions, 1990.

Nicaso, Antonio, and Marcel Danesi. *Made Men: Mafia Culture and the Power of Symbols, Rituals, and Myth*. Lanham: Rowman & Littlefield, 2013.

Oakley, Barbara A. *Evil Genes*. Amherst, NY: Prometheus Books, 2008.

Olsson, John. *Forensic Linguistics: An Introduction to Language, Crime and the Law*. 2nd ed. London: Continuum, 2008.

———. *Word Crime: Solving Crime through Forensic Linguistics*. London: Continuum, 2009.

O'Toole, Mary E. *The School Shooter: A Threat Assessment Perspective*. Quantico, VA: Critical Incident Response Group, National Center for the Analysis of Violent Crime, FBI Academy, 2000.

Pennebaker, James. *The Secret Life of Pronouns: What Our Words Say about Us*. New York: Bloomsbury, 2011.

Philbin, Tom. *I, Monster: Serial Killers in Their Own Chilling Words*. Amherst, NY: Prometheus Books, 2011.

R. v. Sharpe. (2001) 1 S.C.R. 45, 2001 SCC 2.

Reade, W. Winwood. *The Martyrdom of Man*. Reprint, Grove, OR: University Press of the Pacific, 2004. First published in 1872.

Rossmo, D. Kim. *Geographic Profiling*. Boca Raton, FL: CRC, 2000.

Rostand, Jean. *Pensées d'un Biologiste*. Reprinted in *The Substance of Man*. London: Greenwood, 1962. First published in 1939.

Schaub, Michael. "The Bizarre Books by Baton Rouge Shooter Gavin Eugene Long aka Cosmo Setepenra," *Los Angeles Times*, July 18, 2016, http://www.latimes.com/books/la-et-jc-cosmo-setepenra-books-20160718-snap-story.html (accessed July 25, 2016).

Schmid, David. *Natural Born Celebrities: Serial Killers in American Culture*. Chicago: University of Chicago Press, 2005.

Simpson, Philip. *Psycho Paths: Tracking the Serial Killer through Contemporary American Film and Fiction*. Chicago: Southern Illinois University Press, 2000.

Slotkin, Richard. *Gunfighter Nation: The Myth of the Frontier in Twentieth-Century America*. New York: Macmillan Publishing, 1998.

Stewart, Gary. *The Most Dangerous Animal of All*. New York: Harper, 2015.

Sutherland, Edwin H., and David R. Cressey. *Principles of Criminology*. 10th ed. Philadelphia: Lippincott, 1978.

Thomas, Ronald R. *Detective Fiction and the Rise of Forensic Science*. Cambridge: Cambridge University Press, 1999.

Tiihonen, J., et al. "Genetic Background of Extreme Violent Behavior," *Molecular Psychiatry* 20 (June 2015).

van Ornum, William. "The Secret Service on Preventing School Violence," *National Review*, December 17, 2012, http://www.nationalreview.com/corner/335825/secret-service-preventing-school-violence-william-van-ornum (accessed August 28, 2016).

von Krafft-Ebing, Richard. *Psychopathia Sexualis*. Stuttgart: Ferdinand Enke, 1886.

Vronsky, Peter. *Female Serial Killers: How and Why Women Become Monsters*. New York: Berkley, 2007.

———. *Serial Killers: The Method and Madness of Monsters*. New York: Berkley, 2004.

Wells, H. G. *A Modern Utopia*. London: Penguin, 1905.

Wiggins, Bradley E., and G. Bret Bowers. "Memes as Genre: A Structurational Analysis of the Memescape," *New Media & Society* 17, no. 11 (2015): 1886–1906.

Will, George F. *Statecraft as Soulcraft: What Government Does*. New York: Touchstone, 1984.

Williams, Paul. *Almost the Perfect Murder*. London: Penguin Random House UK, 2015.

Wilson, E. O. *On Human Nature*. New York: Bantam, 1978.

Youngs, Donna, David Canter, and Nikki Carthy. "The Offender's Narrative: Unresolved Dissonance in Life as a Film (LAAF) Responses," *Legal and Criminological Psychology* 21 (2016): 251–65.

INDEX